El Gringo

LOWER COVERO.

El Gringo

New Mexico and Her People

W. W. H. Davis

University of Nebraska Press
Lincoln • London

UM

Manufactured in the United States of America

First Bison Book Printing: September 1982

Most recent printing indicated by first digit below:
1   2   3   4   5   6   7   8   9   10

Library of Congress Cataloging in Publication Data

Davis, W. W. H. (William Watts Hart), 1820–1910.
El Gringo : New Mexico and her people.

Reprint. Originally published: New York : Harper, 1857.
"Bison book."
1. New Mexico—Description and travel. 2. New
Mexico—History. 3. Navaho Indians. 4. Davis, W. W. H.
(William Watts Hart), 1820–1910.   I.   Title.
F801.D26   1982   978.9   82-2735
ISBN 0-8032-1665-3   AACR2
ISBN 0-8032-6558-1 (pbk.)

The text of this edition is reproduced from the first edition, published in 1857 by Harper and Brothers.

DEDICATION.

TO

LEWIS S. CORYELL, OF NEW HOPE, PENNSYLVANIA, ESQUIRE,

This Volume is respectfully Inscribed

AS A MARK OF THE AFFECTION AND FRIENDSHIP ENTERTAINED FOR HIM BY

THE AUTHOR.

PREFACE.

THIS volume is mainly written from a diary the author kept during a residence of two and a half years in New Mexico, and the matters contained in it are either drawn from careful personal observation, or other reliable sources. The historical portions are almost wholly obtained from official records in the office of the Secretary of the Territory at Santa Fé, and may be relied upon as correct. The beautiful drawings that adorn the work were executed by Brevet Lieutenant Colonel Eaton, U. S. A., on duty in that territory, and F. A. Percy, Esq., of El Paso, Texas, to whom I am much indebted; and I take this occasion to make my acknowledgments to them for their great kindness. With these remarks the work is submitted to the public, and if, upon perusal, the reader should find any thing in it to instruct or amuse, the author will consider his labors amply rewarded.

W. W. H. DAVIS.

Davisville, Pa., July 28th, 1856.

CONTENTS.

CHAPTER I.

TRIP ACROSS THE PLAINS.

CHAPTER II.

TRIP ACROSS THE PLAINS—*Concluded.*

CHAPTER III.

HISTORICAL SKETCH OF NEW MEXICO.

CONTENTS.

CHAPTER IV.

HISTORICAL SKETCH OF NEW MEXICO—*Concluded.*

CHAPTER V.

THE PUEBLO INDIANS.

CHAPTER VI.

THE PUEBLO INDIANS—*Concluded.*

CONTENTS.

CHAPTER VII.

SANTA FÉ, WITH SOME ACCOUNT OF THE MANNERS AND CUSTOMS OF THE PEOPLE.

CHAPTER VIII.

MANNERS AND CUSTOMS OF THE PEOPLE—*Continued.*

CHAPTER IX.

MANNERS AND CUSTOMS OF THE PEOPLE—*Concluded.*

CHAPTER X.

ARRIVAL IN SANTA FÉ.

CHAPTER XI.

WINTER IN SANTA FÉ.

CONTENTS.

CONTENTS.

CHAPTER XV.

RIDING THE CIRCUIT— *Continued.*

CHAPTER XVI.

RIDING THE CIRCUIT— *Concluded.*

CHAPTER XVII.

TRIP TO THE NABAJO COUNTRY.

CONTENTS.

CHAPTER XVIII.

TRIP TO THE NABAJO COUNTRY—*Concluded.*

ILLUSTRATIONS.

NEW MEXICO AND HER PEOPLE.

CHAPTER I.

TRIP ACROSS THE PLAINS.

I EMBARKED, for the first time, upon the great prairie sea that stretches throughout the central region of North America, in the month of November, eighteen hundred and fifty-three. I arrived at Independence, Missouri, the starting-point, on the twenty-seventh day of the previous month, accompanied by Mr. G. Rodman as traveling companion. The distance between this place and Santa Fé, New Mexico, is nearly a thousand miles, which is traversed monthly by the mule-teams that convey the mail back and forth. As this was our only facility for crossing the Plains at that season of the year, we accordingly took two seats in the mail-wagon, paying one hundred and fifty dollars each, which included board on the way, and transportation of forty pounds of personal baggage. The mail was to leave the first of the coming month, and we employed the time between our arrival and departure in making the necessary preparations for the trip.

When we engaged passage there were no seats taken, and there was every probability of our being the only passengers. We were, therefore, quite delighted when informed by the contractors, two days before the time of starting, that two gentlemen were on their way up the river to go out with us. These were Captain Reynolds, U. S. A., and his step-son, a Mr. Ash, of Philadelphia. They had been delayed coming westward, and, being fearful that the Santa Fé stage might start before their arrival, Captain Reynolds telegraphed the contractors from Jefferson City to wait for them. The dispatch was in the shape of a poetical effusion, and ran as follows:

" Fink's* stages are so rickety,
        His horses are so slow,
His drivers are such drunken sots,
        They scarce can make them go.
Then hold your horses, Billy,†
        Just hold them for a day ;
I've crossed the River Jordan,‡
        And am bound for Santa Fé."

The dispatch had the desired effect ; " Billy" held his horses, and the gallant captain reached the starting-point in due season.

Every thing being in readiness, we left Independence on the afternoon of the first day of November. The morning was beautifully bright and clear, as if smiling upon our setting out, but toward noon the heavens clouded over, and the wind came on to blow almost with the fury of a hurricane. Our little train consisted of three wagons—one for the mail, another for the baggage and provisions, and an ambulance for the passengers. Two of them were drawn by six mules, and the

---

* Name of stage-proprietor from Saint Louis to Independence, Missouri.

† Mr. W. M'Coy, one of the Santa Fé mail-contractors.

‡ A small stream that empties into the Missouri below Jefferson City.

third by four; and, in addition to a driver for each team, there were two outriders to hurry up the lagging animals. All told, our party numbered ten men'; and we carried with us the necessary provisions for the trip, with a moderate supply of oats and corn for the mules. We were well armed to defend ourselves from Indian attacks on the way, and to shoot game, with which the country abounds. Thus equipped, we drove out of Independence at full speed, and commenced our long and somewhat perilous journey.

After traveling some two miles it commenced to rain, which made the roads quite slippery for the mules ; and, as it bid fair to be a stormy night, the conductor thought it most advisable to turn back a short distance, and encamp in a convenient wood. We unharnessed in a grove contiguous to the house of Colonel Hall, one of the contractors, of whose hospitality the passengers partook for the night. The next morning being clear and pleasant, we made early preparations for a final departure. In the mean time we were joined by two additional passengers, Padre Donato, a Catholic priest, and a lay brother, named Carlos, both Italians, and on their way to New Mexico. This addition to our numbers created a necessity for another wagon, which was also drawn by six mules, and arranged to carry passengers in the winter season.

It was two o'clock P.M. by the time we were again under way, and before halting we drove twenty miles to New Santa Fé, a small settlement on the western borders of Missouri, where we encamped upon the prairie. The mail company had an agent at this place, with whom the passengers found accommodations for the night. The family lived in a rude clapboard cabin, but within there was an abundance of good cheer. The evening was dark and cold, and we felicitated ourselves upon being under cover. As we had fasted since morning, the calls of hunger were loud and strong; but in Mrs. White, the agent's wife, we found a ministering angel to our wants. She was a fine specimen of a frontier housewife, and in almost less time than it requires to write it, she had a good supper smoking upon the table. It was a meal that would have done honor to any housekeeper; and if our appreciation of the quality of her victuals may be judged of by the quantity we respectively stowed away under our waistcoats, they received the highest possible commendation. She graced the head of her own table, and, instead of allowing us to eat in moody silence, as hungry men are too apt to do, she maintained a lively conversation the while, and, when the tongue ceased its office, she made use of as pretty a pair of eyes as ever graced a woman's head.

After supper we drew our chairs around the blazing hearth, and chatted with host and hostess until bedtime. Captain Reynolds and myself were favored with the best bed in the house, while the padre and his boy reposed on a soft spot on the floor, and the balance of the party slept in the wagons. In the morning the ground was white with a hoar-frost. The conductor and his men were astir early, and the teams were harnessed and ready for the road before I had shaken off my slumbers. As it was the last opportunity, for some time to come, that we would have to indulge in the luxury of a comfortable bed, we were disposed to prolong our morning nap even at the expense of the conductor's patience; but his stentorian voice quickly called us forth, and we were soon seated in the wagons and on our way across the prairies.

The distance from Independence to Santa Fé may be divided into three stages. The first, from the starting-point to Council Grove, is about a hundred and fifty miles, and passes through the country of the Shawnees,

Caws, and other friendly Indians, and by the roadside is seen the occasional cabin of a frontier settler. The second stage is from Council Grove to Fort Union, some six hundred miles, which lies across the immense plains of the interior of the continent, and is roamed over by the Camanches, Apaches, Arrapahoes, Cheyennes, Pawnees, Kiowahs, and other Indian tribes, and is the home of immense herds of buffaloes and antelopes. The country is generally level, with an occasional roll, and bare of wood, except the few cottonwood-trees found along the streams. Throughout all this region water is scarce. The third stage brings us to Santa Fé through a mountainous and partially settled country, covered with a growth of inferior pine timber, and tolerably well watered.

The sun was just climbing over the eastern tree-tops on the morning of the third instant, as we took our departure from New Santa Fé. The air was keen, and made us shiver, in spite of overcoats and blankets. We drove fifteen miles to the Lone Elm, where we halted to breakfast, the animals being turned out to graze on the prairie grass, while the conductor and his men busied themselves in the cooking arrangements. The kitchen cabinet had not been fairly organized previous to leaving Independence, which had now to be accomplished before any thing could be done in the way of getting breakfast. Jones, a clever Kentuckian, who drove the baggage-wagon, was duly installed chief of the *cuisine*, and Converse and Mitchel—the former in charge of the mail-wagon, and the latter the forage—were nominated assistants. José, a Mexican, and the colored outdriver, were appointed "hewers of wood and drawers of water," and thus the organization was complete. Our kitchen being duly arranged, Jones and his subs set themselves about their useful, and, to the hungry lookers-on, deeply-interesting occupation. The stump of the Lone Elm furnished the necessary fire-wood; and a stagnant creek which runs by this spot—when it runs at all—supplied the necessary water. In due season all the preparations were under way: the ham was being fried; the tin tea-pot was simmering by the fire; and the luxuries, in the shape of butter, cheese, and molasses, were forthcoming from the wagons. Coffee was first voted for breakfast; but, to the regret of the lovers of this narcotic, there was no mill to grind it, and tea was substituted in its place. Matters being in this state of forwardness, Conductor Booth ordered the table to be spread and the victuals placed upon it. The men bustled about in obedience to the command, while the passengers eyed the operations with increased interest.

We expected to see a camp-table brought forth, and a respectable set of tin-ware placed upon it, such as we had been accustomed to in camp-life; but here disappointment met us at the outset. The two subs came from the baggage-wagon, one carrying an India-rubber mule-cover, which he spread upon the ground near the fire for both table and cloth, while the other carried a dirty bag. By the time the mule-cover was duly arranged, the second had his bag untied, which he turned upside down, and poured upon the ground the entire complement of table-furniture, which, being inventoried on the spot, was found to consist of the following named articles, viz. : twelve tin cups, ten tin plates, six spoons, seven knives, two forks, two tin canisters, and two coffee-pots. In addition to the above was one frying and one stew pan; but, as the cooks were not so choice of these, they were not kept in the bag. The eatables were soon upon the table, and the "passengers for Santa Fé" were invited to take seats and help themselves. We sat flat upon old Mother Earth, and fell to work in a manner hardly to be sanctioned any where but on the prairies. As there were but two forks, a question arose as to who should use them; but the matter was amicably adjusted by allotting them to Captain R. and myself in the first instance, on account of conceded seniority in rank, and afterward passed around to the others, each one in his turn. The meal was truly a humble one, and partaken in a republican manner; but nevertheless we ate with as much gusto as though we had been seated at an alderman's board on a reception day.

The spot known to all travelers upon the plain as the Lone Elm is a somewhat noted point, and would afford excellent capital for a romance manufacturer. When all that country was in the possession of the Indians, long before the white man had invaded their dominions, this tree is said to have been a great rallying-point for all the neighboring tribes. It stood solitary and alone upon the prairies, and its top could be seen for many miles around. Here, probably, many a midnight foray was hatched against some distant settlement encroaching too far toward the Indian hunting-ground, and under its widespreading branches many a sage council has been held. It served as a landmark for those seeking the frontiers, and in the early times of the Santa Fé traders it was a place of encampment for the night. Travelers came to look upon it as an old friend—they felt an attachment for the tree that had so often sheltered and shaded them from storm and sun, and no inducement could have made them cut it down. But in the course of time some modern Vandal came along, and laid low this last of its race; and when we passed, it was all gone but a small portion of the stump, and part of that cooked our breakfast. We may be accused of something akin to sacrilege in burning the remains of the old patriarch of the prairie; but with us it was breakfast or no breakfast, and upon such occasions hungry men are not much disposed to give way to romance.

We drove eleven miles to Bull Creek to dinner, where we arrived about two in the afternoon. On a hill near by was a small trading establishment, where divers primitive notions were kept to sell to the Indians. We made a visit to the cabin to endeavor to buy a little milk of the old German woman who ruled over the destinies of the kitchen; but we found her incorrigible, and could not induce her to part with it. Here we saw a young Shawnee squaw, whose tribe inhabit a region of country within a few miles. She was well dressed in semi-American style, and mounted upon a sorrel pony. She galloped across the prairie as we drew up, and in point of horsemanship was a model for any city-trained belle. We remained at the Creek until four, when we harnessed up and drove seventeen miles to Hickory Point, where we encamped for the night.

It was so late in the evening when we reached the camping ground that supper was dispensed with. The mules were secured near the wagons by picketing them to the ground, each one being allowed about twenty feet of rope to graze round. The next care was to prepare our own accommodations for sleeping, and we now found the dormitories as much out of order as was the *cuisine* in the morning. Two slept in the ambulance; the padre and his boy stowed themselves away in the baggage wagon; while the rest of us, who eschewed close apartments and impure atmosphere, made our beds upon the ground. Rodman and myself shared the same blankets, and, as a slight protection from the falling dew, lay down under one of the wagons; but the only advantage we had over those who slept in the wagons was that the quarters had been well aired during the day. Thus arranged, wrapped in our blankets, with our heads pillowed on our watch-coats, we made our most respectful bow to the God of Sleep, and, as soon as the freezing cold would

allow us so to do, we resigned ourselves into the arms
of Morpheus. 'Tis a threadbare saying that "uneasy
lies the head that wears a crown," just as though no other
head has a hard time of it. But I know full well that
upon the night in question, and without a crown upon
it, my poor head had a most uneasy berth. Visions of
well-filled larders and downy beds were traversing my
cranium the livelong night, and when I awoke in the
morning I was fairly stiff with cold, and quite as tired
as when I had lain down the evening before.

We harnessed up about sunrise, and drove eighteen
miles to Rock Creek to graze and breakfast, but continued on to One Hundred and Ten before we halted to dine.
Here flows a small stream of clear water, fringed on either side with cottonwood-trees, and close to the road
were the log cabins of a settler with an Indian wife. In
the timber were encamped a party of discharged soldiers
on their way home to the States from Fort Massachusetts, in New Mexico. They had made their way alone
across the prairies to this point without accident, partly
on foot and partly mounted. They invited us to partake of their homely fare, which we declined, as our own
pot was simmering over the fire, and, besides, we did not
desire to reduce their scanty store, which was no more
than enough to last them into the States. The night
before the prairie was on fire all around us, and at one
time we had fears the wind might change and bring it
down upon our camp. It was the first time I had seen
such a sight, and the spectacle was grand and beautiful.
The heavens were lit up almost as light as day. The
blaze showed a long line of fire, which licked up the dry
grass like so much gossamer, and cracked like the reports of a thousand pistols as the flames ran along with
the wind. The streaks of fire were faint at first, but increased in brightness as it was fanned by the wind, and

moved in its course with terrible rapidity across the prairie. It assumed various forms. Sometimes it shot several feet into the air, like the forked tongue of a serpent; the next moment it would almost disappear, as an opposite breath of wind would arrest its progress; then it starts again into new life, with its fiery tongue licking up every living thing within reach.

We rested that night at Switzer's Creek, ten miles farther on, and, as was our custom, went to sleep without supper or fire. When I awoke the next morning I found that Caw, the mail-dog, had curled up by my side during the night, and as I disturbed his slumbers, he looked at me with an apparent smile, as much as to return thanks for the accommodations my blankets had afforded him. The following day we made a drive of about fifty miles to Council Grove. The wind was piercing cold, and seemed to penetrate the very marrow of our bones. Toward evening it commenced to snow, which, mingled with hail, continued to fall all night and part of the next day. We arrived at the Grove just after dark.

Council Grove is about one hundred and fifty miles west of Independence, and is situated upon the west branch of the Neosho River. At that time it contained some half dozen log cabins and a trading-house, and is the station of the agent for the Caw Indians. Many of the tribe were then there, awaiting the distribution of their annuities. They number about a thousand in all, and were among the most miserable set of beings I have ever seen. They are said to have been in a fine condition at one time, but have sadly degenerated from their intercourse with the whites. They are great drunkards, and a bottle of whisky is potent enough to purchase any thing they possess. They seem to have learned all the vices but none of the virtues of the white man. The men are large and rather fine-looking, but otherwise were squalid enough. The Methodist denomination had a missionary stationed there, but, as the Indians would not allow any preaching among them, he was principally engaged in teaching the children. He had had but little success among them.

The snow was falling fast when we drove up to the Grove, and all felt thankful that we would have a roof to shelter our heads during the night. We took possession of a filthy old cabin, windowless and doorless, and which some of the boys named the "Astor House," in which we ate our supper. As soon as we arrived, the blacksmith was set at work shoeing the mules and mending up the wagons. There was a trip of six hundred miles before us, through a country entirely uninhabited, and it was necessary that every thing should be put in the best possible order. Mr. Withington, the agent for the mail-contractors, treated us in the kindest manner, and while we remained he made our stay as pleasant as possible. We spent the evening around his cheerful hearth, and when bedtime arrived he furnished our party with all the beds he had to spare. The next morning Mrs. W. prepared us a warm breakfast, of which we partook with thankfulness. Just before we arrived, a man belonging to a party on their way from New Mexico came in to the Grove in almost a starving condition, who gave information of the peril of his companions, and desired that food might be sent out to them. Their provisions had given out three days before, when they sent forward the strongest of their number to seek relief. A supply of food was immediately dispatched to them, without which timely aid they would undoubtedly have perished in the severe storm then prevailing.

To this point our road lay across a gently rolling prairie country, with a soil naturally rich, and, wherever placed under cultivation, produced abundantly. The grass is three or four feet high, springing up green in the spring, but drying and withering down in the autumn. To a person who has never been upon the great American prairies, a trip across them can not be otherwise than interesting. Their appearance can hardly be imagined: to be appreciated they must be seen. You find yourself surrounded on every side, and as far as the eye can reach, by a country almost as level as the sea, with an occasional gentle roll, like the ocean swell, to break the universal evenness of the surface. You appear to be standing in the midst of an immense ocean of dry land, and you strain the eye in vain for something to relieve the sameness around you. Out upon these great plains a person experiences different feelings than when confined within cities and forest, and surrounded with the appliances of civilized life. He appears to breathe deeper, and to increase in stature; the sky seems to be bluer and clearer, the air purer, and the sun to shine more brightly. The earth expands in size, and the vastness spread out on every side gives him a higher appreciation of the immensity of God's handiwork. The mind seems to become enlarged also, in beholding the greatness of Nature's works, and a man who is not insensible to such influences can not fail to be made better and wiser by a trip across the prairies. The route traveled is probably the finest natural road in the world, and day after day you roll along with no guide but the beaten track that lies before you. When travelers meet upon the plains it reminds one of ships meeting at sea. The first question is, "Where are you from, and where bound?" and then follows, "How many days out? what kind of weather have you had, and what Indians have you met on the way?" If either party is short of provisions, the other supplies him if he has them to spare, and in all such

things there is a comity between travelers upon the
Plains.

Sunday morning at Council Grove was occupied by
the conductor and his men in making such alterations
and improvement in the team as the nature of the trip
before us seemed to require.   Some of the mules we had
driven to this point were exchanged for better ones, the
former being left behind for the incoming mail to drive
in to Independence.   It was a stormy and unpropitious
day.   It had snowed all the night before, and toward
noon it commenced to rain, which gradually increased as
the day wore away, and the weather became colder.   We
were all disposed to wait there until there was a favorable change in the weather; but as the mail had to be
carried through in a given number of days, and we would
be likely to meet with some detention on the road at
this season of the year, there was no time to be lost at
this end of the route.   We therefore hastened our departure, and, every thing being in readiness, we started
from the Grove between one and two o'clock that afternoon.   We drove seven miles, when we encamped for the
night at a place called Elm Creek.   We had intended
making another drive before we slept, but as it was nearly dark when we reached this point, and the storm continuing with much severity, we concluded to remain until morning.   The prospect for supper and a comfortable
night was dreary enough.   We gathered brush along
the creek, and made a fire, and were thus enabled to cook
a little food; but it rained in torrents while we ate, and
we were all thoroughly drenched.   After supper we sent
out a wood-party to cut a supply of fuel for the night,
who returned in a little while dragging after them a
good-sized cottonwood-tree they had felled.   This was
cut up and piled upon the fire, and soon we had a large
blaze, around which we huddled to warm our chilled

bodies and dry our clothes. Here we sat until quite late, apd in no very cheerful mood, when we made arrangements to pass the night.

To sleep comfortably upon the ground such a night as this required more than ordinary management, and called into requisition all our ingenuity. The balance of the party slept in the wagons, but I preferred lying out to being cramped up among the baggage and mailbags, and accordingly made my bed under one of the wagons. I wrapped myself up in a buffalo robe and blankets, and, with as much resignation as possible, laid me down to sleep. I discovered, when too late to remedy the difficulty, that I was reposing in a little hollow, and soon became aware that the water was running toward me; but there was hardly a choice left, and I must either run the risk of being drenched there, or go elsewhere with every prospect of doing worse. I therefore determined to stand my ground and take the chances. In the course of time I fell asleep, and while in troubled dreams about Noah and the ark, I awoke to find a considerable pool of water by my side. It now required straight and steady lying to keep out of the water, but this I managed to do, and again passed into the land of dreams. In the course of the night I awoke a second time, and found the condition of things much worse; the water had collected in the hollow in which I was lying, and I was wet to the skin. This seemed like a determination to drive me out, but I resolved not to beat a retreat so long as I could keep the head above water; but all sleep was at an end, and I spent the balance of the night in moody reflection.

The morning at last dawned, rainy and unpleasant. We drove eight miles to Diamond Spring to breakfast. The rain came down in torrents while we were around the fire eating, and all were obliged to seek shelter in the wagons, plate in hand. We remained here but a short time, when we harnessed up and drove to the Cotton Wood, twenty-nine miles, where we made camp for the night. By evening the weather cleared up, and the moon came out bright and clear from under the heavy clouds. The country was now becoming less rolling, and appeared more like an extended plain. On the ninth of the month we reached the Little Arkansas, where we breakfasted, and stopped for the night at Plumb Bute. While breakfasting, we espied a fine old buffalo bull feeding a little way up the creek, and having a hankering after some of his flesh, Captain Reynolds and myself took our rifles and started in pursuit. I followed up the winding of the stream, which here runs through a deep ravine, while the captain held directly across the prairie. I had lost sight of the buffalo, and was anxiously seeking his whereabouts, when I heard the crack of a rifle, and, upon looking up the stream, saw the animal standing under a cottonwood-tree, shaking his head as though about to make a charge. The captain gave him a little more searoom, but he did not advance; when another shot caused him to beat a retreat, and he was soon lost to sight over a roll of the prairie.

We encamped for noon and dined at Cow Creek. Here I received my first alarm from the Indians. Seeing a small herd of buffaloes feeding up the creek, Rodman, Ash, and myself started off in pursuit, two being armed with rifles, and the third with a small six-shooter. We followed them some distance from the camp, but finding they were moving off without a prospect of being able to overtake them, we concluded to return. We were on the point of retracing our steps, when one of the party cried out, "Look at the Indians!" and, turning to the north, we espied three mounted warriors, just out of rifle-shot, standing upon a roll of the prairie. The cry of "Indians" is at all times startling upon the Plains, but particularly so when you encounter them away from your main party; and, under such circumstances, the market value of good white scalps will naturally occur to the mind.   We held a council of war, and resolved unanimously that it was advisable to return to camp; we considered ourselves a pretty fair match for the three Indians in sight, but did not know how many more there were behind the ridge.   We knew it would not do to let the Indians see that we were alarmed, and therefore did not run; but we managed to do some of the handsomest kind of walking, now and then looking back to see if our red brethren were coming on.   They gradually moved toward us, which caused us to lengthen our steps a *little*. We made a straight line for the ravine that lay in front of us, and, when once in it and hid from the Indians, we made some very respectable running.   We soon increased the distance between us and them; and when we emerged from the ravine upon the plain, we were out of all danger, and walked leisurely into camp.   The Indians followed slowly, and came in while we were eating dinner, and turned out to be three old Caws; and, if the truth was known, they were probably as badly frightened as ourselves.   As usual, they were upon a begging expedition.   We filled a pipe for each, which they smoked with much gusto before the fire, and then gave them a moderate drink of brandy apiece, which was the most acceptable thing we could have given them.   The youngest of the party was not satisfied, but wanted more; he made many signs to show how dry he was, and offered all the buffalo-meat he had on his pony for another dram.   We gave the old man a few things to carry home to his squaw; and when we drove on, we left them hovering over the expiring embers of our fire.

The next day we passed the Great Bend of the Ar-

kansas, and made our camp for the night eight miles beyond the Pawnee Fork.   Here we struck the region of
buffalo grass, and saw herds of the animal grazing upon
the surrounding plains.   They were very shy, and we
could not get near enough to shoot any of them.   We
breakfasted upon the meat we had procured from the
Caw Indians, which I found quite delicious, being sweeter and more juicy than beef.   We made the crossing of
Pawnee Fork about nine o'clock at night, with a bright
moon shining upon us.   This is considered among the
most dangerous ground on the road, and, before we attempted crossing, Mr. Booth made a reconnaissance of the
ford, and up and down the stream some distance.   The
banks are high and steep, and afford an excellent situation for an Indian ambuscade.   When he returned to
the wagons he reported that he " smelt Injins," and directed us to have our arms ready for an emergency.   We
therefore shouldered our rifles and buckled on our pistols, to be ready to defend the passage of the wagons if
it should be necessary ; but we crossed in safety, and
continued on to camp, where we arrived at a late hour.

In crossing Coon Creek the following day we met
with an accident that came nigh putting some of us *hors
du combat* for the rest of the trip.   The wagon in which
four of us were riding had been given into the care of
the Mexican a little while before, and, as he was not
much skilled in driving, the mules ran away with us.
They plunged at full speed down the steep bank into the
creek ; and the wagon body, with its human load, was
thrown off the running gears, and landed at least ten feet
distant in the dry bed of the stream.   The concussion
seemed like a young earthquake.   People may talk about
seeing stars upon such occasions, but, as near as my recollection serves me, I had the pleasure of beholding a
score or more of full-sized moons.   I was pitched out of

the wagon head foremost on to the hard earth, stunned but not much hurt. On looking after my companions, I found them to be alive and kicking, and scrambling out of the wagon with all possible speed, apparently fearful it was about to make another summerset. We were all more or less bruised. Rodman was more seriously injured than the others, and the blood was streaming down his face from an ugly cut over the left eye, produced by falling against some sharp instrument. The wagon was in a worse condition than the passengers. When the mules had rid themselves of the body, they dashed across the Plains with the running gears in fine style, apparently pleased with the operation as a most capital joke. They dropped the wheels here and there as the linch-pins came out, and then dragged the axles about on the ground until they were stopped by the men. This accident detained us about an hour, when the wagon was pronounced in running order once more, and we resumed our journey.

At this time our road lay across what is known as the Dry Route, where for the distance of thirty miles there is no water. We last filled our kegs at the Pawnee Fork, which supplied us with water to drink, but we had none to cook with, and the mules were obliged to thirst until we reached the Arkansas. We made our last meal at Coon Creek, the scene of our disaster, where we cooked with buffalo chips in place of wood, of which latter there was none to be had. They burn with a bright warm flame, much the same as Irish peat. We passed through immense herds of buffaloes all day, but did not stop to kill any of them, being anxious to reach the river as soon as possible, as the mules had not been watered for twenty-four hours. Soon after dark we saw a fire ahead, which we supposed was the camp of a party of Indians, but when we drew near we found it to be the down mail from Santa Fé, a single wagon in charge of four men. We halted a while to graze our wearied animals, but they refused to eat until a smart shower of rain had moistened the grass.

Soon after we arrived at the camp of the down mail a large herd of buffaloes came toward us on their way to water. We could hear them some distance by the rumbling noise they made, and when they appeared in view they resembled a great black cloud moving close to the earth. Two of us sallied out, rifle in hand, hoping to be able to bag one of them, and laid ourselves down in a ravine near which we knew they must pass. They came slowly toward us in a great moving mass, fairly making the earth tremble with their tread, and the leader now and then stopping to snuff the air, as if apprehensive of danger. They were almost within rifle-shot, when they became alarmed at a noise in our camp, and turned and scampered off as rapidly as possible. This evening the wolves came around us in great numbers, and kept up a most dismal howling the while. They and the buffalo are sworn enemies, and have many fierce encounters. They chase the herds in droves and singly until they run some one of them down, which they hamstring, and afterward dispatch at pleasure. The oldest bulls sometimes fall a prey to them in this manner, and the bones of their victims lie scattered over the Plains. When the cows are attacked, the bulls, like gallant fellows, come to their rescue; and they farther exhibit their devotion to the gentler sex by forming a ring around them in time of a storm to shelter them as much as possible from its severity.

We resumed the drive at half past eleven o'clock at night, with twelve miles before us to the Arkansas, the first point at which we could reach water. The night was dark as pitch, and before we had driven a mile the mules refused to go faster than a walk through sheer fatigue, and neither whipping nor coaxing would induce them to hasten their speed. After traveling a few miles along the beaten road we turned to the left, hoping to reach the water by a shorter route through the hills, Captain Reynolds and myself leading the teams on foot. We followed the buffalo-paths, as we knew these animals always reached the water by the most direct route. The moon and stars had now come out, and the night was beautiful and clear. We followed down a narrow valley inclosed on either side by a ridge of broken hills. Several times we saw ahead what all supposed to be water, but as we approached it vanished into air, and turned out to be no more than the *mirage* of the Plains, which had oft before deceived the weary traveler. Thus we trudged along several weary miles, hoping every moment to see the stream, when the fatigue of the day would come to an end. At length, when man and beast were well-nigh worn down, the sparkling Arkansas was seen directly in front, and but a few hundred yards distant. The mules at once snuffed the water and increased their pace, and in a few minutes we were on the banks of the shining river, now about three o'clock in the morning. The thirsty animals could hardly restrain their impatience to be in the stream until they were unharnessed ; and, when once free, they rushed pell-mell into the water, and drank long and deep. We arranged our little camp without ceremony, and were soon in sweet repose amid the high prairie grass.

We did not leave camp until ten o'clock the next day, and then continued our journey up the east bank of the Arkansas. The river here is not more than three hundred yards wide, with low banks, and filled with numerous beds of sand. The water is very shallow, clear, and pleasant to the taste, but in regard to navigation there is no hope of its ever being able to bear upon its bosom a larger craft than an Indian canoe. As you ascend the river the banks become more broken, as a general thing the ridges following the course of the stream. We passed old Fort Atkinson, now in ruins, and halted a few miles beyond to dine. During the preparations for dinner each man seemed metamorphosed into a cook, ready and willing to lend his aid. 'Tis said "many cooks spoil the broth," but the quality of the victuals that day gave the lie direct to the old adage, for the soup was never more palatable, and the fried buffalo-meat was delicious. The cooking scene around the fire was amusing. Here one was seen with a large potato on the end of a stick, which he was roasting in the ashes, and there another with a slice of buffalo-meat broiling upon the coals, while a third was stirring the soup and adding the condiments. The gallant, poetical captain gave his entire attention to a buffalo-steak which he was broiling upon a piece of old iron he had found at the fort. The meal was truly a joint-stock concern, and each one helped himself according to his inclination. Flap-jacks were in the bill of fare to-day for the first time, and the maker received praise enough to satisfy any reasonable mortal. We saw a number of buffaloes during the day, but they had too much good sense to come within range of our rifles. We encamped that night at the middle crossing among the sand-hills.

We forded the river the next morning opposite our camp-ground, and stopped on the other side for breakfast. There were herds of buffaloes and antelopes grazing near, but we did not succeed in killing any of them. A large number of the former came down to the river to cross over about the time we encamped, but, becoming alarmed at our presence, they scampered off to the sand-hills, and a few only succeeded in getting across. The antelope is a most beautiful and graceful little animal, and, when running across the plains, has almost the appearance of a thing of air. We gave chase to a large herd, but they soon placed themselves far beyond the reach of danger. Here the road leaves the river and strikes off toward the southwest, with a stretch of nearly sixty miles without water.

We left camp at ten, and resumed our journey after filling our water-kegs and jugs from the river. For about four miles the road gradually ascends among the low sand-hills, when we strike the *Jornada*, a stretch of nearly fifty miles of dead level, without a tree, or bush, or hill to break the evenness of the surface, and covered with buffalo-grass. We dined near the spot where Colonel Cook disarmed the Texans a few years ago, which one of the passengers christened the Jornada Hotel. We made a night-drive of twenty-five miles, and encamped upon the open plains. The next morning we drove to Sand Creek for breakfast, completing the passage of the Jornada in fifteen driving hours.

To day our friend the padre complained of being *mui enfermo* in his *cabeza*, which means, in plain English, that the poor fellow had the head-ache. As a traveling companion we found him much more agreeable than many who understand our language and manners better. He greatly improved upon acquaintance, and his good qualities, which were gradually developed, more than overbalanced his eccentricities ; and in all things we left a wide margin, because he was a stranger in a strange land. He was generous to a fault, and appeared to have in his heart an abundance of that desirable fluid the world calls the milk of human kindness. He was a man of learning and extensive travel, having been five years a missionary in the Holy Land, and had passed much time among the Arabs, whose language he spoke with fluency. Though he and I were far asunder in matters of religion, I could but have some respect for the faith he professes, and for which he sacrifices all the charms of life, and buries himself from the world in the middle of the continent. We may speak about the tenets of the Romish Church, but we must unite in giving the priesthood credit for great self-denial, and a meek forbearance with all the trials that beset them in their lonely path through life.

CHAPTER II.

TRIP ACROSS THE PLAINS—*Concluded.*

Camp at Sand Creek.—First Buffalo killed.—Cimmarron River.—Indian Fright.—Padre and his Pistols.—Mishap.—Country.—Stranger's Grave. — Flap-jacks. — Prairie Dogs : their Habits — Appearance. — Rock Creek. — Geological Formation.—Buffalo Hunters.—Murder of Mrs. White. — Mountains in View. — Murder of a Mail Party.—Fort Union.—Las Vegas.—Tecalota. — Old Pecos.—Ruins of Pueblo.—Cañon.—Arrival at Santa Fé.

THE reader left us, at the close of the last chapter, encamped at Sand Creek for breakfast. Here we shot and made captive our first buffalo. As we were sitting around our camp-fire, discussing the remains of our morning's meal, five buffaloes were seen approaching a small pool of water a little way in front. Booth seized his rifle as soon as he saw them coming toward us, and, stealing along the edge of the pond until he obtained a good position, waited for them to come up. They advanced with stately dignity, ignorant that an enemy was concealed so near. They were led, some yards in advance, by a noble-looking old bull, who had probably piloted the herd across the Plains for many years. When they had approached within a hundred yards, Booth fired, and struck the leader under the fore shoulder. He wheeled around and staggered, but did not fall; then braced himself, and turned his head with an angry look in the direction whence the shot came. The others trotted off a few yards, but soon returned and took their stand beside their wounded companion. Booth, in the mean time, remained lying close to the ground where he had fired, while the buffaloes kept looking in that direction, and seemed disposed to keep their position until they had discovered their enemy. Seeing our companion in rather a dangerous situation, three of us sallied out from camp, rifle in hand, to raise the siege and relieve him. We ran along the edge of the pond toward the place of concealment, and when within a hundred yards of the animals we opened a fire upon them. Captain R. struck the wounded buffalo in the fore leg, and brought him to the ground, while my ball took effect under the fore shoulder of one of the others. The latter did not fall, but with his three comrades moved slowly off, stopping now and then to look back at the fallen bull. I pursued them some distance, but not being able to get within rifle-shot again, returned to the place where the wounded animal had fallen. He was not yet dead, and we fired three more balls into him before he yielded up the ghost, when we fell upon him with our knives, and cut out the choicest pieces, leaving the balance to the vultures and wolves.

The same afternoon we drove fifteen miles to the Cimmarron, or Lost River, where we halted for dinner. The only evidence of a river to be seen was the dry bed of the stream which wound before us across the Plain. In some parts there is running water in the old channel, while in other places it sinks into the sand, and does not make its appearance for some miles. The storms upon the Cimmarron are terrific, and apparently as much dreaded as were the "fierce Bermotha" that Shakspeare wrote about in times of yore. Sometimes the hail comes down as large as hens' eggs, and the wind blows with the fury of a West India hurricane. The mail-men had often spoken of the fierce storms we might expect upon the Lost River, and we were therefore rejoiced to see it for the first time beneath a clear sky.

While we were waiting dinner, our little camp was startled by the cry, " Look at the Indians !" when, casting our eyes toward the west, we saw what we supposed to be a party of some thirty savages just rising a swell in the prairie. The anticipations of dinner were at an end for the present, and all hands stood to their arms. Then there was "mustering in hot haste"—all was bustle and confusion. Each man was putting himself upon a war footing : one was hallooing, "Where is my rifle ?" another asking for his six-shooter; while a third was crying out, " I have lost my knife." Our friend the padre was a good deal alarmed, and some of his actions were quite amusing. When the alarm was first given he ran for the baggage-wagon and called for his box, which was at the bottom of the load. We did not know but that he was after a crucifix to confess the whole party, and therefore one of the men got the box and placed it before him. He opened it, and took therefrom a pair of old shoes, in which were stowed away a brace of pocket pistols about six inches long. His weapons were duly loaded, and the man of peace was prepared to stand upon the defensive. The arms being placed in order, we next caught up the mules and hitched them to the wagons ; and I venture to say that the same number of animals were never harnessed in quicker time, nor the dinner fixings cleared away with less ceremony. About the time we were ready to drive on, we discovered the supposed Indians to be a party of teamsters on their return to the States, having conducted a train of wagons to Santa Fé. Of course we were a good deal relieved to find that the imaginary foes were friends, but for the time being they answered the purpose of bona fide Indians, and caused us a genuine alarm.

After a few minutes' chat with the strangers we resumed the road and drove to the " Barrels," where we

halted for the night. A short time before we reached
camp one of the hind wheels of the passenger wagon ran
off, and let one side of the body down. At first we
thought something serious had happened; but, upon examination, we found there was no other damage done
than a skeen drawn out and a linch-pin lost, and in a
short time we were in running order again. The padre
considered himself beneath an unlucky star, inasmuch as
all the accidents to the wagon happened on his side.
After the turn-over in Coon Creek he made his boy Carlos change seats with him, believing his was the unfortunate side of the wagon; but now, as the wheel ran off
on the side to which he had changed, he fully believed
that misfortune followed him. We reached camp at a
late hour, when, turning the animals out to graze, we
cooked a hasty supper and lay down to sleep, some in
the wagons and some upon the Plains.

The country along the Cimmarron is very sandy.
Wood is scarce, and the only water to be had for a great
distance is found in stagnant pools in the old bed of the
river. The following day we drove some fifty miles, and
encamped in the evening at a place that bears no name.
We breakfasted and supped upon buffalo-meat, and many
thanks were given to the cook for the savory dishes.
The night was cold and frosty, and sleeping upon the
ground was very uncomfortable. We continued the next
day through the same barren country, and again struck
the Cimmarron. We dined at a place known as the
" Stranger's Grave." Here lie the remains of some
poor fellow, who probably died on his way home after a
long absence. The grave is near the road, and a plain
board has been erected by some friendly hand to mark
the spot where the stranger sleeps. Upon one side the
letters "J. M.," and upon the other the name of " Isam
B. Monson" have been cut into the wood. What a lone-

ly place for the last resting-place of a human being! In the afternoon we passed the spot known as "Mule Head." It is a modern Golgotha, and marks the place where a hundred and twenty mules perished in one night a few years ago. The bleached bones are piled up by the side of the road. We are now beyond the region of buffaloes, and are passing through herds of antelopes, which skim the Plains upon all sides of us. The night was cold and damp, and when I arose in the morning my bedding was dripping with water. The poor chambermaid was again blessed—" over the left"—for not shaking up the feathers, which seemed to have become knotty for want of use.

We harnessed up early, and drove sixteen miles to breakfast, to Cedar Spring. The padre made himself useful to-day, and in a manner that was pleasing to the whole party. We had flap-jacks for breakfast, and the cook had tried in vain to turn them without the aid of a knife. Our priestly friend watched with attention, and, seeing him at fault, came to his assistance. He understood the operation well, having probably been taught the same in some lonely cell in the Holy Land, and turned them with ease, making them perform sundry gyrations in the air before they struck the pan again. Ever after, when the pan and batter were brought into requisition, they were turned over to him, with the polite request that he would make himself useful, and his kindness of heart never permitted him to refuse. As we looked westward to-day, we could see away in the distance, like fleecy clouds hanging in the atmosphere, the faint outlines of what proved to be the Mesa Mayor, the first of a succession of table-lands we were approaching. At dinner one of the mail-men seriously shocked the feelings of our spiritual friend by asking him if the Pope had a wife. The question was asked with such a sober countenance that the padre was at a loss to determine whether it was done in jest or earnest; but he replied good-humoredly that "the Pope never marries," with a look that implied that he was imparting knowledge to an ignorant heretic.

We were now traveling through the region inhabited by the "prairie dog," and the whole country seemed one continued village. They are a curious and interesting little animal, and deserve a passing notice. For miles the Plains are dotted with the piles of dirt before their holes, which resemble large ant-hills. They dig a deep hole in the ground, four or six inches in diameter, and carry up the dirt and place it in a heap at the mouth in the shape of a cone, and about a foot high. Their holes are unequal distances apart, and are arranged without order. It is said by some that they live on friendly terms with the owl and rattlesnake, but, from the best information I could obtain of their manners and habits, I do not think such is the case. It is quite amusing to see the little canine citizens manœuvre when a party of strangers invade their dominions. In the first place you will observe some of the little fellows, in various parts of the settlement, putting their heads out of their holes and peeping over the sand-hills in front to see what is going on. Next they venture all the way out, and sit on their hind legs upon the top of the sand-hills in order to obtain a better view of matters and things. After having made a satisfactory reconnaissance, you will see them running in different directions as though giving intelligence through the village. They skip from hole to hole with great agility; soon the whole population is aroused, and "heads out" seems to be the order of the day.

Those that first discerned your approach seem to have been sentinels, stationed to sound the alarm to the main body. Now the town is aroused, and every able-bodied

citizen comes out of his hole to be prepared for any
emergency that may arise. As you approach nearer
their activity increases, and frequent communication is
held between different quarters of the town. Now you
notice three or four in close conclave, as if holding council upon the affairs of the nation, at the end of which
they separate, each one returning to his own home. Now
you observe a single dog run across to his neighbor, hold
a moment's confab with him, and then skip back again.
In another part of the village you will see them assembled in grand council, in considerable numbers, apparently holding a solemn debate upon the state of public affairs. They are formed in a circle, each one sitting erect
upon his hind legs, and in the middle is seated a grave
old patriarch, who has the required wisdom to preside
over and direct their deliberations. Apparently some
important question has been discussed and decided, for,
when they adjourn, messengers are seen hastening to all
parts of the town to announce the result. Thus the little rascals keep up their operations until you draw very
near, when every fellow disappears in his hole, and you
see nothing more of them while you remain in the village. In point of size they resemble a common gray
squirrel, and look not unlike that little animal with the
ears cut off and the tail bobbed. They are seldom caught,
and will not even leave their holes when water is poured
in upon them. We dined at M'Nese's Creek, named
from an old hunter who was killed there by the Indians
a few years ago, and slept at Cotton Wood, twelve miles
beyond.

The next day we made Round Mound, and encamped
upon the open plain. It began to rain soon after we left
camp in the morning, and continued all day and night.
We halted on the Rabatier Creek for breakfast, fourteen
miles from where we had slept the night before, and

while eating we sought shelter under a ledge of overhanging rocks from the pelting of the storm. We remained at this point until three o'clock in the afternoon,
when we harnessed up and drove on. The rain came
down in torrents while we ate dinner, and our humble
camp-fire did but little toward keeping us warm and
dry. Our night drive was exceedingly unpleasant; it
was as dark as pitch, the roads were deep with mud,
and the rain still came down with great violence. As
usual, I made my bed upon the ground, and when I
awoke in the morning I found myself almost submerged
in water.

The camp was astir early the next morning, but we
did not leave until about eight o'clock. We breakfasted
at Rock Creek, the rain holding up while we ate. The
geological formation of the rocks along the stream is
rather interesting. The banks are abrupt, and in many
places perpendicular. The rocks were originally formed
by deposition in water, and the strata can yet be distinctly traced, as though they had been laid by a stone-
mason. The layers have not been disturbed from their
horizontal position, and the attrition of water in times of
freshets has worn many of the softer stones away, and
left the harder ones projecting over the bed of the stream.
The formation appears to have been subjected to the action of fire at a subsequent period, as it bears evidence
of having undergone intense heat. Many of the rocks
are partially crumbled, and in places they are almost a
blood red, caused by the action of the atmosphere upon
the chemicals in their composition. In places they exhibit seams and ridges upon their flat surface, probably
caused by a softer overlying stone having been reduced
to a liquid state, portions of which remained and became
hardened.

Soon after we encamped the advance of a large party

of Mexican buffalo-hunters came in, and stopped just above us upon the stream. All told, they numbered a hundred and fifty men, near five hundred animals, and some fifty carts. They were upon their annual buffalo-hunt, which they make each fall, when they remain upon the Plains six weeks or two months. They dry the meat in the camp, and sell it when they return to the settlements. They made as mottled and uncivilized an appearance as can well be imagined; no two wore the same costume, and, upon the whole, they looked not unlike a party of gipsies migrating to some new field of action. They showed their friendly feeling by offering us *aguardiente* to drink, as barbarous an alcoholic compound as ever was made, and gave us a few loaves of bread, of Taos flour, dark and coarse, but sweet.

The rain set in again soon after we were under way in the afternoon, and continued nearly all night. We had traveled but a few miles when it became dark, and, as the storm increased, we concluded to halt and encamp until morning. The mules were picketed near the wagons, and also well blanketed to keep them from freezing; but the rain came down in such torrents that it was out of the question to cook. We all passed the night in the wagons, as it was too wet to lie out: some dozed upright on their seats, while others had the privilege of lying down. I was one of the perpendicular snoozers; and to keep the rain from beating in the wagon, I hung an India-rubber cloth up in front. The night seemed of an interminable length, and we were all greatly rejoiced when the morning broke, and showed a clear sky looking down upon us.

During the travel of yesterday, between Whetstone Branch and Rock Creek, we passed the spot where a small party of Americans were killed, a few years before, by the Jicarilla Apache Indians. Mr. White had been a merchant in Santa Fé, and was now returning to New Mexico with his family, in company with the train of Mr. Aubrey. All danger was considered at an end when they arrived at this point in the road, and Mr. White and family left the train and started on ahead. His party consisted of himself, wife, and child, a German named Lawberger, and an American whose name is not known, a Mexican, and a negro servant. There is a difference of opinion as to the manner of attack, but I was informed by Major John Greiner, then Indian agent at Santa Fé, that the following relation of the affair was made to him some time afterward by the Jicarilla chief Chacow. While the Americans were in camp, a small party of Indians came up and demanded presents. These Mr. White refused to give them, and drove them out of camp; they returned shortly, and were again treated in the same manner. This time they did not go away, but commenced an attack upon the party by shooting the negro and Mexican, the latter falling upon the fire. The others made an attempt to escape, but were all killed except Mrs. White and child, who were made prisoners. The dead bodies were then laid beside the road, but were neither scalped nor stripped. A short time afterward a party of Mexicans came along and began to plunder the wagon, when the Indians, who had concealed themselves, fired upon them and wounded a boy, who was left for dead. He laid still until the Indians had left, when he got up and started toward the settlements, with an arrow sticking between the bones of his arm. He came up with a party of Americans the same day, and got in in safety. The Indians who committed the outrage are said to have been a party on their return from the South; that they struck the trail a short distance east of the place where the attack was made, which the main body followed, while a few were sent back to watch the train.

When the affair was known in Santa Fé, a company
of dragoons, with Kit Carson as guide, were sent in pursuit.   They struck the trail, and followed it for three or
four days, when they came up with and attacked the Indians.   They succeeded in killing several of the savages,
but during the fight the latter murdered both Mrs. White
and her child.   Several of the women and children of
the Indians perished in a severe snow-storm that came
on.   The troops came nigh sharing the same fate, but
their guide, who was well acquainted with the country,
conducted them to timber, where they obtained shelter
from the storm and wood to keep them warm.

The morning of the twentieth was clear and cold, and
the mountains within sight were covered with snow.
We drove to the Point of Rocks to breakfast, dined ten
miles beyond, and encamped for the night on the west
bank of the Canadian Fork of the Arkansas.   To-day we
crossed the first of the series of mesas that terminate the
western boundary of the Plains, and came within range
of the mountainous regions.   Captain Reynolds and myself walked two miles across this beautiful stretch of table-land.   The road ascends in a winding course until
the plateau is reached, when it runs away toward the
west in nearly a straight line.   When fairly upon the
mesa, we halted to admire the prospect that opened before us.   The country is almost as level as a floor for
miles in every direction.   A rim of mountains, broken
and serrated, but not high, bounds it in the distance on
three sides, while toward the east you look upon the
boundless plain stretching away until the earth and sky
appear to meet.   At that elevation, near seven thousand feet above the level of the sea, the sky shone as
bright and clear as crystal, and there seemed hardly a
limit to the vision.   The rarity of the atmosphere sensibly affected our respiration, and the least exertion cre-

ated an unpleasant sensation upon the lungs. After crossing the mesa, we entered upon a more rolling country,
and followed the winding course of the valleys to the river.

The last few miles of the road was wet and muddy,
and we did not reach the crossing of the river until
nearly midnight. The stream is narrow but rapid, and
the banks steep and rather difficult of descent. The
crossing was in bad repair, but we made the passage
without accident. The place of camping was damp and
soft from recent rains, but, as there was no choice of
lodgings to one who had an outside ticket, I threw myself upon the wet ground, and soundly slept away the
fatigues of the day.

When we awoke in the morning the ground was white
with a heavy frost. We breakfasted at the Ocaté, where
we consumed the last of our rations except a little ham
and coffee, and halted at four in the afternoon to graze
the animals. There was no wood to be obtained, and we
were obliged to fast for the remainder of the day. The
mules were grazed upon the grass that abounded; and
one of the passengers remarked that the landlord of the
hotel was liable in damages because he did not furnish
entertainment for man as well as beast. The road was
bad, and we made but little progress.

Near this point is the Wagon Mound, in the vicinity
of which the United States mail-party was cut off by
the Indians in the winter of 1850. They were en route
from Fort Leavenworth to Santa Fé, and were ten in number, all of whom were killed, together with their mules,
and the wagon rifled of its contents. From information
afterward obtained, it was the combined work of a party
of Apache and Utah Indians. The first attack was made
in the morning, and the fight lasted all day, without
much damage being done, only a man or two wounded.
This was by the Apaches alone. In the evening they

were joined by a party of Utahs, who told them they did not know how to fight Americans, but that they would show them. The attack was renewed the next morning, when the combined force of Indians rushed upon and overpowered them after a short resistance. The final struggle took place at a pass between the hills, where the savages had every advantage. When intelligence of the fight reached Santa Fé, a party of soldiers were sent out to bury the dead. Two men were found dead in the wagon, having probably been wounded early in the engagement, and placed there by their companions, where they were afterward killed. The mules, and the remainder of the party, were lying dead near by. The men had been shot with arrows, and the animals with balls. The former were partly stripped, but none were scalped. A great quantity of arrows covered the ground, and the mail matter was scattered round about.

We encamped for the night in a little wet valley, and again lay down to sleep, supperless, and without fire. We were astir early the next morning, and got under way in good season. The distance from this point to Fort Union is ten miles, and the remainder of our journey to that post lay mostly through the mountain valleys. In a drive of five miles we came to a region of snow, which lay three or four inches deep upon the ground. As we crossed the ridge some three miles distant, the fort came into view, which at first sight appeared like a cluster of dark spots upon the white surface, close to the foot of a range of mountains. As we drew nearer we could distinctly see the quarters of officers and men; soon the flash of the sentinels' muskets caught the eye, and objects could be distinctly seen moving about. We reached the fort about eleven o'clock, and were landed at the suttler's store, that being the post-office.

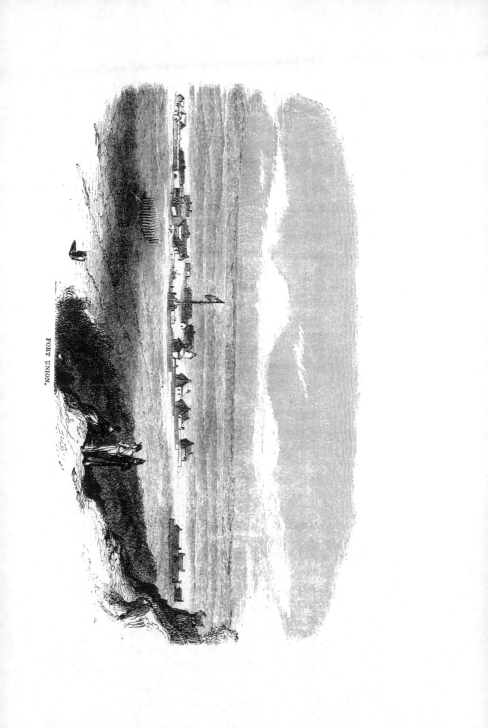

FORT UNION.

Fort Union, a hundred and ten miles from Santa Fé, is situated in the pleasant valley of the Moro. It is an open post, without either stockades or breastworks of any kind, and, barring the officers and soldiers who are seen about, it has much more the appearance of a quiet frontier village than that of a military station. It is laid out with broad and straight streets crossing each other at right angles. The huts are built of pine logs, obtained from the neighboring mountains, and the quarters of both officers and men wore a neat and comfortable appearance. I had the pleasure of making the acquaintance of several of the officers, and among others Lieutenant-colonel Cook, of the dragoons, commanding the post. I dined at the hospitable board of Colonel Cook, and, after having eaten but one meal for the past forty-eight hours, the reader will readily believe that I did full justice to the repast.

We left the fort about three in the afternoon, and drove two miles beyond Barclay's Fort, where we encamped for the night. This is a private trading-post, and was built during the war with Mexico. It is a large adobe establishment, and, like the immense caravansaries of the East, serves as an abode for men and animals. From the outside it presents rather a formidable as well as a neat appearance, being pierced with loop-holes and ornamented with battlements. The rooms within were damp and uncomfortable, and all the surroundings looked so gloomy, the hour being twilight, that it reminded me of some old state prison where the good and great of former times have languished away their lives. As we were now in a country abounding with wood, and no danger to be apprehended from the Indians, we built up a large fire at our place of camping, and slept with some degree of comfort.

The next morning we drove to Las Vegas to break-

fast, sixteen miles. About midway between our camp
and this place we crossed a ridge that is called the Grand
Divide, separating the waters that flow east into the
Mississippi from those that flow west into the Rio del
Norte. The country around is diversified with hill and
dale, but there lacked the appliances of civilized life to
make the landscape pleasing to the sight. Las Vegas
is a dirty mud town of some seven hundred inhabitants;
many of the houses were in ruins, and most of the others
wore an exceedingly uncomfortable appearance. We
halted our teams in the Plaza, but which more resembled
a muddy field than a public square, and all sorts of four-
footed domestic animals were roaming at large over it.
We made a sumptuous meal on fried ham, bread and
molasses, eggs, goats' milk, etc. A few Americans were
living here, who seemed to control the trade of the place.
In company with Padre Donato I paid a visit to the an-
tiquated mud church, which looked as though it had
stood the wear and tear of more years than was likely
to be meted out to it in the future. It stands upon the
Plaza, and over the entrance hangs an old cracked bell,
the tones of which fell in doleful sounds upon the ear.
The form is that of a cross, with a damp earthen floor,
and void of seats, or other accommodations for worshipers. In the nave is the altar, with a few rude and primitive decorations, and in the rear of it are three daubs
of paintings, one of which is intended to represent Christ
nailed to the cross; while a rough image of the Virgin
Mary stood in the north transept. The old man in attendance showed us the sacred vestments of the priests;
and as he laid article after article before us, and explained their respective use, a smile of proud satisfaction appeared to light up his countenance.

Our next drive was to the Mexican village of Tecalota.
As we leave Las Vegas the road ascends slightly, but

soon descends again to a narrow valley, which we follow some four miles, when we suddenly turn to the right and pass a mountain ridge through a deep cañon. On the right of the valley, a chain of serrated hills, rather than mountains, run from northeast to southwest, while on the left the country is more open, and a few miles to the east lie the open prairies. The ridge appears to have been cloven asunder by some great convulsion of nature, and a beautiful road made through it wide enough for four wagons to pass abreast. The sides of the cañon are formed of immense masses of rocks nearly perpendicular. The original formation was deposition in water, but there has been a subsequent upheaval, as well as a subjection to intense heat, which has displaced the strata, which now lie at an angle of about 45°, with the dip toward the east. The ridge exhibits no other vegetation than a growth of scrubby pine-trees, and a few blades of grass starting up among the rocks. Passing the cañon we entered another narrow valley, wedged in between opposite hills, down which we traveled for some miles. Just within the cañon a clear spring bubbles forth from the side of a sand-bank, at which I quenched my thirst, as no more water was to be found for some distance.

It was near two o'clock in the afternoon when we reached Tecalota, where we halted long enough to feed the animals and dine. This place looks enough like Las Vegas to be a twin sister, and has a population of some five hundred, living in miserable mud houses. As we drove into the town, a lad was in the belfry of the old mud church, tolling the bell for the death of one of the inhabitants, which he effected by striking the clapper against the opposite sides of the bell with the hand. Here a teacher of the Methodist Church had just located, and was about to open a school for the instruction of the

rising generation. I crossed the Plaza to his room for a
few moments, and listened with pleasure to the recital
of his bright anticipations for the future. May God
smile upon all his labors, and may his hopes never grow
dim! Mr. Moore, an accommodating and intelligent
American, is located here, who appears to be pushing
business with the usual energy of our countrymen,
wherever found. We encamped for the night at Bernal
Spring, six miles beyond, at the intersection of the Independence and Fort Smith roads. The country between these two points is mountainous, and mostly covered with a scrubby growth of pine. The water of the
spring is strongly impregnated with carbonate of soda,
and both unpleasant to the taste and unhealthy. Almost overlooking our camp rises up a mountain peak
high above all its fellows. The sides slope gradually
until within a few hundred feet of the top, when they
become perpendicular, and rise up like walls of masonry,
showing the natural layers of stone with perfect distinct-
ness. We procured eggs and onions from a small hamlet near by, and tried to buy milk, but the goats were
abroad, and cows they had not.

We drove fourteen miles the next morning before day-
light, and halted for breakfast near the little village of
San José. In the route we crossed the Pecos River, a
beautiful stream, and abounding in trout. While we
were eating, a Mexican and his boy came to our camp
with a few articles to sell, and as they were both cold
and hungry, we shared with them our food and fire, and
sent them away with well-filled stomachs. We dined
at old Pecos on a fine sheep which one of the mail-men
was fortunate enough to purchase. Within a short distance of our camp are the remains of the old Indian
pueblo of Pecos ; and while the men were harnessing up
the mules, I started across to examine the ruins. The

church was roofless, and altarless, and fast going to decay. It is in the form of a cross, built of adobes, with
the main entrance looking toward the southwest; it is
of much more recent construction than the rest of the
ruins, and was undoubtedly built by the Spaniards after
the Indians had been converted to Christianity. All
the wood-work about the building showed conclusive
evidence that it had been fashioned by Europeans. Just
in the rear of the church, and covering the slope of
the hill for two or three hundred yards, are the ruins
of the village. Large blocks of stone, some oblong and
others square, and weighing a ton and upward, lie about
upon the surface of the ground, some of which show
signs of having been laid in mortar. While I was ex-
amining the ruins the wagons left camp and started on,
and I was subjected to a run of about half a mile before
I overtook them. That afternoon we drove ten miles
farther, and encamped for the night at *El Boca del
Cañon*—the mouth of the cañon. This cañon is another
pass through the mountains, and appears to have been
formed by Nature expressly for a wagon road. It is
about three miles in length, and in many places is only
wide enough for one wagon; the sides are formed of
ledges of rocks, in some parts two or three hundred feet
high, and almost perpendicular. The place of our camp
was at the western terminus of the cañon, and near where
the Mexicans took up their position to oppose the march
of the American troops under General Kearney in 1846.

We congratulated ourselves that this was the last
night before reaching Santa Fé, and were quite rejoiced
that our long journey was so nearly terminated. The
cañon serves as a great funnel, and at all seasons of the
year a current of air draws through it from west to east.
We left camp next morning at eight o'clock, and drove
to the Arroyo Hondo for breakfast, where we remained

long enough to graze the animals. We had now six
miles to travel, and after we had resumed the road we
drove along leisurely through a hilly and barren country
covered with pine-trees. We had gone about two miles
of the distance when from the top of a hill we saw before us in a valley the long-looked-for Santa Fé, the terminus of our travels for the present, and in a short time
we were within the limits of the city of the Holy Faith
of Saint Francis.

CHAPTER III.

HISTORICAL SKETCH OF NEW MEXICO.

Country little known.—Situation.—First Knowledge of Spaniards.—
Bacá and Companions.—Their Adventures.—Negro goes to Cibola.
—Nizza.—Coronado's Expedition.—Arrives at Cibola.—Tignex.—
Cicuyé.—Querechos.—Quivira.—Fate of Expedition.—People of the
Country.—Route of Coronado.—Situation of Cibola.—Espejo.—His
Description of the People.—Oñate colonizes the Country.—His Peti-
tion and Grants.—Treatment of Natives.—Rebellion of 1680.—Popé.
—Santa Fé taken.—Retreat of Spaniards.—Otermin attempts a Re-
conquest.—Fails.—Bargas.—Revolution quelled and Peace restored.

THERE is no country protected by our flag and subject to our laws so little known to the people of the
United States as the territory of New Mexico. Its very
position precludes an intimate intercourse with other sections of the Union, and serves to lock up a knowledge
of the country within its own limits. The natural features differ widely from the rest of the Union ; and the
inhabitants, with the manners and customs of their Moorish and Castilian ancestors, are both new and strange to
our people. For these reasons, reliable information of
this hitherto almost unknown region can not fail to be
interesting to the public.

This territory occupies that central region of North
America lying between the rivers Arkansas on the east
and the Colorado on the west, and is bounded by Texas
and Mexico on the south, and Utah and Kansas on the
north, and contains an area of two hundred and seven
thousand square miles. It was obtained from Mexico
under the treaty of Guadalupe de Hidalgo, with the exception of a narrow strip along the southern border, pur-

chased under the late Gadsden treaty. The physical formation is a type of the whole of that extensive region known as the Great American Central Basin, whose distinguishing features are extensive and arid elevated plains, lofty and barren mountains, and narrow valleys along the water-courses. The middle portion is drained by the Rio del Norte and its branches, and the other principal streams are the eastern tributaries of the Colorado, and some of the western tributaries of the Arkansas. A continuation of the great rocky chain runs through the eastern part of the territory, and numerous isolated peaks and spurs are found in other sections. A large portion shows very evident traces of recent volcanic action, and in many places the surface is seamed and cut up by immense ravines and cañons.

It is not my intention to write a history of New Mexico in this volume, but merely to give the reader, in the present and the next succeeding chapter, a sketch of the leading historical incidents that have transpired in the course of more than three hundred years, since its first discovery and exploration by the Spaniards.

The first knowledge the Spaniards of Southern Mexico had of this country was about the year 1530, when it was known as the country of the seven cities. At that time Nuño de Guzman, the governor of New Spain, had in his employ an Indian, said to be a native of the province of Tejas, who gave him information of an extensive and rich country to the north, of which he related the most marvelous accounts. He said that his father had formerly traded there as a merchant, and that the country abounded in the precious metals, and contained seven large and beautiful cities. Guzman was so much interested in the account of the Indian that he immediately organized an expedition for the exploration of this new region. The adventurers marched from the city of Mexico to Culiacan, but they encountered so many hardships by the time they had reached that point that they abandoned the enterprise and returned home. The governor remained in Culiacan and colonized the country.

About the year 1538 the Spaniards received further information of the country of the seven cities from Alvar Nuñes Cabeza de Baca, who, with three companions, arrived in Culiacan, and were the first Europeans who passed through the country. They were the survivors of the unfortunate expedition of Pamfilio Narvaez, who sailed from San Domingo the eleventh day of April, 1528, for the conquest of Florida. They landed in safety and proceeded some distance inland, leaving instructions for the fleet to follow along the coast, and to await their coming at some safe and convenient harbor. Instead of obeying these instructions the vessels sailed for Habaná, and left Narvaez and his companions to their fate. The adventurers returned to the coast after a brief absence, but neither finding the vessels nor hearing any thing of them, they constructed boats in which they intended coasting along the gulf to the River Pacuno, whence they hoped to be able to reach the Spanish settlements in Mexico. They converted their stirrups, spurs, and every other piece of metal into saws, nails, &c.; they cut up and sewed together their shirts for sails, and made cordage of the tails and manes of their horses; and they killed their horses, and dried the flesh for provisions for the voyage. Thus equipped, they launched their frail barks upon the almost unknown waters of the gulf. They coasted in safety beyond the mouth of the Mississippi, when they encountered a furious storm, which wrecked some of the boats, and drove others out to sea, which were never heard of afterward. The boat commanded by Baca was thrown upon a low, sandy island near the shore, whence he and his companions were fortunate enough to

reach the main land.   Of those who escaped drowning,
all were killed by the savages except Baca, two other
Spaniards, and an Arab negro.

The survivors directed their course toward the interi-
or, and, after wandering about the country for several
years, they reached the Spanish settlement of Culiacan,
in New Galicia, on the eastern shore of the Gulf of California.   Their route across the continent can not be
traced with accuracy at the present day.   They are supposed to have been wrecked on one of the low, sandy
islands that skirt the coast of Louisiana or Texas, and
to have pursued a northwesterly course until they reached the plains frequented by the buffalo, on some of the
western tributaries of the Arkansas, whence they took a
southwest direction toward the frontier settlements of
New Spain.   Coronado, in his subsequent expedition
through the country, visited a point where Baca and his
companions had probably passed, being told by the Indians that a small party of white men had been there
some time before, who had blessed their buffalo-skins.

The relation of their adventures by Baca and his companions created a deep interest among the Spaniards in
Mexico, and raised a desire to penetrate these unknown
regions, as well to seek adventure as to possess the country for the crown of Spain.   In order to obtain a better
knowledge of the country, Vasquez Coronado, at that
time Governor of New Galicia, sent three monks, with
the Arab negro who had accompanied Baca, in the direction where the country of the seven cities was said to
lie.   The negro went in advance of the monks, and crossed the desert to Cibola in company with a party of friendly Indians.   He was kindly received, and treated in the
best possible manner; but, presuming upon their mild
disposition, he began to make very unreasonable demands
upon them.   His conduct finally became so bad that they

were obliged to place him in confinement. They held a council over him, and resolved to put him to death—fearing he intended to do them some great harm—which they carried into execution. Some of the Indians who accompanied him were detained as prisoners, while the remainder were set at liberty, and directed to return to their own country. On their way back the Indians met the three monks in the desert, to whom they related all that had happened to them and the negro in Cibola. This alarmed the monks so much that they hastened back with all possible speed to inform the governor of the result of their explorations. Among the monks was one named Marcos de Nizza, a shrewd and unscrupulous man, who gave Coronado a most exaggerated account of what they had seen and heard, representing the country as rich and populous. This account inflamed anew the minds of the Spaniards, as it more than confirmed the marvelous stories told of it previously. Coronado desired to explore the country in person, and for that purpose requested and obtained permission of Mendoza, the viceroy, to organize and lead an expedition thither.

In a short time an army of three hundred Spaniards, horse and foot, composed of the adventurous cavaliers of the times, and eight hundred friendly Indians, was raised for the expedition and duly organized, the whole being placed under the command of Coronado, with the title of captain general. The troops assembled at a place called Compostella, whence they marched to Culiacan, where they arrived the day after Easter, in the year 1540. After remaining here a few days to complete their arrangements, they resumed their march for Cibola, driving along with them one hundred and fifty head of European cows and a large number of sheep for the support of the troops, and also to assist in the colonization of the country.

Coronado, with an escort of sixty men under the command of one Jaramillo, and accompanied by the monk Nizza as guide, set off in advance of the main army. They took a northwest direction, nearly parallel with the shore of the Gulf of California, and at the end of thirty-eight days they came to the edge of a desert bordered by a chain of mountains. They crossed the mountains, and entered upon the desert, over which they marched for thirteen days in a course a little to the east of north, crossing several rivers on the way, at the end of which time they reached the first village of what was called the country of the Cibola. The villages were six in number, situated in a valley six leagues long, and the houses were three and four stories high, built of mud and stones, with terraces running around them. The whole province was subjugated. From this place Coronado continued his march to a neighboring province called Tignex, a few leagues to the northeast. Here he was soon afterward joined by the main army, when they went into winter quarters, and remained there until the following spring. The winter was a very severe one; snow lay upon the ground three and four feet deep, and the river which ran by the town was frozen so that horses could cross upon the ice. When the main army reached Tignex, the inhabitants were in a state of rebellion, caused by the heavy tribute Coronado had levied upon the province, and the bad treatment their women received from the Spaniards. The arrival of the additional force enabled the general to subdue them in a short time, when their villages were captured, and a large number massacred and made prisoners.

When the spring opened they resumed the march, but not before the neighboring provinces had been brought to submission. The army left Tignex on the twenty-fifth day of May for the province of Cicuyé, twenty-five leagues distant to the northeast. They reached Cicuyé without accident, and the inhabitants immediately made terms with the Spaniards, and remained peaceable. Here they encountered a large and deep river, which detained them several days to build a bridge before they could cross over. Thence they continued their march in a direction northeast for six or seven days, when they came to the buffalo-plains, where these animals abounded in great numbers. Here they met with a race of people different from any they had before seen—they were called Querechos—who inhabited lodges made of the skin of the buffalo, and lived upon the flesh. They had a great number of large dogs, which they obliged to carry their baggage when they moved from place to place. These people appeared friendly, and offered no resistance to the Spaniards. From this point Coronado ordered the main body of the army to return to Tignex, while he continued on some distance farther to the north with a small escort. In his march he saw another tribe of natives distinct from the Querechos—they were called Teyas—who made their home in the valley of the Tignex, and frequented the plains to hunt buffaloes. They were also friendly, and furnished guides to the main army, by which means they were enabled to reach Tignex, on their return, by a much shorter route than the one by which they had marched to the plains.

When Coronado marched from Tignex in the spring, it was with the intention of visiting the country of Quivira, which had been represented as abounding in gold and silver, and where was situated a beautiful city with broad streets, and houses three and four stories high; but he was deceived by his guide, and conducted out upon the plains. He obtained a new guide from some of the roving tribes, who professed to be acquainted with Quivira, and determined to march that way on his return to Tignex. After the main army had taken up their march, himself and escort placed themselves under the direction of the Indian guide, and started for Quivira; but when he arrived in that country he found things very different from what they had been represented. There was neither gold nor silver, nor a magnificent city. The country was without interest, with only a few small villages, and the inhabitants differed in no particular from those they had already seen. Being greatly disappointed in not finding gold and other riches, he returned thence to Tignex, where the whole army spent the winter of 1541 and 1542.

It was the intention of Coronado to renew his explorations in the following spring, and penetrate farther into the country of which the Indians had spoken so much and given such flattering accounts, but several causes operated to prevent an expedition of the kind. Soon after they went into winter quarters he was severely hurt by a fall from his horse, which confined him to his bed for some weeks, during which time the discipline of his troops had, in a measure, been relaxed, and they became discontented. He was also becoming home-sick. He had left behind him a young and lovely wife, and great wealth; and having been sadly disappointed in not finding the rich and populous countries he had expected to discover, he began to pine to return home. The dissatisfaction among the officers and men increased as their hardships multiplied, and they desired to be led back to the pleasant valleys of New Galicia. A council of war was held to determine what should be done under the circumstances, and it was thought best to evacuate the country, which they carried into effect as soon as spring opened, when they returned to Culiacan. The returning adventurers were received without favor by the viceroy, and the conduct of Coronado was so highly censured that he was deprived of his government, thereby lost his reputation, and died in obscurity.

An account of this expedition to the Cibola country was afterward written by one Castañeda, who accompanied it, in which he gives an interesting description of the country they passed through, with the manners and customs of the inhabitants. The villages were all built on the same plan, and consisted of one or more blocks of houses in the form of a parallelogram, and were from two to four stories in height, with terraces. There were no doors on the ground floor, but they were entered several feet above, by means of ladders, which the inhabitants pulled up after them and secured. The ascent was made in this manner from one terrace to another, there being no internal communication between the stories. Some of the houses had balconies of wood, and opened upon an interior court, which added to their strength in time of an attack. The houses were large, and some of them could accommodate three and four hundred persons. They were built of mud, made hard by drying in the sun, and for lime they made use of a mixture of ashes, earth, and coal. In each village there were well-constructed baths, the males and females using separate ones. Some of them were built with considerable taste, the roof being supported with large wooden pillars and the floor paved with stone. In each village was also an *estufa*, built under ground, and which was used for both political and religious purposes. They assembled here to discuss all the affairs of state, and for all other matters of grave deliberation. Their sacred fires were kept burning within the *estufa*, and were never allowed to go out.

In their manners the inhabitants were mild and amiable, and, when not molested, always received the Spaniards kindly. Their customs were extremely simple. The men dressed in cotton cloth and tanned skins, which was the dress of the women in some of the provinces, while in others they went naked winter and summer. Their food consisted mainly of maize, beans, and pumpkins, and they also manufactured bread from the berry of the mesquit tree. In some of the valleys the soil is said to have been so rich that it was not necessary to break up the ground before sowing the seed, and that the produce of one year was sufficient for the consumption of seven years. They raised cotton, from which they made much of their own clothing. They were armed with bows and arrows, clubs and bucklers, which were their weapons of war. They manufactured a great quantity of pottery, which they glazed in a very neat manner with some shining metal; they also made ornamental vases, beautiful in finish and curious in form. The villages were governed by a council of old men, and by the *caciques* and renowned warriors. The people were comely in person, and intelligent.

The route of Coronado can be traced with much greater accuracy than the previous trip of Baca and his companions across the continent. Leaving Culiacan on the river of the same name in the Mexican state of Sinaloa, they marched about parallel with the Gulf of California, passing through what is now the State of Sonora, until they arrived nearly at the head of the gulf, when they changed their course toward the northeast. They continued in this direction, and are supposed to have struck the Gila River near the present ruins known as *Casas Grandes*, as Castañeda mentions, in his journal, that just before they entered the desert they passed a large ruin called Chichilticali; and the barren region which leads to the point where I locate Cibola begins on the north side of the Gila. Leaving these ruins, they crossed this desert, and reached the country of the seven cities, or

Cibola, in a march of thirteen days. Thence they continued their march to Tignex and Cicuyé, and so on until they arrived upon the plains where they encountered buffaloes.

There has been much speculation in reference to the situation of the Cibola country, some locating it where are now found the seven villages of the Moquis, and others in a still different region of country; but after a careful investigation of the subject, with the aid of some old manuscript documents found in the archives in Santa Fé, I believe the valley of Zuñi to have been the true location of Cibola. In giving an account of the march of the Spaniards in 1540, Castañeda mentions that a few miles before they arrived at the first village, which bore the name of the province, they came to a small river, which, on account of the reddish hue of the water, they called Rio Bermajo. The present pueblo of Zuñi is on the north side of the Rio Colorado Chiquito (Little Red River), which name was probably given to it on account of the color of the water. He also describes the village as being situated upon a high rock, which was the case with the old pueblo, and the distance of it from the river is about that mentioned by the Spaniards, while the new village is immediately upon the bank of the stream. Zuñi is northeast of the point where they are supposed to have crossed the Gila, with several hundred miles of barren country intervening; and it is the first Indian village, or the ruins thereof, to my knowledge, to be met with after you pass that river coming northeast. He also speaks of the province of Tusayan, twenty-five leagues from Cibola, and on the route to the great cañon of the Rio Colorado; from which province they took a guide, and marched in a westerly course to the cañon. Placing Cibola in the valley of Zuñi, it makes the location of Tusayan, both as to direction and distance, agree

with that of Moqui of the present day; and there are no
other two localities in the whole territory that stand so
nearly in the relation to the great cañon as that described by Castañeda. Among the records of the early
explorations of New Mexico by the Spaniards that fell
into my hands in Santa Fé was the manuscript journal
of Captain General Don Domingo Jeronso Petriz de Cruzate, who marched into the country in 1688 for the purpose of reducing the Indians to subjection. He mentions, among other things, that in the time of Philip the
Second of Spain, Zuñi was known as the Buffalo Province.* Now, as Philip was upon the throne within
twenty years after the expedition of Coronado, and some
of the men were still living who engaged in it, and that
before his death other Spaniards visited the Cibola country, which was afterward named Zuñi, I think the evidence in favor of the latter province being the Cibola of
Castañeda is quite conclusive. This location of Cibola
aids us much in tracing the further course of Coronado,
and also throws additional light upon an interesting point
in history.

A party of Coronado's men, as before mentioned, visited, toward the west, a large river that flowed through
a fissure in the rocks which was so deep that from the
top the stream appeared like a thread of silver. This
was undoubtedly the cañon of the Rio Colorado, which
is looked upon as one of the most remarkable things in
nature, and which, on account of its great depth and
steepness of the sides, has never been descended to the
water. The province of Tignex was most probably situated in the valley of the Puerco, as this is the first river
you come to traveling northeast from Zuñi, and answers
very well to the description given of the river of Tignex,

* The word cibola means buffalo, and is undoubtedly of Indian instead of Spanish origin.

which ran in front of the village of that name. The banks are said to have been high and steep, and the current rapid, and that before it emptied into the Cicuyé the river disappeared. The Puerco is a stream of this character, and at certain seasons of the year it sinks into the sand before it reaches the mouth, and afterward appears again. It empties into the Rio del Norte some hundred and fifty miles below Santa Fé. The river the natives called Cicuyé, and which the Spaniards were obliged to bridge before they could cross it, was, I believe, the Rio del Norte. Castañeda mentions that, six or seven days after leaving the river, they reached the plains where the buffalo abounded, which would be about the time required, at their rate of marching, to reach the plains east of the Canadian River from the crossing of the Del Norte any where in the latitude of Santa Fé. But we have further confirmation. The village of Jemez is mentioned as having been visited by the Spaniards, and that before they reached the Cicuyé, in going east from Tignex, they crossed another smaller stream and a range of mountains. The River Santa Ana lies between the Puerco and the Jemez Mountains, which must be the smaller river referred to; and this chain of mountains lies between the River Santa Ana and the Rio del Norte, and from the position the Spaniards were in when in the valley where Jemez is situated, they could not reach the River Cicuyé (Del Norte) without crossing that river and chain of mountains. On his return from the plains, Coronado must have passed by the salt lakes near Manzana, which answer tolerably well to the location of those mentioned in the journal of Castañeda. After leaving Quivira, they continued toward the west to the River Cicuyé, which they struck about a hundred miles south of the point where they had crossed it going east. They followed up the river until they reached the

province of Cicuyé, whence they proceeded to Tignex
and joined the main army.

The exact location of the Quivira mentioned by Castañeda has never been satisfactorily determined, and the
question is still one of speculation. There are to be
seen, some distance south of the salt lakes mentioned,
the ruins of a village now called Quivira, which has been
in its present condition since the memory of the oldest
inhabitant of the country. The ruins of a large church
and convent are still in a good state of preservation, but
they are evidently the work of white men, from the style
of building and material, and the carving found upon the
beams. They are probably the remains of an early
Spanish mission, or the ruins of a pueblo where a priest
was stationed after the Europeans took possession of
the country, and which was abandoned by the Indians
during some of the early wars between them and the
Spaniards, and the village allowed to go to ruins. The
Mexicans have traditions among them concerning Quivira, but they partake so much of romance that they are
not worthy of narration.

After the unsuccessful expedition of Coronado, it was
some years before another attempt was made to explore
and take possession of New Mexico. During this time
a few friars, who always formed the vanguard in the discoveries and explorations in Spanish America, penetrated
the country, and made an effort to Christianize and civ-
ilize the Indians. In the reign of Philip the Second of
Spain, a Franciscan friar, named Marcos de Niza or Nizza, with a few companions, penetrated the country as far
as the province of Zuñi, which I have already located as
the ancient country of Cibola. This priest is said to
have been a native of New Mexico, and may have been
a son of the same friar Marcos de Nizza heretofore mentioned, who, it will be recollected, attempted to reach

Cibola with the Arab negro, and afterward accompanied the expedition of Coronado. The first arrival of Niza and his people caused much surprise among the natives, who were astonished at seeing white men, and at first thought them to be gods, and respected them as such. But after their surprise had worn off a cruel war broke out, in which most of the priests were killed, a few only making their escape to the pueblos of El Paso. Among those who escaped was a friar, who went to Mexico, and carried with him an image of Our Lady of Macana, which was preserved for a long time in the convent of that city. The precise time of this outbreak I have not been able to determine from the data in my possession, but suppose it to have been about the year 1580, or shortly afterward, as I have evidence that a Franciscan missionary, named Augustin Ruiz, entered the country in the year 1581, and was murdered by the natives, a victim of his own religious zeal. The Viceroy of Mexico, hearing of the new discoveries made in the country, and the progress of the missionaries, sent one Don Antonio Espejo into the territory with men and provisions to protect and supply the missions. After his arrival there was an outbreak among the natives, which compelled him to send for a re-enforcement of troops to defend the settlers and found new presidios, which were accordingly furnished him.

Espejo gives an interesting account of the country; and I have translated the following extract from De Larenaudière's History of Mexico:

"The people were somewhat advanced toward civilization, with many manners and customs similar to those of the Aztec. Many of the men and women wore long gowns of cotton, tastefully painted, and some had coats of cloth colored with blue and white, similar to the manner of the Chinese. They were adorned with feathers of different colors.   One of the chiefs gave him four thousand bolls of cotton.   One of the tribes, called Jumanes, painted the face, arms, and legs in ridiculous figures. Their arms were great bows, with arrows terminated with sharp-pointed stones, very hard, and wooden swords armed on both sides with sharp-cutting stones, similar to the swords of the Aztecs.   The latter they use with great dexterity, and could cut a man's body in two at a single blow.   Their shields were covered with untanned bullhide.   Some of the nations lived in houses of stone four stories high, and walls very thick to keep out the cold of winter.   Others slept under tents during the heat of summer, or lived in them all the year.   There were found villages where luxury and comforts were noted. The houses were whitewashed, and the walls covered with pictures.   The inhabitants used rich mantles with similar pictures, and subsisted on good flesh and cornbread.   Other tribes were somewhat more savage: they covered themselves with skins of animals, the product of the chase, and the flesh of the mountain bull was their principal food.   Those nearest to the banks of the Del Norte, whose fields appeared well cultivated, obeyed chiefs whose orders were announced by public criers. In the pueblos of all the Indians were seen a multitude of idols, and in each house there was a chapel dedicated to the genius of mischief.   They represented, by means of pictures, the sun, moon, and stars as principal objects of their worship.   When they saw the Spanish horses for the first time they were no less astonished than the Mexicans, and were on the point of worshiping them as superior beings.   They subsisted them in their most beautiful houses, and entreated them to accept the best they had.   There were found in that great region abundant harvests of corn, flax similar to that of Europe, vines loaded with grapes, and beautiful forests filled with buffaloes, deer, stags, and every species of game."

These flattering accounts of the province received from Espejo determined the Viceroy of Mexico to take permanent possession of, and colonize the country. For that purpose he sent a new supply of provisions and a re-enforcement of troops to Espejo, under the command of Don Juan de Oñate, toward the close of the sixteenth century.* Oñate was a native of Zacatecas, and appears to have been a man of some note in his day. He conceived the idea of planting Spanish colonies in New Mexico; but whether he moved in the matter before or after he conducted the re-enforcements for the protection of the missions I have not been able to determine. For this purpose he presented a petition, dated September 21st, 1595, to the Viceroy of New Spain, asking permission to colonize the country. He pledged himself to introduce into the country two hundred soldiers, horses, cattle, merchandise, and agricultural implements. As a remuneration for these services he demanded large grants of land; the ennobling of his family; a considerable loan of money, a fat salary, and to be furnished with arms and ammunition; besides the permission to reduce the natives to obedience, which meant to make slaves of them. He also stipulated that the government should supply the colony with "six priests, with a full complement of books, ornaments, and church accoutrements." The petition was granted, with the exception of some of his most extravagant demands, and in accordance therewith he introduced the colony into the country. The decree of the King of Spain, Philip the Third, is dated the

* There is a discrepance in the records as to the time that Oñate arrived in New Mexico. Padre Frejes, in his history of the conquest of the country, published in Mexico in 1830, states that Oñate arrived there in the year 1595; Mariana mentions that he set out from Mexico in 1598; while De Larenaudière, in his History of Mexico, published in Barcelona in 1844, states that he took possession of the country the last year of the sixteenth century—1599.

eighth day of July, 1602, and, among other things, specifies that himself and his descendants shall hold and enjoy the rank of hidalgos. Five years were granted him to make the conquest of the country; but if he should die in that time, or before he should have finished the conquest, his descendants were authorized to complete the same with its colonization.

For three quarters of a century after the first permanent settlements were made, I have not been able to obtain any reliable history of the operations of the Spaniards. Several villages and missions were established, principally in the valley of the Del Norte; and the settlers turned their attention to the cultivation of the soil and the means of living, while the priests occupied themselves in converting the natives to Christianity. The first mission is said to have been established at a place called El Teguayo, and up to the year 1608 as many as eight thousand Indians had been baptized. All the territory conquered from the natives was united in one province, and was at first called New Granada, but afterward the name of New Mexico was given to it. In the year 1611 Oñate made an expedition of exploration toward the east, and discovered the Cannibal Lakes, and also a red river which was called the River of the Cadaudachos, or that of the Palisade. The situation of these lakes is not known at the present day, but the river spoken of is probably the Canadian fork of the Arkansas; and the name Palisade was given to it because of the deep rocky fissure it flows through, in some parts of its course, and which they must have seen.

The Spaniards entered the country by the way of El Paso del Norte, and thence extended their settlements up the valley of the river toward the north. They were at first well received by the simple-minded inhabitants, for they were of an amiable disposition, and averse to war; but when they found that the strangers desired to reduce them to a state of slavery, they rose in rebellion, and fierce and bloody wars were waged for several years before they were finally subdued.   With that inordinate thirst for gold that marked the Spanish pioneer in all parts of the New World, those of New Mexico soon neglected agriculture and turned their attention to mining. Many valuable mines of gold and silver were discovered, and worked with considerable profit.   The Indians were compelled to labor in the mines, where, year after year, they dragged out a life more miserable than they had ever before experienced.   This bad treatment sunk deep into the hearts of these people, and from generous friends it turned them into bitter enemies.

The natives had other cause of complaint.   It has always been the policy of the Spanish government to change the religion as well as the political institutions of every people whom they conquer.   In accordance with this rule of action, as soon as Oñate had established himself in the country, he ordered the Indians to give up the faith of their fathers, to which they were deeply attached, and embrace that of himself and his followers— Catholicism.   This was a compliance cruel in the extreme, but force obliged them to submit; and in a short time they saw their ancient rites prohibited, their temples of worship closed, and their heathen gods destroyed.   They could not understand the religion of the white man, and considered it a great hardship to be obliged to profess what they did not believe.   This, united with the physical sufferings they were compelled to endure in the mines, was more than they could bear, which caused wide-spread discontent, and made them ripe for rebellion. They made several attempts at revolt, but the watchful care of the Spaniards prevented any of them being carried into effect until the year 1680, when success, for a time, crowned their efforts.

In the latter year, a deliverer from the yoke of their hard task-masters came in one of their own number. An able and eloquent Indian, said to have belonged to the pueblo of Taos, named Popé, planned a general rising against the Spaniards, and united all the villages in its execution.* He pretended the gift of supernatural powers, and made his simple-minded brethren believe that the devil had ordered all the whites in the country to be massacred. He was obliged to resort to great secrecy and much cunning to elude the vigilance of the Spaniards, but he was fully equal to the occasion. He communicated with distant pueblos by means of knots tied in a rope made of the fibres of the palm-tree, which was carried from village to village by their fleetest runners. All their arrangements were made without exciting the suspicion of the Spaniards, and they were so fearful of betrayal that not a woman was admitted into their confidence. The time fixed upon for the rising was the tenth day of August, 1680, when an indiscriminate slaughter was to be made of all the Spaniards in the country.

Their secret, through treachery, became known to the authorities two days before the time agreed upon. Two of the San Juan Indians divulged the whole plan to Governor Otermin, and thus placed him upon his guard. As soon as the rebels knew that their conspiracy had been exposed, they immediately flew to arms, fearing further delay would endanger all. The authorities took every possible means to place themselves in a posture of defense. The Spaniards in the north were ordered to repair at once to Santa Fé, and place themselves under the orders of the governor, while those in the south were

---

* It is said that the pueblos of San Juan and Pozos remained faithful to the Spaniards, for which the former was afterward styled San Juan de los Caballeros, or San Juan of the Gentlemen.

directed to rendezvous at Isleta. The capital was fortified, and all the inhabitants retired from the suburbs to
the Plaza. The Indians did not delay the commence-
ment of hostilities, but immediately marched upon Santa
Fé, putting to death all the Spaniards that were not able
to make their escape. On the thirteenth, a large body
of savages were seen approaching the town, which they
surrounded and placed in a state of siege. They yelled
defiance to the Spaniards; they said that the God of the
Christian was dead, but that their god, the sun and
moon, never died, and that they only awaited the coming
of their confederates to commence the work of extermi-
nation.

The governor and authorities were alarmed, and endeavored to conciliate the savages. Messengers were
sent out with offers of peace and the promise of kind
treatment in the future; but the Indians treated all their
overtures with contempt, and refused to make any terms.
They told the messengers that they had brought with
them two crosses, one painted red, which signified war,
and the other white, which signified peace; that they
might have their choice, but if they should select the one
that indicated peace, it must be upon condition that they
retire immediately from the country. The Indians saw
a day of deliverance and retribution for nearly a century
of grievous wrongs at hand, and they were not willing to
place themselves again in the power of their cruel masters. Governor Otermin declined to accede to the con-
ditions they imposed, but determined to attack them, and,
if possible, defeat them before they received re-enforcements. He sallied out with his troops early in the morning, and made an impetuous assault upon the enemy,
who received him with great bravery. The battle continued all day, with considerable loss on both sides,
when, toward nightfall, their allies, the Teguas and oth-

er tribes, were seen approaching the town, which induced the Spaniards to cease the combat and retire within their fortifications.

The Indians were now in great force, and closely invested the place, shutting the garrison and inhabitants within their earthen defenses. The siege had continued nine days, and much suffering been caused among the Spaniards; the enemy had cut off the supply of water, and their provisions were also becoming scarce. In the night the garrison made a sortie from the town, cut their way through the enemy, and caused them to fall back a little distance, partially raising the siege. The Spaniards the next day held a council of war, composed of the military and principal citizens, to determine what course they had better pursue under the circumstances. There was no hope of succor from below, nor a probability of their being able to withstand the repeated assaults of their numerous enemy: they therefore deemed it to be their duty to retreat to El Paso del Norte, and leave the capital to its fate. They therefore made the necessary arrangements to evacuate the place as soon as possible, which they carried into effect on the twenty-first of the month, and took up the line of march for the south. The inhabitants followed the army on foot, and carried most of their baggage on their backs. Their sufferings on the march were very great, and it was with difficulty they could procure food enough to eat. As they advanced through the country they found the pueblos deserted and the farms laid waste, but no enemy opposed their march. They reached San Lorenzo, near El Paso, in the latter part of September, completely broken down by the hardships they had endured.

As the Spaniards evacuated Santa Fé, the savages watched them closely from a little distance, but they did not attempt to molest them, probably rejoiced that they were getting rid of them with so little trouble. When they had disappeared, the enemy entered and took possession of the place. They held great rejoicings in honor of the victory, accompanied with many of the rites of their heathen worship. They assembled in the Plaza, where they danced the *Cachina*, their favorite idolatrous dance, and paid adoration to the devil as the supreme object of their reverence. The country being now freed from the Spaniards, the Indians every where re-established their ancient religious rites. The Christian churches, and the articles used in the Catholic worship, were destroyed, and the priests were either driven away or killed. Estufas were erected in every pueblo, and all their ancient customs, both civil and religious, were again placed in full force. They endeavored, as much as possible, to obliterate every trace of their Spanish conquerors, and in every respect sunk back into all the idolatrous practices of their heathen ancestors.*

Governor Otermin reported the rebellion in New Mexico to the viceroy, and asked for a re-enforcement to reconquer the country. The desired aid was furnished, but was tardy in arriving; and it was not until the month of November of the following year, 1681, that he was able to take the field against the enemy. He took

---

* It is said that the priest stationed at Zuñi neither was killed nor fled, but saved himself by abjuring his faith and turning Indian. That when the Spaniards went there at the time of the reconquest, about the year 1690, they inquired for the *Padre*, who answered in person that he was there; but, being dressed and painted like an Indian, they failed to recognize him, and asked him if he could write. He answered that he could, but had no paper. The Spaniards then passed up to him upon the rocky height where the pueblo then was situated a skin, upon which he made letters with charcoal. This satisfied them of his identity, when they demanded and received a surrender of the place. This is the tradition of the Indians, but is not correct, as I find, by an examination of the manuscript record of the times, that the Zuñians killed their priest at the time of the rebellion.

up his march from El Paso on the eighth of the month, with a force of several hundred men, composed of Spaniards and friendly Indians. They continued up the valley of the Rio del Norte without meeting with any serious resistance until he arrived at the pueblo of Isleta, where he found a body of some three thousand Indians assembled to oppose his farther advance. By this time his provisions had nearly all been consumed; the greater number of his animals were dead, and the weather was cold and the snow deep. He was surrounded by a numerous and savage foe, and was without the hope of assistance in this most trying emergency. Under these circumstances, a council of war was held and a retreat determined upon, and the army retired to El Paso, followed and harassed on their march by the Indians.

Soon afterward Otermin was removed from office, and the reconquest of the country was intrusted to Don Diego de Bargas Zapata, who was appointed the governor and commandant of the province. The contest was continued, with varied success, for several years, the Indians making a determined resistance. In the year 1693, Bargas entered the country with a strong force, and, attacking pueblo after pueblo, finally whipped them into submission. Several thousand Indians had assembled in and around Santa Fé, which they made their headquarters. He advanced against them with his whole army, and after an obstinate battle, which continued the whole day, he drove them from the place, and entered and took possession of it. The Indians every where sued for peace, and for the time being seemed completely subdued. In the year 1698 another revolution broke out, but, as it was only participated in by a few of the pueblos, it was soon put down by the energy of Bargas, and without much bloodshed, and thus the reconquest was rendered complete.

CHAPTER IV.

HISTORICAL SKETCH OF NEW MEXICO—*Concluded.*

Result of Rebellion of 1680.—Interval of Peace.—War with Camanches.—Conspiracy of 1814.—Nabajos killed at Jemez.—Expulsion Law.—Revolution of 1837.—The Cause of it.—Plan of Rebels.
—Authorities defeated.—Death of Governor Perez.—Cruel Conduct
of Indians.—Rebel Governor.—General Armijo.—General Kearney
marches for New Mexico.—Country conquered.—Revolution of 1847.
—The Leaders and their Plans.—First Conspiracy discovered.—The
People taking up Arms.—Revolution put down.—Territory organized.—Organic Law.—Mexican Courts.—Baston de Justicia.—Fueros.—Will New Mexico become a Slave State?—History of State
Government in New Mexico.

THE result of the Indian rebellion of 1680 taught the
Spanish government a useful lesson, and which it had
the good sense to profit by. It became evident that the
natives must be treated with greater leniency, which
course was finally adopted when the authorities saw
there was no other alternative. Although they were, as
formerly, compelled to embrace the Catholic religion,
yet in other respects the yoke of the conqueror was
rendered more easy; they were better secured in their
social rights, the grants of land were confirmed to the
pueblos, and they were not compelled to undergo the
same severe labor in the mines as before. But while this
state of things had a tendency to neutralize their hostility, it by no means rendered them entirely contented
with the Spaniards as masters.

After the re-establishment of the Spanish power in
New Mexico, a period of nearly a hundred and fifty
years rolled away without any serious disturbance be-

tween the two races. Now and then the murmurs of
an approaching storm were heard in the distance, but
by good management on the part of the government the
troubled waters were quieted from time to time, and the
apparent friendly relations were not disturbed.

While peace was maintained with the Pueblo Indians,
there was hostility between the Spaniards and some of
the wild tribes living in and around the territory almost
up to the time the country fell into the hands of the
Americans. Among others, the Camanches, one of the
most warlike and numerous of the neighboring tribes,
kept up a desperate war upon the country from the reconquest of Diego de Bargas up to near the close of the
eighteenth century. During this time several severe
battles were fought between them, among which may be
mentioned the action of Green Horn, about the middle
of the last century, and that of *El Rito Don Carlos*,
which took place in 1783. The last and most desperate
action was fought at Rabbit Ear in 1785. The Camanches were on their return from an expedition against
the village of Tomé, in Valencia county, and had met in
grand council for the purpose of having a war-dance
over the scalps they had taken. They had also obtained
a large amount of booty, and made prisoners two sisters
of the name of Pino. The territorial troops, numbering
two hundred and fifty men, commanded by Lieutenant
Guerrero, made an attack upon the Indians while they
were assembled in council. The Camanches kept up
the fight for three hours, when they were forced to retire, with the loss of a large number in killed and wounded, with all their spoils, the captives, and their animals.
The Indians drew off to a short distance and held a
council of war, after which they renewed the fight, when
they retook their own horses and compelled the troops
to retreat. The loss of the Camanches in these two ac-

tions was so great that they sued for peace soon after, when a treaty was made with them, which they have kept up to the present time, with the exception of an occasional slight depredation.

In the year 1814, a rebellion against the authority of Don Aberto Maynes, then governor of the province, was put on foot by Corporal Antonio Armijo and Dionicio Valdez. The conspiracy was discovered before they had time to arrange and establish well all their plans, and they were arrested, tried, and sentenced to ten years' imprisonment at Ensinillas (known as the Trias farm, twenty-five miles northwest of Chihuahua).

In 1815, a soldier of the name of Cora stole a few articles from the public store-house at Santa Fé, then under the charge of the paymaster of the place, Lieutenant Don Valentino Moreno. He was arrested, tried, and sentenced to be shot, and, notwithstanding some of the most influential persons of the province interceded in his behalf, the sentence was carried into execution. This is given as an evidence of the iron rule that prevailed in those days in the country. No influence was able to shield the culprit from the punishment that had been awarded him, but the law, with all its rigor, was carried into effect; and even this species of tyranny was not wholly without a good influence upon the population of the country.

In the year 1820, a most cruel and brutal outrage was perpetrated upon a party of Nabajo Indians in the village of Jemez. They had been hostile, but at this time they came in for the purpose of making peace. After their arrival, having been received in a friendly manner by the inhabitants, the corporation of the village, headed by one Juan Antonio Baca, the alcalde, assembled in council and resolved to put them to death. For this purpose the people were collected, who fell upon the defenseless

Indians and killed them with clubs. A complaint of the outrage was made to the government, and the ringleaders were arrested and brought to trial; but the case was kept in court until 1824 without any decision being made upon it, when the parties were set at liberty. Ten years after, in 1834, these same men fell by the hands of the Nabajos, by which it almost appears that Divine Providence inflicted upon these murderers the punishment the authorities of the country had failed to mete out to them.

In 1826, while a large number of Utah and Jicarilla Apache Indians were assembled in the town of Don Fernandez de Taos, a Camanche warrior and two boys of the same tribe came into the Ranchos, a village within about three miles. When the Utahs and Apaches heard of the arrival of the latter, they demanded them of the authorities in order to put them to death. Upon this becoming known to the inhabitants, they opposed their being given up, and insisted upon their being protected. The Indians were very angry at the people because they opposed the surrender of the Camanche and boys, and told them that unless they were given up to them they would take them by force. This alarmed the alcalde, Juan Antonio Martines, and he resolved to surrender the warrior to appease the wrath of the savages; and to make his conduct more dastardly, he caused the gun of the Camanche to be discharged and loaded with dirt, thus depriving him of the means of self-defense. He was then turned over to his enemies, who fell upon him with great fury; he defended himself as well as he could with his bow and arrows, but was soon overpowered by numbers and put to death.

In order to rid the country of all native-born Spaniards, the Mexican Congress, in the year 1828, passed what is known as the Expulsion Law, which expelled all of this class of persons from the republic. There were at that time several Franciscan friars residing in the territory, who were subject to this decree, but two of them, Alvino and Castro, were excepted and permitted to remain, in consequence of their great age, and by paying each the sum of five hundred dollars. The motive was rather that of avarice than charity, and the officers in power violated the general laws of the country for the sake of money. This arrangement was brought about by the agency of a priest named Leyva, who obtained the money from the two friars, which is said to have gone into the pockets of Don Francisco Sarasino, then acting governor, and who is now living in the Rio Abajo, and Santiago Abreu, the chief justice of the territory. At that time anarchy and misrule prevailed throughout the country, and avarice had such a strong hold upon the officials that money would buy off almost any delinquent. In the case of the expulsion, the other Spaniards had not enough money to satisfy the demands of the authorities, and therefore the law was carried out against them to the very letter.

The next and only serious disturbance that has taken place in New Mexico since the revolution of 1680 was the rebellion of 1837, which for a time was crowned with complete success, and promised an entire change in the administration of the country. The rebellion broke out in August of that year, and resulted in the murder of Governor Perez and his executive officers. A combination of circumstances, among which is included the intrigue of a party in the territory who desired to ride into power regardless of the means, led to the outbreak. The first cause of discontent was created in 1835 by Santa Ana sending into the country a new governor, named Perez, a creature of his own, which caused great dissatisfaction among the people, as they had been accustomed to be ruled over by native governors. No open opposition was manifested, but the change of rulers gave the designing demagogues a pretext to prepare the minds of the people for what followed. The following year an event happened which gave a new stimulant to the leaders of the discontented spirits.

In the year 1836, the disbursing officers of the territory were charged with peculation, and were arrested and brought to trial. At that time there was a district court in the territory composed of Judges Nafere, Santiago Abreu, and Juan Estevan Pino, before which the case was brought for hearing; but Nafere and Abreu, being both accused as accomplices, were not permitted to sit upon the trial, and Pino alone composed the court. The disbursing officers were found guilty, but before sentence was passed upon them the case was removed from the court by Governor Perez. This arbitrary act caused great dissatisfaction throughout the territory, and greatly increased the opposition to the administration. During the suspension of the principal disbursing officer, his duties were discharged by General Manuel Armijo, and when the former was restored to his office, the latter returned to his residence in Albuquerque, but was full of discontent. He was much pleased with the office the short time that he held it, and he determined to possess himself of it again, if possible. He first attempted to get it by intrigue and bribery, but, failing in this, he changed his plans, which resulted favorably, being materially aided by circumstances which produced terrible consequences. He took into his confidence Juan Estevan Pino and Juan Rafael Ortiz, declared enemies to the administration, and who had the influence of wealth and standing in the territory. They took advantage of a favorable event which happened about this time, and which was the means of giving success to their operations.

In 1837 the Congress of Mexico passed a general tax law, which made it the duty of the governor to carry it into effect in New Mexico. As soon as this was known, the opposition took strong ground against it, and denounced it in the most violent terms. They represented the measure in the most objectionable manner possible, and, among other obnoxious features they said it contained was that of compelling husbands to pay a tax for the privilege of sleeping with their own wives; and they exhorted the people not to submit to such an unjust law. This appeal to a people who had never been accustomed to a tax of any kind, and too ignorant to inquire into the truth of the matter, served to arouse them to the highest pitch of exasperation against the government. The leaders dispatched secret agents into all parts of the country to excite the populace and induce them to resist the law, while they themselves matured their plans for the rebellion. The people of the northern part of the territory were the most active in their opposition, and the leaders had the promise of large assistance from the Pueblo Indians of that section. About the same time, the prefect of the northern district caused an alcalde to be imprisoned for some real or pretended misdemeanor in office by order of the governor. This brought matters to a crisis ; the alcalde was released by a mob, and the Indians and other malcontents flew to arms.

The revolutionary movement began about the first of August, and extended through several of the northern pueblos, and differed from all previous outbreaks in that it had the countenance and support of the disaffected portion of the Mexican population. The rebels made the village of La Cañada, twenty-five miles north of Santa Fé, the centre of their operations, where they placed on foot their active measures. Among the Indian villages which took part in the revolution were San Yldefonso, Rancho, Jacoma, Pojuaque, Cuyo, Monque, and Nambé. On the third day of August a large number of the malcontents assembled in La Cañada in order to organize their means of resistance, when they adopted the following as their "plan" of government, and which they caused to be published to the people.

"Viva, God and the nation, and the faith of Jesus Christ; for the principal points which we defend are the following:

"1st. To be with God and the nation, and the faith of Jesus Christ.

"2d. To defend our country until we spill every drop of our blood in order to obtain the victory we have in view.

"3d. Not to admit the departmental 'plan.'

"4th. Not to admit any tax.

"5th. Not to admit the disorder desired by those who are attempting to procure it.　God and the nation.*

"ENCAMPMENT.

"Santa Cruz de la Cañada, August 3d, 1837."

When news of these proceedings reached Santa Fé, the authorities were in great alarm, and took immediate steps to quell the insurrection.　The governor called upon the alcaldes to assemble the militia, but few of them showed any disposition to turn out.　Among those who took up arms to sustain the government were the warriors of the pueblos of Santa Domingo and San Juan, the latter of which, it will be remembered, remained faithful to the Spaniards in the general rebellion of 1680.

The governor hastily collected all his disposable

* The above "plan" is a true translation from an original manuscript copy in Spanish in possession of the author.

troops, and at their head marched from Santa Fé, on the seventh of August, to meet the enemy assembled at La Cañada. They encamped that night at Pojuaque, and the next day they encountered the rebels upon the mesa of San Yldefonso. When the government troops came in presence of the enemy, nearly all deserted to them, and the few that remained faithful to the governor were obliged to turn and flee with him. He returned to Santa Fé, where he arrived between two and three o'clock the same afternoon. He remained in the capital until ten o'clock the same night, when he left, with a few trusty followers, for the Rio Abajo. When the Indians had put the troops to flight, and saw the day was their own, they sent instructions to all the villages through which the fugitives would be obliged to pass to apprehend and put them to death, while they took up the march toward Santa Fé. That night the governor, in his flight, slept at the Alamo, and on the following day, the ninth, his farther retreat was stopped by some of the pueblos in the valley of the Del Norte. His party being routed, they separated and fled in different directions, each one bent upon saving himself. He returned toward Santa Fé on foot for greater security, having sent his saddle-horse forward by one of his followers. He reached the house of Don Salvador Martinez (one league below the town, on the road to Albuquerque), where he took refuge, and where the Indians, who were following upon his trail, overtook and killed him before sundown.

While the pulse of life was yet beating in his body they cut off his head, which they carried in triumph to the camp of the rebels, which was now established near *La Capilla de nuestra Senora del Rosario* (about five hundred yards west of the Plaza of Santa Fé). The same day the Indians captured and killed Don Jesus Maria Alaria, secretary of state, whom they took in his own house, stripped, and then lanced him to death; Don Ramon Abreu; Don Mariano Abreu; Lieutenant Hurtado and two soldiers, Escoto and Ortega. Don Santiago Abreu, former governor of the territory, was taken the same day near Los Cerillos, and carried to the pueblo of Santa Domingo, where he was kept in the stocks that night, and was killed the next day in the most cruel manner; they cut off his members one at a time, and shook them in his face, taunting him the while with the offenses of which he stood accused. The head of the governor was used as a foot-ball, and kicked around the camp of the rebels; and all the bodies of the slain were left exposed where they fell until some Christian hand gave them burial. Thus perished the most obnoxious and influential supporters of the administration, and for the time being all opposition to the rebellion was at an end.

On the tenth instant the rebel force entered and took possession of Santa Fé, when they repaired to the parish church and offered up thanks for the victory they had achieved. The same day they elected one of the boldest of their number, a Taos Indian named José Gonzales, governor, who was duly installed into office, and began the administration of public affairs. The property of the murdered officials was confiscated and distributed among the rebels, and of the effects of the late Governor Perez a large portion fell to the share of Gonzales. The same afternoon the insurgents left town and returned to their villages, the new governor and a few of his most confidential friends remaining. A general assembly, composed of the alcaldes and other leading men of the counties, was now called, which convened in the palace in Santa Fé on the twenty-seventh day of August, and proceeded to deliberate upon the condition of the country. One of their first legislative acts was the confirmation of the confiscation of the property of the late officials who had been killed, and which left some of their families destitute in the world.

At this stage of the proceedings General Armijo stepped forth upon the theatre of action, to play out the part he had commenced, and for which purpose he had to resort to more intrigue and bad faith. Having thus far contributed to the success of the rebellion, he now changed his tactics, and in order to secure for himself the supreme power of the country, which he had aimed at from the first, he projected a counter-revolution in the Rio Abajo, and marched to Santa Fé with a considerable body of troops. When Gonzales received information of the approach of the troops from below, he left the capital and retired to Rio Ariba, where there was still a considerable body of the rebels under arms in La Cañada and the neighboring pueblos. No sooner had Armijo reached Santa Fé than he glided into the vacant chair of state, and assumed the control of the government, causing himself to be proclaimed *Comandante General* of the province. He immediately dispatched a courier to the supreme government at the city of Mexico with an account of affairs, not forgetting to rate his own services at their full value. For the part he played and the treachery he exhibited to his co-conspirators he was subsequently confirmed in the office he had seized upon, which he maintained for eight years, ruling the country with a rod of iron.

In the mean time, the supreme government of Mexico took proper steps effectively to crush the rebellion. A re-enforcement of troops, numbering four hundred men, were sent up from Chihuahua and Zacatecas, who reached Santa Fé the beginning of the year 1838. The rebels, meanwhile, had been kept in a state of comparative peace by the authorities, under the pretext of desiring to treat with them, but the moment the new troops arrived, open hostilities were proclaimed against them. The whole force, under the command of General Armijo, marched against the rebels at La Cañada in the month of January, where they had again assembled in considerable numbers, when a battle ensued, which resulted in the entire defeat and route of the latter. The chief Gonzales and some of the other leading men of the rebellion fell into the hands of the authorities. General Armijo now played out the last act in this bloody drama. Having the supreme power in his own hands, he concluded to put out of the way those of his confederates whom he could not reward, and therefore ordered a court-martial for the trial of many of the persons who had aided him with money and arms, and had been instrumental in placing him at the head of affairs. This court sentenced to death Desiderio Montoya, Antonio Abed Montoya, the Alcalde Esquebel, and the late governor José Gonzales, and Armijo is said to have caused many others to be privately assassinated. He was much censured for his cruelty toward the Montoyas and Gonzales. Many persons of influence exerted themselves to procure a remittance of the sentence, but Armijo was deaf to every appeal on behalf of his former confederates. The only answer he made to these intercessions was, that the court had found them guilty, and that he had no authority to pardon them. They were shot within two hundred yards of the Plaza of Santa Fé, on the north side, in from the *garita*.

These briefly-narrated facts form the leading historical events of the country from the first explorations by the Spaniards down to the year 1846, when it was taken possession of by the United States troops, since which time it has formed a portion of our Union.

Soon after war was declared against Mexico in May,

1846, the government of the United States determined to organize an expedition for the conquest of the province of New Mexico. The troops, to be called the "Army of the West," were to assemble on the frontier of Missouri, and to be placed under the command of Colonel Stephen W. Kearney, of the first regiment of dragoons. A requisition was made upon Missouri for volunteers to compose this expedition, who were ordered to rendezvous at Fort Leavenworth, on the right bank of the Missouri River, twenty-two miles above the mouth of the Kansas. The citizens turned out with great promptitude, and in about a month the number called for were assembled at the fort, and being organized preparatory to the march. The whole force consisted of sixteen hundred and fifty-eight men, and sixteen pieces of cannon, being mainly composed of mounted volunteers.

The troops took up the line of march for Santa Fé on the sixteenth day of June. Their course lay across the almost boundless plains that stretch westward to the eastern slope of the Rocky Mountains, a distance of nearly a thousand miles. The little army was about fifty days making the march, and, on the eighteenth of August, they entered and took possession of Santa Fé without opposition. The enemy had assembled, in some considerable force, a few miles from the city to resist our troops, but they fled on their near approach without firing a shot, and the conquest was a bloodless one. Kearney took possession of the country in the name of the United States, and issued a proclamation to the people, assuring them that they would be protected in their persons, property, and religion, and that henceforth they would be considered American citizens. He immediately organized a form of territorial government, had a code of laws drafted to suit the wants of the people, and appointed suitable persons, Americans and Mexicans, to administer the same.   Many of the inhabitants took the oath of allegiance, swearing to support the Constitution of the United States.   Thus was a complete change made in the institutions of the country, and the people passed from the old to a new order of things without the shedding of a drop of blood.

Notwithstanding the people had apparently submitted with good grace to the rule of the Americans, and appeared to be well satisfied with the condition of things, there was much discontent among a portion of the population, who resolved not to give up the country without a struggle.   These were principally of the wealthy class, with the addition of a few unquiet spirits, who saw their dreams of ambition dashed to the ground should the Americans retain possession of the country, and incorporate it permanently into the Union.   These discontented ones soon began to mature their plans of rebellion, and, like Catiline and his co-conspirators, held meetings in retired places at the dead hour of night to plot the expulsion of their conquerors.   The two leading spirits in the enterprise were Tomas Ortiz and Diego Archuleta, men of talent and enterprise, and of great ambition, whom gambling and intemperance had rendered desperate.   They had the countenance and support of Manuel Chavez, Miguel E. Pino, Nicolas Pino, Pablo Dominguez, and Tomas Baca of Peña Blanca, all men of influence.   A number of the priests joined in the conspiracy, and some even preached rebellion in the pulpit.   The two who took the lead were the Vicar Juan Félipe Ortiz and Padre José Manuel Gallegos.   Priest Ortiz, upon pretense of going to the town of Jolla, in Rio Ariba, in order to celebrate the feast of Our Lady of Guadalupe, visited the upper country to excite the people to rebellion.   The same day that he left Santa Fé, Priest Gallegos arrived in town from Albuquerque, by agreement with the co-conspirators, to arrange their operations. Every thing was conducted with the most profound secrecy, and only a few of the leading men were made acquainted with their plans. The secret was not to be intrusted to a woman for fear it would be divulged.

The first meeting was held on the twelfth of December, 1846, and the nineteenth of the same month was fixed upon as the time of rising, which was to be general all over the Territory. All the Americans were to be either killed or driven from the country, as also those Mexicans who had accepted office under General Kearney. This accomplished, they were to seize upon the government and establish themselves in power. To each of the ringleaders a distinct duty was assigned, and they mutually pledged themselves upon the cross. So confident were they of success that they had even named the chief officers of the new government, among whom Tomas Ortiz was fixed upon for governor, and Archuleta to be the commandant general. The master spirits went into different sections of the country to stir up the people to resistance. Every thing looked propitious, and promised success to the enterprise.

A final meeting was held in Santa Fé on the evening of the eighteenth to arrange the plan of attack upon the garrison, but not finding their organization complete, they agreed to postpone the time of taking up arms until Christmas eve. This was considered a more fitting time to make the attempt, inasmuch as it would be a season of amusement, when the soldiers would be generally off their guard, scattered about the town unarmed, and could be easily overcome. The following was the plan of attack as agreed upon, and as sworn to before the court upon the trial of some of the conspirators: " On Saturday evening, the nineteenth of December, all were to assemble with their men at the parish church.

Having divided themselves into several parties, they were to sally forth, some to seize the pieces of artillery, others to go to the quarters of the colonel, and others to the palace of the governor (if he should be there), and if not, to send an order to Taos to seize him, because he would give them the most trouble. This act was also agreed upon by all. The sound of the church bell was to be the signal for the assault by the forces concealed in the church, and those which Diego Archuleta should have brought near the city; midnight was the time agreed upon, when all were to enter the Plaza at the same moment, seize the pieces, and point them into the streets."

The conspiracy was discovered in time to place the troops upon their guard, and prevent it being carried into effect at the time agreed upon. Three days before the time of rising, Augustin Duran informed Governor Bent of the plan of rebellion, who immediately caused several of the leaders to be arrested.* The conspirators, being aware that their movements had been made known to the Americans, made no attempt at outbreak, and, for the time being, the rebellion was suppressed.

The discovery had only smothered, not quenched the revolutionary spirit, and a new and more extended conspiracy was almost immediately placed on foot. Religious fanaticism was made use of to excite the people against the Americans, and they were called upon to arm themselves in defense of their holy faith, their homes, and their country. Some of the Pueblo Indians were enlisted in the cause, which added greatly to its strength. Great secrecy was observed, and no suspicion was entertained that another outbreak was so near at hand.

* It is said by some that the conspiracy was divulged by a mulatto girl. She is alleged to have been the wife of one of the conspirators, and gradually drew from him their plan of operation, which she communicated to General Price in season to prevent the outbreak.

The time fixed upon was the nineteenth day of January, 1847, when the people took up arms in various parts of the country.   Governor Bent, supposing that the rebellion was quelled, left Santa Fé for his home at Don Fernandez de Taos, where he arrived about the middle of the month.   A large body of the rebels, composed mainly of Pueblo Indians, and incited to the act by Priest Martinez and others, attacked his residence, and murdered him and several others in cold blood.   The same day seven Americans were attacked at the Arroyo Hondo, who, after defending themselves for two days, were most cruelly butchered.   Four were killed at the Moro, and two on the Rio Colorado.   A large rebel force had assembled at La Cañada for the purpose of advancing upon Santa Fé, but General Price, being aware of their movements, marched against them with four hundred men and four pieces of mountain howitzers.   He attacked them on the afternoon of the twenty-fourth, and routed them with the loss of near a hundred men.   They retreated toward Taos, closely followed by our troops. They made a stand at El Embudo, where they were again defeated with loss.   They continued their retreat to Taos, followed by the Americans, who arrived there on the third day of February.   They found the Mexicans and Indians strongly fortified in the pueblo of the latter, the main body having intrenched themselves in the church. An attack was made upon them the next morning, and the action continued all day with great fierceness and considerable loss.   The following morning they capitulated, and surrendered the place into the hands of the Americans.   In these actions the enemy lost some three hundred killed and wounded, while our loss was about sixty.

The rebels were equally unsuccessful in other parts of the country.   Captain Hendley, who was stationed on the Rio Pecos in command of the grazing parties, as soon as he heard of the insurrection, took possession of Las Vegas, where the enemy were beginning to collect. Here he soon assembled about two hundred and fifty men, and prepared to operate against the rebels. Learning that the Mexicans were in considerable force at the Moro, he marched for that place on the twenty-second instant with eighty men. He arrived there on the twenty-fourth, and found the enemy some two hundred strong, and prepared to defend the town. He attacked them with gallantry, and was already in possession of part of the town, when a considerable body of the Mexicans threw themselves into an old fort, from which they could not be dislodged without artillery, and our troops were obliged to retire, with the loss of one killed (Captain Hendley) and three wounded. The loss of the enemy was about forty. On the first day of February the Moro was again attacked by Captain Morin, the enemy defeated, and the village destroyed.

The success of the American arms quelled the rebellion and restored the country to a state of peace. Most of the leaders fled and could not be captured. Ortiz and Archuleta succeeded in reaching the city of Mexico, where they remained until the close of the war. Montoya, one of the chiefs of the conspiracy, was tried by a court-martial, convicted, and on the seventh of February he was executed in presence of the army. He styled himself the Santa Ana of the North, and was a man of influence. At Taos fourteen were tried for the murder of Governor Bent, convicted, and executed. Several others were convicted of treason and sentenced to be hung, but were pardoned by the President upon the ground that, as actual war was existing between the two governments, a Mexican citizen could not commit treason against the United States.

New Mexico was made a portion of the American

PUEBLO OF TAOS.—NORTH PUEBLO.

Union by the treaty of Guadalupe de Hidalgo, and a territorial government was erected over it by the Act of Congress, approved September 9th, 1850. The first Legislative Assembly was convened in Santa Fé in June of the next year, when the different departments of the new government were organized and put into operation. This act of Congress, known as the Organic Law, is the fundamental law of the Territory, and stands in the place of a Constitution in the respective states of the Union. All the political power conferred upon the people is derived from this source, and it is quoted both in the halls of legislation and in the courts of justice as the *ultima thule* beyond which they can not go. It provides, among other things, for the appointment by the President, by and with the advice and consent of the Senate, of a governor for the Territory, who shall hold his office for four years, unless sooner removed. He is *ex officio* superintendent of Indian affairs, and is also the commander-in-chief of the militia. He has an absolute veto on all laws passed by the Legislative Assembly, and is empowered to grant pardons for offenses against the laws of the Territory, and reprieves for offenses against the laws of the United States until the pleasure of the President can be made known. His annual salary is three thousand dollars.

There is also a secretary of state for the Territory, appointed in the same manner, and for the same length of time as the governor. His general duties are about the same as those that pertain to that office in the respective states, with the addition of some others that belong exclusively to the territories. By virtue of his office he is made the disbursing agent of the United States for the Territory, as far as the money annually appropriated by Congress for legislative expenses is concerned. The amount thus appropriated is twenty thousand dollars, for which he gives bond, with approved securities, to the United States. His accounts are rendered twice a year to the Treasury Department, where they are carefully examined, and all payments stopped against him that are not "proper and reasonable in amount." The secretary alone is responsible for the expenditure of this fund, and neither the Legislature nor the governor has the least control over it. In case of the death, removal, or necessary absence of the governor from the Territory, the duties of the executive and superintendency of Indian affairs devolve upon the secretary, but without the additional pay of these two offices. His salary is two thousand dollars annually, together with fees of office.

The second branch of the territorial government provided for in the Organic Law—the law-making power— is vested in the governor and the Legislative Assembly, the latter consisting of the Council and House of Representatives. The Council consists of thirteen members, and the House of Representatives of twenty-six; the former being elected for two years, and the latter annually. The qualification of voters, as prescribed in the Organic Law for the first election, embraces all free white male inhabitants above the age of twenty-one years who were residents of the Territory at the time of the passage of the act, but the Legislature subsequently fixed the time of residence at one year.

The judicial power of the Territory is vested in a Supreme Court, District and Probate Courts, and justices of the peace, the jurisdiction of which tribunals, both original and appellate, is limited by law. Justices of the peace have no jurisdiction where the title to land comes in question, nor where the amount in controversy exceeds one hundred dollars. Appeals and writs of error are allowed from the District to the Supreme Court of the Territory, and from the latter to the Supreme Court

of the United States. The organization of the Probate
and Justices' Courts is by virtue of statutory provision,
and their more particular powers and jurisdiction will be
hereafter mentioned. To the United States Courts belong a marshal and a district attorney, who have the
same tenure of office as the judges, during the pleasure
of the President. The marshal fills an important and
laborious office, and the compensation is but a mere pit-
tance for the services rendered. The United States
pay all the expenses of the District Court for the first
six days of each term, and the marshal, as the disbursing officer, handles the money; but if the court should
continue longer than six days at any one term, the jurors receive no pay for their services, as the Territory has
never made any provision for that purpose. The district
attorney is the representative of the United States in all
matters in which the general government is a party in
interest, and in all criminal offenses against the laws of
Congress he conducts the "pleas of the Crown." The
office is not worth the having. His time is occupied between five and six months in the year in making the circuit of the Territory, attending upon the United States
Courts, during which time he is obliged to travel about
two thousand miles, crossing high mountains, barren
plains, and fording rivers. For all his labor and time the
government allows him the *liberal* salary of two hundred
and fifty dollars annually, together with fees of office,
which will amount to some six or eight hundred more.

The jurisdiction of the Probate Court, as well as that
of the alcaldes, or justices of the peace, is conferred by
statute, except in the two instances already referred to,
in connection with the latter tribunal, as being contained
in the Organic Law. The judge of probate, known as
the prefect, is elected for two years, and holds six terms
of his court annually. He has original jurisdiction in

all cases of the probate of wills, and settlement of accounts of administrators and guardians ; and, in general, the same duties pertain to him as belong to the offices of surrogate or register of wills, and clerk of the Orphans' Court in the States of the Union. He has also a supervision over the public roads of the county, and the control of vagrants and others who have no visible means of support, whom he has authority to have arrested and tried, and, if convicted, to bind them out to labor upon public works. He can try appeals from alcaldes where the amount in controversy is over fifty dollars ; and appeals are taken from the judgment of the prefect to the District Court. Each county in the Territory is entitled to one prefect.

The alcaldes are elected annually in the respective counties, each precinct being entitled to one. The civil jurisdiction is substantially the same as that which usually belongs to justices of the peace, but the criminal jurisdiction is more extensive. They have cognizance of all larcenies, except the stealing of horses, asses, hogs, and goats, where the goods stolen do not exceed one hundred dollars in value ; of the offense of buying, receiving, or aiding in the concealment of stolen goods within the same amount ; and also of all assaults, assaults and batteries, and breaches of the peace. These several offenses are tried before a jury in the alcalde's court, and, upon conviction, he has the power to punish by fine and imprisonment ; but the accused has the right to appeal to the District Court. A sheriff is elected in each county for two years, who is also *ex officio* collector of taxes. There are likewise an auditor of public accounts, treasurer, and attorney general for the Territory, all of whom are appointed for the term of two years by the governor, by and with the advice of the Legislative Council.

The administration of justice in New Mexico, before the country fell into the hands of the Americans, was rude and uncertain, and the people had very little security for their persons and property. The system of government they were made subject to was, in all its bearings, a miserable tyranny; and in the various changes that took place in the central government no relief was given to this and other provinces. On the establishment of the republic, New Mexico was erected into a separate province, and was allowed a political organization that made some little pretension to a regular government, but the pretension was about all. The chief executive officer was called *gefe politico*—political chief; and a kind of Legislature was allowed—a poor affair at best—known as the *Diputacion Provincial*. When the central system was adopted, the names of the respective branches of the government were changed, but their power remained about the same as before. A governor was appointed by the President of Mexico for the term of eight years, and the legislative power was vested in a kind of executive council called the *Junta Departamental*. The powers of this body were very limited, and, in fact, they were no more than the creatures of the governor, who was the lord and master of the whole department. He imitated the early kings of England, and whenever he saw the members were disposed to become troublesome, he would "prorogue" the *Junta* and send them to their homes, the country, for the time being, having no further need of their services. In this easy manner he got rid of those who might have become unwelcome advisers.

The only tribunal of justice was the alcalde's court, none of whom were ever accused of knowing any thing about law. Under certain restrictions, appeals were carried up to the Supreme Court in the city of Mexico; but the distance was two thousand miles, and the expense so

great that few could afford it. The practice before the
alcalde in these days was exceedingly primitive, and
whenever justice was obtained it was quickly meted out.
A man, with his cause of complaint, went in person before that officer, and made a plain statement of the action,
when the alcalde directed the complainant to bring the
defendant before him. When the parties appeared, the
alcalde allowed each one to give his own version of the
case, and occasionally examined witnesses sworn upon a
cross made by crossing the finger and thumb. Sometimes the matter in dispute was left to the decision of
third persons, but a trial by jury was unknown. The
decision of the alcalde was seldom made up according to
the merits of the case, and much too frequently the judgment was purchased with money.

When the defendant failed to appear at the verbal
summons of the plaintiff, the alcalde dispatched after him
the regular process of the court. This was a large cane,
dignified with the name of *baston de justicia*, or staff of
justice, which was held in much more dread than a modern warrant. If he did not respond to the mandate of
the cane, he was considered in contempt of court, and
was sure to be punished accordingly. The jurisdiction
of the alcalde was very limited, and certain persons were
beyond the pale of himself and his cane. These were
called *fueros*. According to the Spanish ecclesiastical
law, no member of priesthood, of the rank of *curate* and
upward, could be made to appear before a civil tribunal,
but they were alone to be judged by their peers—the
clergy. The military were also exempt from trial before
a civil tribunal, which extended to both officers and men.
These exemptions maintained privileged classes in the
community, which proved a dead weight against any advance toward freedom.

The mode of punishment was fine and imprisonment;

but it was not always meted out in proportion to the offense, nor inflicted with a view to avenge the outraged law or reform the criminal. In a case of debt, the debtor was not sent to jail if the creditor was willing to accept his services to work out the amount of the judgment; by which means he was saved from prison, but for the time being was plunged into a state of servitude. He worked for a fixed sum, some five or six dollars per month, and was supplied with the necessary goods from his employer's store. His wages were not sufficient to support himself and family, and enable him to discharge his former indebtedness, and therefore the customs and laws of the country reduced him to a state of peonage, and the unfortunate debtor found himself a slave for life. This same system is continued in the modern servitude known as peonism, of which I will take occasion to say more in a subsequent chapter.

The second section of the Organic Law provides that whenever New Mexico shall be received into the Union as a state, she may be admitted with or without slavery, as her Constitution may prescribe at the time of admission. This is fair and just, and allows the people to determine for themselves what shall be the nature of their domestic institutions, and, moreover, is in accordance with the principles of our government. In spite of the fears of the abolitionists, and others who wish to prescribe the institutions the territories shall have at the time of their admission into the Union, there is every probability of New Mexico becoming a free state. The whole matter has been more wisely regulated by Nature than can be ordered by man. The greater portion of the country is not adapted to slave labor, which would be found too unprofitable to warrant its introduction. The main branch of agriculture which the Territory at present supports— and the same must be the case in future—is grazing. In the northern and middle section the climate is too cold for the growth of any crops that would yield a profitable return to slave labor. A greater barrier than climate is the cheapness of peon labor, which is less expensive to the proprietor; and even in the southern parts, where more tropical productions could be raised, their labor would fully supply the place of the negro. A peon can perform as much work, and can be hired for about what it will cost to clothe and feed a negro, with the further advantage of the master having no capital invested in him, which he must lose at the death of the slave. The present labor of the country is so much cheaper than any that could be introduced, that a person would hardly be justifiable in risking his capital in slaves with so little prospect of profitable return. The peons have been train- ed to the management of flocks and herds, and are much better adapted to this pursuit than the negro could pos- sibly become; and there is no other employment which would yield so much profit to the master for the labor of the slave. Hence, for these reasons, the climate, cheap- ness of the present labor, and the nature of the produc- tions, will all have a tendency to exclude slave labor, and particularly so when it can be employed with so much greater profit elsewhere in the cultivation of hemp, tobacco, cotton, rice, and sugar. At the same time, the people have no particular dislike to the institution of negro slavery, and I do not believe they would hesitate to introduce it, if found to be necessary to their agricul- tural prosperity. But if it should be introduced, my opinion is that the institution would never flourish with any degree of vigor, and that in a few years it would gradually die out, as in the northern states of the Union.

I will conclude this chapter by giving a brief account of the efforts made in New Mexico, at the close of the war, to obtain either a state or territorial government for that province, some portion of which forms an unwritten page in the history of the times. A movement of the kind was first induced by the letter of the Hon. Thomas H. Benton to the people of California and New Mexico, advising them to found governments for themselves without waiting for the action of Congress. In the fall of 1848, William Z. Angney, Esq., a lawyer of very considerable talent, and late a captain in the army, commanding a battalion of volunteers, returned from Missouri full of the idea set forth in Mr. Benton's letter, and endeavored to induce the people of New Mexico to follow the course he recommended. Colonel Washington, then the civil and military governor of the province, finding that an excitement was growing up upon the subject, issued a proclamation, dated the 23d of November, 1848, commanding the inhabitants to abstain from " participating in or being movers of seditious meetings ;" after which public meetings ceased for a time, and all things went on quietly. In December of the same year, a convention, composed of delegates from all parts of the Territory, assembled in Santa Fé, and memorialized Congress for a territorial government, but none was granted during that session. The memorial was bitterly attacked in the Senate, because of the provisions it contained in reference to slavery, which was probably the reason it was not acted upon.

New Mexico not having a representative in Washington to look after the interest of the country, the people resolved to send an agent there for that purpose. A movement to this effect was put on foot in May, 1849, which resulted in Hugh N. Smith, Esq., being sent to the federal capital to watch over the affairs of the Territory, his expenses being borne by an association of private individuals. This movement begat an opposition on the part of certain gentlemen, who coveted the position for one of their own number, and they took immediate steps to counteract it. Those mainly instrumental in the matter were Major R. H. Weightman, late a paymaster in the army, and Mr. Angney, before mentioned, who stirred up the public mind, and held several meetings in Santa Fé upon the subject. Lieutenant Colonel Benjamin Beall, the then military commandant in the absence of Colonel Washington, issued a proclamation for the election of delegates to a convention to assemble in Santa Fé in September, 1849, for the purpose of adopting a plan for a territorial government, and to elect a delegate to Congress to urge its adoption. A satisfactory plan was agreed upon, and Hugh N. Smith, Esq., was elected as delegate, who went to Washington, and remained nearly the whole session, but was refused his seat by a majority of four votes.

In the mean time the country became greatly agitated as to the terms upon which California and New Mexico should be admitted into the Union, the slavery question having been thrown in as a bone of contention. Texas also began to assert her claim anew to all that part of New Mexico east of the Rio del Norte; and to carry out this purpose, that state sent Spruce M. Baird, Esq., under the appointment of judge, into the Territory, to erect all that portion of the country into the county of Santa Fé, and to extend the jurisdiction of the laws of Texas over it. The people of New Mexico being averse to Texas rule, they disregarded this assumed jurisdiction, and refused obedience thereto; and the mission of Mr. Baird being barren of consequences, he returned again to Texas. Early in the spring of 1850, Texas sent a commissioner, Robert S. Neighbors, Esq., into New Mexico, with instructions to divide the country east of the Rio del Norte into several counties of that state, and to hold elections in them for county officers. Upon the mission of Mr. Neighbors being known, it was loudly denounced in public meetings throughout the Territory, and a very strong opposition was raised against him and the objects he had in view.   He issued a proclamation fixing time and places for an election, but nobody went to the polls, and the matter fell to the ground.

About this time two opposite parties sprang up in New Mexico, one being in favor of a state, and the other a territorial government, which engendered a deal of excitement and ill feeling.   Several large public meetings were held by the respective parties in Santa Fé.   The state party took sides with Mr. Neighbors, while the territorial party, composed of the mass of the people, were opposed to the dismemberment of the Territory by Texas. At one of these meetings the excitement ran so high that it almost led to bloodshed.   The agitation of the question of a state government originated with the then national administration.   President Taylor and his cabinet desired to avoid the responsibility of acting upon the slavery question, which would be required of them if Congress should establish governments for the new territory acquired under the treaty of Guadalupe Hidalgo from Mexico.   Hence the desire, on their part, to induce the people of California and New Mexico to form governments for themselves, and, in so doing, to settle the vexed question, so far as they were concerned, in their own way.   In the spring of 1849, James S. Calhoun, Esq., went to New Mexico, under an appointment as Indian agent, but upon his arrival he declared that he had secret instructions from the government at Washington to induce the people to form a state government.

For a time the plan of a state government received but little support, but in the course of the summer and fall an excitement was raised upon the subject, and both parties, state and territorial, published addresses to the peo-

ple; the former being headed by Messrs Calhoun, Alvarez, and Pillans, and the latter by St. Vrain, Houghton,
Beaubien, and others.   The matter continued to be discussed without much effect in favor of the state organization until the spring of 1850, when Colonel George
A. M'Call arrived in Santa Fé from the States, upon a
like mission as Calhoun.   He informed the people that
no territorial government would be granted by Congress,
and that President Taylor was determined that New
Mexico should be erected into a state government, in order to settle the question of slavery, and also that of
boundary with Texas.   The delegate in Congress, Mr.
Smith, wrote home to the same effect; and things appeared very much as though the general government had
left the people of the Territory to shift for themselves.

In view of the present condition of political affairs—
Congress neglecting to organize a territorial government
on the one hand, and Texas threatening to dismember
the country on the other, with the presence of military
rule daily becoming obnoxious to the people—the territorial party at last yielded their preference, and joined
in the advocacy of a state government.   Accordingly, res-
olutions to that effect were adopted at a meeting held in
the city of Santa Fé on the 20th of April, 1850, and also
requesting Colonel John Monroe, the civil and military
governor, to issue a proclamation calling upon the people
to elect delegates to a convention to be convened on the
15th of May following at that place.   The delegates, elected in pursuance of the proclamation, assembled in convention on the day therein mentioned, and remained in
session for ten days, during which time they adopted, with
great unanimity, a Constitution, which had been drafted
by Joab Houghton and M. F. Tuley, Esquires.   It assimilated, in its general features, to the Constitutions of the
new states of the Union; and, among other things, contained a clause prohibiting slavery, in order to meet the

views of the Mexican population. The Constitution was adopted on the 20th of June with little, if any opposition, and, at the same time, state officers were elected. The Legislature assembled on the 1st of July of the same year at Santa Fé, when they elected two senators in Congress, Francis A. Cunningham and Richard H. Weightman.

At the state election Henry Connelly was elected governor, and Manuel Alvarez lieutenant governor. Dr. Connelly being absent in the States, Mr. Alvarez was acting governor for the time being, who, backed by the Legislature then in session and the newly-elected officials, attempted at once to put the state government into full operation without awaiting its adoption and approval. This movement caused a lengthy and quite angry correspondence between Mr. Alvarez and Colonel Monroe, who forbade any assumption of civil power by the new officials.   Among other things, the Legislature provided for the election of county officers, which Acting Governor Alvarez attempted to carry into effect by issuing writs of election, which Colonel Monroe also forbade by proclamation to the people, in which he declared all such elections null and void.   In consequence of this opposition on the part of the military authority, the elections were not held, and matters moved on for some months the same as before the state organization was effected.

In the mean time Mr. Weightman, one of the senators elect, went to Washington to present the Constitution of New Mexico, ask for her admittance into the Union, and claim his seat.   Upon his arrival, he found that the Compromise Bill of 1850, in which was included the act organizing a territorial government for New Mexico, had just passed Congress, and which at once took precedence of the state organization.   The new territorial government went into operation the 3d of March, 1851, Mr. Calhoun being sworn in as governor. Thus originated, and ceased to exist, the state government of New Mexico.

CHAPTER V.

THE PUEBLO INDIANS.

Pueblos most interesting Class of Inhabitants.—Origin of Name.—Religion.—Number of Villages.—Their Names.—Moqui Villages.—Different Nations and Languages.—Tagnos Nation extinct.—Did the Spaniards reclaim these Indians?—Cibola and the People.—Tignex and Jemez.—Cicuyé and the Buildings.—Pueblo Indians same People the Spaniards found in the Country.—First Decree of Charles V.—Subsequent Decrees.—Title of Indians to Land.—Ruins of Pueblos.—Abo.—Quarra.—Quivira.—Other Ruins.—Scarcity of Water.—Cause of Villages deserted.—Wager of Battle.—Who are the Pueblo Indians?—Opinion of Mr. Gallatin.—Are they Aztecs?—The Question an interesting one.

THE most interesting class of the inhabitants of New Mexico are those known as the *Pueblo Indians*. They are the descendants of the ancient rulers of the country, and are so called because they dwell in villages and subsist by agriculture, instead of living in lodges and depending upon the chase as the wild Indians of the mountains and plains. The word pueblo is the Spanish for village, and hence the origin of their name. They are semi-civilized, and in part have conformed to the manners and customs of their Mexican neighbors, from whom they have drawn the little civilization they possess. The greater number of them have embraced the Christian religion, and worship after the forms of the Catholic Church.

Within a few years this people have attracted considerable attention among the learned, who have made an effort to unravel the mystery that hangs around their origin and early history, as also to obtain a more correct knowledge of their present manners and customs. The interest manifested in this primitive race will warrant me in devoting a few pages to them, in which I will give the reader all the information I have been able to obtain concerning them, derived from personal observation and other authentic sources.

The number of inhabited pueblos in the Territory is twenty-six, the majority of which are situated in the valley of the Del Norte, extending, from Taos in the north to Isleta in the south, some two hundred miles. In ancient times they were much more numerous than at present, and the ruins of many are now to be seen in various parts of the country. Their names are Taos, Picoris, Nambé, Tezuque, Pojuaque, San Juan, San Yldefonso, Santo Domingo, San Felipé, Santa Ana, Cochiti, Isleta, Silla, Laguna, Acoma, Jemez, Zuñi, Sandia, and Santa Clara. Besides these there are the seven villages of the Moquis in the western part of the Territory, well toward the Rio Colorado of the west, which are the least known of all the pueblos. They have not had a priest stationed among them since the revolution of 1680, and, being far removed from the Mexican population, they have remained to the present day in a very primitive condition, and retained most of their ancient manners and habits. When Cruzate visited the Moqui country in 1692, he saw five inhabited pueblos, which were then called Aguatubi, Gualpi, Jongopavi, Monsonavi, and Orayvi. Five of these villages now bear the names of Moqui, Oraybe, Una Vida, Cuelpe, and Towas; the names of the other two I do not know, and, not having visited that country, I am not able to say how the situation of the modern agrees with that of the ancient pueblos. A few miles to the south of Isleta is what was once an Indian pueblo, but the inhabitants have intermarried with the Spaniards to such a degree that it has become almost merged into a Mexican village. In Texas, a short distance below the southern boundary of New Mexico, and in the valley of the Del Norte, is a pueblo called Isleta of the South, but neither it nor Los Lentes is included in the twenty-six named as being in the Territory.

In ancient times the several pueblos formed four distinct nations, called *Piro*, *Tegua*, *Queres*, and *Tagnos* or *Tanos*, speaking as many different dialects or languages. The languages of the first three, the remains of former nationalities, are still extant, but the fourth, that of the Tagnos or Tanos, is said to have become extinct. The pueblos that still speak the Piro language are Taos, Tezuque, Sandia, Isleta, and Isleta of the South; those that speak the Queres language are Santa Ana, Jemez, San Felipe, Cochiti, Santo Domingo, Laguna, Acoma, Picoris, and Silla. It is maintained by some that Zuñi speaks the Piro language, and that four of the Moqui villages speak a dialect very nearly the same as that of the Navajos, while a fifth speaks that of San Juan, which is Tegua; but as Cruzate, in his journal, places both Zuñi and Moqui as belonging to the Queres nation, such designation of them is most probably correct. In the days of their greatest strength this was the most powerful of all the Pueblo nations; and in their conflicts with the Spaniards, Queres sent forth the most able warriors into the field, and had the most cunning prophets in the estufas. The *Tegua* language is still spoken by San Juan, Santa Clara, Nambé, Pojuaque, and San Yldefonso. The pueblos that once composed the powerful nation of *Tagnos* have been harshly dealt with in the course of time, and it is not certainly known that even a remnant of this people now remain, although it is said that some of the western villages speak that language. The once populous pueblo of Pecos, those on the Galestio, and others to the southward, were of this nation, but they have long

since fallen to decay, and time-stained ruins only mark
the former homes of these dusky warriors. The distance
from Picoris to the Moqui villages is about four hundred
miles, and from Taos to Isleta of the South still farther,
and yet these widely separated pueblos speak, each two,
the same language, and, in all probability, are from the
same parent stock. This identity of language, as evidence in favor of their having originally been one people,
also supports the supposition that they were from some
cause dispersed from a common locality, and obliged to
seek new homes in distant regions. Most of the Pueblo
Indians have picked up a smattering of the Spanish language, but their native tongue is always used in their
conversation with each other.

It has been and still is the opinion of many persons
that the Pueblo Indians of New Mexico were reclaimed
from a wild state and placed in villages by the Spaniards. This is an error, as can be shown by abundant
evidence. They were living in villages long before Europeans landed upon the shores of America. The first
Spaniards who penetrated into New Mexico found them
in substantially the same condition as at the present
day, and when Cortez entered Southern Mexico, he encountered a race of men inhabiting that country almost
identical with the Pueblo Indians in style of living,
manners, and customs. The earliest and most positive
testimony we have upon this subject, so far as New
Mexico is concerned, we find in the journal of Castañeda
de Nagera, the chronicler of the expedition of Coronado
of 1540, already referred to. He noted the provinces
they passed through, with a description of the country,
and the people, and all of interest that was seen during
their march. This journal has been preserved, and now
lies before me. In order to prove that the people then
inhabiting New Mexico were the same race of men as

the Pueblos of the present day, I will make a few extracts from Castañeda upon the subject. In speaking
of Cibola, the first province at which they arrived, he
gives the following brief account of it :

" The province of Cibola contains seven villages. The
largest is called Muzaque. The houses of the country
are ordinarily three or four stories high, but at Muzaque
there are some which reach seven stories. The Indians
of this country are very intelligent. They cover the
natural parts and the entire middle of the person with
pieces of stuff which resemble napkins ; they are gar-
nished with tufts and with embroidery at the corners,
and are fastened around the reins. These natives have
also kinds of pelisses of feathers or hare-skins and cotton stuffs. The women wear on the shoulders a sort of
mantle, which they fasten around the neck, passing it
under the right arm. They also make garments of skins
very well dressed, and trick off their hair behind the ears
in the shape of a wheel, which resembles the handle of
a cup."

Speaking of the villages of the province of Tignex, forty leagues to the north of Cibola, he says, "They are governed by a council of old men. The houses are built in
common ; the women temper the mortar and raise the
walls ; the men bring timber and construct the frames.
They have no lime, but they make a mixture of ashes,
earth, and charcoal, which answers very well as a substitute ; for, although they raise their houses four stories
high, the walls are not more than three feet thick. They
make great heaps of thyme and rushes, which they set on
fire ; when the mass is reduced to coal and ashes, they
throw upon it a great deal of earth and water, and mix all
together. They then knead it in round masses, which are
dried, and which they employ as stones ; the whole is
then coated with the same mixture. The work thus re-

sembles somewhat a piece of masonry." He also mentions that contiguous to this province lay that of Jemez,
seven leagues to the northeast, which also contained
seven villages. The pueblo of Jemez is still in existence, and contains several hundred inhabitants, and, from
its location, is probably a village of the province of that
name mentioned by Castañeda. In the same valley are
three or four other inhabited pueblos, and several in
ruins.

In giving a description of the same province, he remarks, " The houses are well distributed and very neat.
One room is designed for the kitchen, and another to
grind the grain. This last is apart, and contains a furnace and three stones made fast in masonry. Three
women sit down before these stones ; the first crushes
the grain, the second brays it, and the third reduces it
entirely to powder. Before entering, they take off their
shoes, tie their hair, cover their head, and shake their
clothes. While they are at work, a man, seated at the
door, plays on a bagpipe, so that they work keeping time:
they sing in three voices. They make a great deal of
flour at once. To make bread, they mix it with warm
water, and make a dough which resembles the cakes
called *dubles*. No other fruit than pine-nuts* are seen
in the country. The men wear a sort of shirt of dressed
leather, and a pelisse over it. In all this province was
found pottery glazed, and vases of really curious form
and workmanship."

Farther toward the northeast the Spaniards came to
the village of Cicuyé, which is described as follows : " It
is built on the top of a rock, forming a great square, and
the centre is occupied by a public place, under which are
vapor baths. The houses are four stories high, the roof
in the form of a terrace, all of the same height, and on

---

* Probably *piñones*, which are found all over the country.

which the circuit of the village may be made without finding a street to obstruct the passage. To the first two stories there is a corridor, in the form of a balcony, on which they can circulate round the village, and under which they can find shelter. The houses have no doors below, but they ascend to the balconies within the village by means of ladders which may be removed. Upon these balconies, which serve as streets, open all the doors by which the houses are entered. Those which front upon the country are supported against those which open upon the court. These last are higher, which is very useful in time of war."

The evidence here cited from the journal of Castañeda seems sufficient to satisfy an impartial reader that the present race of Pueblo Indians is identical with the people the Spaniards found in the country in 1540. Their mode of building, manners and customs, and style of dress, are all substantially the same. They were found living in detached villages, scattered over the country, as at the present day, and subsisted by cultivating the soil; and at that early day they were distinguished from the roving tribes of the mountains and plains, who dwelt in lodges made of buffalo-skins. It is not probable that in about half a century, the time intervening between the coming of Coronado and the settlement of the country by the Spaniards, the numerous and populous villages seen by that officer had ceased to exist, and the inhabitants gone back into a wild and nomadic state. This is the only reasonable supposition upon which to base the hypothesis that the Pueblo Indians were found in a roving state when the Spaniards permanently settled the country at the close of the sixteenth century, and were placed by them in villages as we now find them. If this hypothesis be true, to what cause are we to attribute the breaking up of the organized communities of a country, and the dispersion of the inhabitants as wanderers upon the face of the earth? And if these people are not the same race that the first European explorers found inhabiting the country, how is the singular fact accounted for that the village of Jemez answers exactly, in name and location, and similarity of population, to the Jemez of the present day? These points can not be reconciled except upon the admission that the modern Pueblo Indians are the aboriginals of the country, living as their forefathers lived when the white men first made their appearance. In all essential particulars there can be no doubt that they are the same people the Spaniards found in the country more than three centuries ago, with the exception of having undergone some slight changes in manners and dress, consequent upon living contiguous to and mingling with an antagonistic race.

As further evidence upon this subject, I will briefly notice the course of the Spanish government toward the Pueblo Indians, and which also goes to prove that they were found by the first settlers living in fixed communities. Soon after the conquest by Cortez, the government became sensible of the policy of conciliating a people so numerous and powerful as the aboriginals of the country, and hence grants of land were made to the respective pueblos for purposes of agriculture. The first decree upon this subject is that of Charles the Fifth, given in 1523, only three years after the conquest, which authorizes the viceroys and governors to grant to each village as much land as might be necessary for agricultural and building purposes. The next decree upon the subject is that of 1533, which makes the mountains, pastures, and waters common to both Spaniards and Indians. On the twenty-first of March, 1551, the Emperor Charles promulgated a third ordinance touching the Pueblo Indians, but which concerned their spiritual more than their temporal welfare. This provides that they shall be reduced to pueblos; but as they were already living in villages, as the two former decrees would prove, without seeking for other evidence, the true intent of this latter ordinance must have been to fix them in larger communities, as a greater convenience in matters of religious instruction, as the spiritual welfare of the Indians was the sole object embraced in the decree. The decree of Felipe the Second, of June, 1587, confirmed to the different pueblos a grant of eleven hundred varas square of land, to be measured from the last house of the village toward the four points of the compass. The quantity was afterward increased to a league square. Some of the decrees, as well before as after this time, mention the nature of the title the Indians were to have in the land granted under them, which in no instance appears to have been of a higher grade than the right of possession. The ordinance of Felipe the Fourth, of March the sixteenth, 1642, provides that the lands which the Pueblo Indians have in any manner improved by their industry shall be reserved to them, but that they shall neither have power to sell or in any manner alienate the same. The decree of the Royal Audience of Mexico of February twenty-third, 1781, confirmatory of that of Felipe the Third of October twentieth, 1598, prohibits the Pueblo Indians from selling, renting, leasing, or in any other manner disposing of their lands, either to each other or to third persons, without the permission of the said Royal Audience; and the same decree also expressly provides that the Indians have no direct right in the land set apart for them. In 1816 the Royal Audience of Guadalajara refused to confirm the sale of a rancho belonging to the pueblo of Cochiti, and which sale was not confirmed until the year 1827, when it was done by the Mexican Congress.

These authorities are evidence in support of two facts

of some importance. The first is, that the Spaniards, at the conquest of Southern Mexico, found the Indians in pueblos, and granted them lands in order to conciliate them. The second point established is the fact that the Pueblo Indians held their grants by a possessory title only, the fee-simple remaining in the crown of Spain in the first instance, and afterward in the government of Mexico by virtue of her independence, which, by the treaty of Guadalupe Hidalgo, passed to the United States, so far as the pueblos of New Mexico are concerned.

We have abundant evidence that the Pueblo Indians were in ancient times much more numerous than at the present day, as is attested by the ruins that lie scattered over the country, and the manuscript journals of the early Spanish officers still preserved in the archives of Santa Fé. One nation, the Tagnos or Tanos, once powerful and warlike, has become entirely extinct, and many of the villages of the four remaining nations have gone to ruins. Of those now in decay, and a long time abandoned by the inhabitants, and whose names have come down to the present day, can be mentioned Pecos, San Lazaro, San Marcos, San Cristobal, Socorro, and Senacu, besides others whose names have been forgotten, all of which were peopled as late as 1692, when Cruzate marched through the country. In the palmiest days of the Pueblo Indians, the valley in which Santa Fé is situated was the centre of the four nations, and here were located their most populous pueblos. Their villages were built upon both sides of the Santa Fé River for several miles, extending from the mountains down to the little town of Agua Fria. In this distance down the valley there are seen to this day pieces of painted pottery, and other remains of the pueblos that have passed away. There may also be mentioned the ruins of Abo, Quarra, and Gran Quivira, which are undoubtedly the remains ot pueblos, although I have not been able to find any notice of them among the old archives. From all the information I have been able to obtain concerning these latter ruins, from their location, I am of the opinion that they were villages of the Tagnos nation, and were destroyed and deserted at the time of the rebellion of 1680. This people inhabited the country to the southward of Santa Fé, including some villages upon the Galestio Creek, and the ruins referred to are the only evidence in all that section of country of pre-existing pueblos. They are almost due south of Santa Fé, and no other locality is found to correspond so well with the situation of the ancient Tagnos villages ; and the ruins themselves give evidence that the towns that formerly stood there were not unlike the pueblos of the present day. As these ruins have attracted considerable attention, I will notice them with some particularity.*

The ruins of Abo are in the county of Valencia, a few miles south of the town of Manzana, and consist of the walls of a church, and heaps of stones that mark the site of ruined houses. The church was evidently the work of Christian hands, as it was built in the form of a cross, and some of the timbers show marks of the axe upon them. The dimensions are one hundred and thirty-two feet for the long arm, and forty-one feet for the short arm of the cross. The height of the walls still standing is about fifty feet: they are of great thickness, and the material of construction is a dark red sandstone found in the neighborhood. The stones are in small pieces, undressed, and were laid in mud. There are no remains of an arch about the building, and the roof, though now in ruins, was probably composed of earth, as at the pres-

* I am indebted to the highly interesting report of Brevet Major Carleton, U. S. A., for the greater part of my information in reference to the ruins of Abo, Quarra, and Gran Quivira.

ent day, and supported by large beams.   The remains
of an outer wall, which probably inclosed the town, can
still be traced, about nine hundred and fifty feet from
north to south, and four hundred and fifty from east to
west.   These distances would indicate that the population was considerable, with the compact mode of building
practiced by the Pueblo Indians.   The country around
is barren and rolling, covered with piñon and pine trees,
and without evidence of ever having been under cultivation.   Twelve miles and a half north of Abo is Quarra,
situated upon a small stream that soon sinks into the
sand and disappears.   The ruins are substantially the
same as those found at Abo, and are evidently the remains of the same people.   The church is rather smaller
in dimensions, and some portions of it are in a better
state of preservation.   Near by are two groves of apple-
trees, which tradition says were planted when Abo and
Quarra were inhabited.   Two of the trees are six and
eight feet in circumference, and most of them still bear
fruit.   As apple-trees are not indigenous to the country,
they were probably planted by the Spanish priests, and
belonged to one or both of these villages when inhabited.

The Gran Quivira is about forty miles east of south
from Quarra, situated in the midst of an elevated and
barren country.   The ruins consist of " the remains of
a large church or cathedral, with a monastery attached;
a small church or chapel, and the ruins of the town extending nine hundred feet in a direction east and west,
and three hundred north and south.   All these buildings
have been constructed of the dark blue limestone which
is found in the vicinity."   The church is about the size
of the one at Abo, and in pretty much the same condition.   Some of the beams are elaborately carved, and
exhibit considerable mechanical skill.   Major Carleton,
U. S. A., in giving an account of his visit to these ruins

in December, 1853, says, "The walls of the cathedral are now about thirty feet in height. It was estimated, from the great quantity of stones that have fallen down, forming a sort of talus both with the walls and the outside of them, that originally this building was all of fifty feet in height. There is a small room to the right as you enter the cathedral, and another room, which is very large, and which communicates with the main body of the building by a door at the left of the transept. There was also a communication between this large room and the monastery, or system of cloisters, which are attached to the cathedral. This building is one hundred and eighteen feet long outside, and thirty-two in width. Its walls are three feet and eight inches in thickness. It is apparently in a better state of preservation than the cathedral, but yet none of the former wood-work remains in it." Among the ruins are found great quantities of broken earthenware, some of which had been handsomely painted and glazed. An old road runs toward the east, which can be plainly traced for some distance, and in which are growing cedar-trees of a large size. The country round about shows no traces of ever having been cultivated, and the nearest water, at the present time, is at the base of the mountain called *La Sierra de las Gallinas*, fifteen miles off.

From the earliest knowledge we have of New Mexico, we find the Gran Quivira spoken of as a place of remarkable interest, and the most fabulous accounts are related of it. It will be borne in mind by the reader that one of the objects of the expedition of Coronado into New Mexico was to discover the grand city of Quivira, which was said to be built upon a scale of great magnificence, and to abound in the precious metals. A town bearing this name was reached after a long and fatiguing march, but they found it very different in every particular from what it had been represented. Castañeda speaks of the town and the surrounding country as follows: " Up to that point the whole country is only one plain; at Quivira mountains begin to be perceived. From what was seen, it appears to be a well-peopled country. The plants and fruit generally resemble those of Spain: plums, grapes, nuts, mulberries, rye, grass, oats, pennyroyal, origanum, and flax, which the natives do not cultivate because they do not understand the use of it. Their manners and customs are the same as those of Tegas, and the villages resemble those of Spain. The houses are round and have no walls; the stories are like lofts; the roofs are of straw. The inhabitants sleep under the roofs, and there they keep all they possess." This description of the country around the Quivira visited by Coronado is very different from that in which the present ruins are found, and yet there is a possibility of the two localities being the same. It will be recollected that when Coronado left the main army to search for the Gran Quivira they were some considerable distance out upon the plains east of the Rio del Norte, and that in his march he took a southwest direction until he arrived in that country. He mentions passing some salt lakes, which are yet to be found in that region. There are no other ruins, that I am aware of, any where in the section of the country in which he locates Quivira, or passed through on his march. In three centuries and more, the country may have undergone such changes as to reduce it from a fertile and populous region, as the Spaniards then describe it, to an uninhabited and barren waste. These ruins are now pretty well stripped of the romance that hung around them for so long a time, and are generally acknowledged to be no more than the remains of Indian pueblos.*

* Since the above was written, I have come in possession of some

Similar ruins are found in various other sections of the territory. Near the pueblo of Zuña are the ruins of the ancient village inhabited by the forefathers of the present race. They are upon a high rock; the situation is an admirable one for defense, and in Indian warfare must have been impregnable. In the valley of Jemez there are seen the ruins of several villages; and in various sections of the country inhabited by the Navajo Indians still more extensive ruins are found. There is one feature connected with these ruined towns worthy of note, and that is the great scarcity of water near them. In some instances, the nearest water, at the present day, is several miles off, and difficult of access. This could not have been the case when these towns were peopled, as it is well known that nearness to water is the first consideration with all mankind in locating their habitations. We can come to no other conclusion, then, than that the springs and streams have dried up and ceased to flow since these villages were deserted. This would argue that the face of the country since that period has undergone great physical changes, of which there seems great probability, as exhibited by the traces of recent volcanic action in different parts of the country.

The cause of the desertion of so many villages, and where fled the inhabitants, would be a natural inquiry

facts which throw a little light upon the early condition of Quivira, obtained from the old manuscript journal of Don Diego de Bargas, found in the secretary's office at Santa Fé. On the second day of May, 1694, while he was the governor and captain-general of the province, the war captain of the Pecos pueblo, accompanied by eight "Farreon Apaches," made him a visit in Santa Fé. During the interview Bargas asked them the distance from their country to that of the Quivira, to which they replied that the distance was from twenty-five to thirty days' travel—that they knew this country well, for the reason that they went to the Quivira country for captives to buy horses with. This proves that Quivira was inhabited at that time, as were probably Abo and Quarra, and that they were subsequently depopulated.

on the part of the reader. Many of them, without doubt, were depopulated during the rebellion of 1680, or, more properly, during the reconquest from 1692 to 1696. When Bargas returned to the country in the spring of 1694, he distributed the lands deserted by the Indians among the Spaniards, leaving their quaint-looking houses to fall into decay and go to ruins. It is also related, but more as a matter of tradition than from any authentic source, that after the Indians had driven the Spaniards from the country, a quarrel took place between them about their lands. It soon became general, and nearly every pueblo in the country took part with one side or the other. Seeing it was likely to lead to a fatal division among themselves, which would enable the enemy to make an easy conquest of the country, they agreed to have the matter decided by wager of battle. Two hundred warriors were chosen upon each side, who were to contend for their respective parties, and those whose representatives should be worsted in the contest were quietly to withdraw from the country, and leave the others in possession. The combatants met upon a plain, and decided the contest after a long and bloody struggle. The defeated party left their villages and sought new homes, many, it is said, taking up their abode in California. If this occurrence actually took place, we can very easily account for the ruins of so many villages now found scattered over the territory; and probably it was the lands of the unsuccessful party that Bargas divided among his followers after the reconquest. Whatever was the cause of the abandonment of their villages, the ruins themselves must always remain an object of interest, as the mute memorial of a once powerful race of people now almost extinct.

The question would naturally suggest itself to the mind of the reader, "Of what race are the Pueblo In-

dians, and whence did they come?" Upon this subject
different opinions have been expressed by those who
have examined the question. Some contend that they
are of Aztec origin, while others believe them to be the
remains of an ancient Toltec colony; and among those
who hold the latter view of the question was the late
Albert Gallatin. According to tradition, the Aztecs,
when they peopled Mexico, came from the north or
northwest, and only reached their location in the valley
of Anahuac after a period of a hundred and fifty years.
From time to time they halted in their migration toward
the south, remaining several years in a place, where they
founded villages and cultivated the earth. Castañeda
was of opinion, from what he could learn of these people
during his sojourn in the country with Coronado, that
they had come from the northwest. If such was the
case, some probably remained behind in their new abode
when the main body continued their migration southward, and it is possible that many of the ruins found
in the country are the remains of the villages they deserted when they moved on. The present race of Pueblo Indians have a tradition among them that they are
the people of Montezuma; and the Pecos pueblo are
said to have believed that he would come back some
time to deliver them from the Spaniards. To the present day the Indians of Laguna worship an object they
call by the name of the Aztec king, and which is fashioned to resemble him, as they suppose. They keep up
the estufa because, as they say, it was instituted by
Montezuma, and, as far as I have been able to learn,
they still number the sun among the objects of their
heathen worship. Lieutenant Simpson states in his
journal that a Jemez Indian told him that God and the
sun are one and the same. Baron Humboldt, upon the
authority of missionaries who were well acquainted with

the Aztec language, contends that it differs essentially from that spoken by the Indians of New Mexico, and hence argues that they are not the same race of people. It also appears from the evidence of Castañeda that the Indians of New Mexico were entirely unknown to the people of Southern Mexico, and that their first information respecting them was obtained from Cabeza de Baca and his companions. If they are the same race as the Aztecs, and left behind in their migration southward, the latter would have had knowledge of them, and the Spaniards would have learned of their location long before Baca passed through the country. These facts are in opposition to the hypothesis that they are the same people, while the similitude between the manners and customs, and also the mode of building of the Pueblo Indians and the ancient Aztecs would argue an identity of race; and if, upon careful investigation, their language should be found substantially the same, the evidence would seem much more conclusive upon the subject.

In whatever light the question is viewed, it presents points of deep interest, and can not fail to create a desire in the mind of every intelligent person to know more of this singular people who inhabit the very heart of the American continent. Who they are and whence they came must always remain shrouded in mystery, unless a modern Œdipus should spring up to unravel their romantic history.

CHAPTER VI.*

THE PUEBLO INDIANS—*Concluded.*

History of Pueblo Indians.—New Religion forced upon them.—At-
tempts at Rebellion in 1640 and 1650.—Their Failure.—First gen-
eral Conspiracy.—Rebellion of 1680.—How organized.—Popé.—His
Plans.—Time of Rising.—Plot discovered.—Indians take up Arms.
—Santa Fé besieged.—Spaniards retreat.—Country reconquered.—
Population.—Their Buildings.—Estufa.—Government.—Officers.—
Confirmation of Governor.—Council of Wise Men.—The Cachina.—
How the Land is held.—Weapons.—Dress.—Arts.—Food.—Not Cit-
izens.—Sacred Fire.—The Serpent.—Tradition of the Eagle.—Green
Corn Dance.—Vocabulary of Words.

THE history of the Pueblo Indians presents many
points of interest, and as the subject is one with which
the readers of our country are almost entirely unacquainted, I will briefly narrate a few of the leading incidents connected with their early intercourse with the
Spaniards. These facts are drawn from official documents, and may be relied upon as correct.

When the Spaniards first came to the country and
made permanent settlements, now more than two centuries and a half ago, they found these Indians numerous
and powerful, living peaceful and happy lives in their
villages, and supplied with the comforts and necessaries
of life. The Europeans overran and took possession of
their mountains and valleys, and reduced the inhabitants
from independence to a state of servitude; the pleasures
of their simple and primitive life were at an end, and
they saw themselves, in a few years, "the hewers of wood

---

* The reader will observe in this chapter some repetition of facts
mentioned in Chapter III., which could not be well avoided, but was
required in order to make each subject complete in itself.

and drawers of water" for a new and more powerful race
of men. They were obliged to give up the faith of their
fathers, which they had worshiped from time immemorial, and embrace the Catholic religion. They saw their
estufas closed, their articles of religious ceremony destroyed, and all their ancient rites entirely interdicted.
This treatment begat a feeling of hatred toward the
Spaniards, whom they began to regard as intruders in
their country and usurpers of their lands, and deemed it
their duty to expel them by force of arms. Neither the
teachings of the priests nor the punishment inflicted
upon them from time to time was able to extinguish the
hostility that filled their bosoms, and they only awaited
a proper occasion to take up arms and drive out the in-
vaders.

They made several attempts at rebellion before they
met with success, their plans being either discovered by
the watchful care of the Spaniards, or divulged by trai-
tors in their own ranks. The first effort of the kind
was about the year 1640, while Governor Arguello was
at the head of affairs in the province. The immediate
cause of this attempted outbreak was the whipping and
hanging of forty Indians, who refused to give up their
ancient religious worship and become good Catholics.
The conspiracy was discovered and nipped in the bud.
In the year 1650, while General Concha was governor,
they made a second attempt of the kind, which likewise
proved unsuccessful. This was placed on foot by the
leading men of the pueblos of Ysleta, Alameda, San Felipe, Cochiti, and Jemez. The time fixed upon for the
rising was the Thursday night of Passion Week. The
Indians were to rise while the Spaniards were in the
churches engaged in religious exercises, and fall upon
them by surprise, when all were to be massacred or
driven from the country. A party had been sent out to

secure the horses of the Spaniards, to prevent their escape; but, being arrested and examined by the order of the governor, the whole plot became known, and the ringleaders were secured. Those arrested were afterward tried: some of them were hanged or otherwise put to death, and others were sold into slavery for a term of years. There were several other attempts at rebellion between the years 1640 and 1680, and although the Indians were unsuccessful in every instance, they were not discouraged from making subsequent efforts to free themselves from the yoke of the Spaniards. The first general conspiracy among all the pueblos of the country was that put on foot while General Villanueva was the governor and captain-general of the province, the head and front of which was one Estevan Clemente, the governor of the Salt Lake pueblo. He was a man of note among the Indians, and aroused up his brethren to resistance. The plan of operations was about the same as those fixed upon in the time of General Concha. The Thursday night of Passion Week was again to be the time of rising, and the Indians were to seize all the horses to prevent the escape of the Spaniards. The conspiracy was discovered in time to prevent its being carried into effect, and thus failed, as in former attempts.

The first rebellion which met with even partial success was that which broke out in the year 1680, while Don Antonio de Otermin was governor and captain-general. In this attempt they were fully successful for a time, and not only succeeded in driving the Spaniards from the country, but maintained their independence for twelve years, in opposition to all the force the government could send against them. The conspiracy was placed on foot in the first place by the Taos Indians, who made an effort to unite all the pueblos in a common cause. The method of communicating information of the proposed rising was simple in the extreme. Two deer-skins were taken, upon which were made drawings representing the manner of the conspiracy and the object of it, which were sent round to all the villages by trusty hands, with an invitation to join in the rebellion and assist in the expulsion of the Spaniards. All acquiesced in the plan except the seven villages of the Moquis, for which reason the matter was dropped for the time being.

A second attempt was made the same year, soon afterward, which led to successful results. The leading spirits in this enterprise were Popé—by some said to have been a native of the pueblo of Taos, and by others a native of San Juan—and Catiti, a Queres Indian. They were shrewd and able men, and knew well the means to take to rouse up their countrymen to resistance. Popé seized upon the superstition of his untutored brethren, and turned it to a good account. He shut himself up for a time in the estufa, and would neither see nor hold any intercourse with his companions. When he appeared again in the village, he informed them that he had held communion with the devil, and through him feigned to have received messages from the infernal regions. These revelations directed him as to the course he should pursue to meet with success. He was to unite all the pueblos in a common league against the Spaniards, and the method of giving them information was also pointed out. He was to make a rope of palm-leaf fibres, in which were to be tied a number of knots. This was to be forwarded from pueblo to pueblo by the swiftest runners, and each village that joined in the conspiracy was to untie a knot. The number of knots remaining in the rope when it should be returned whence it was sent would signify the number of days before the outbreak was to take place. The rope was sent round as the devil had directed, and all the villages to which it was carried showed their approval of the plan by each one untying a knot.

The organization was effected with the greatest secrecy, and every possible means taken to prevent a discovery·and insure success; and they were so fearful their conspiracy might be divulged to the enemy, it is said they did not let a woman into the secret. Even those who fell under suspicion were put to death; and Popé caused his own son-in-law, Nicolas Bua, governor of the pueblo of San Juan, to be killed, for no other reason than because he was suspected of treachery by some of the conspirators. The day fixed upon for the breaking out of the rebellion was the tenth of August (1680), and the poor Indians looked forward to its arrival as the period that was to deliver their necks from the yoke of the Spaniards. They had newly bent their bows, and tipped their arrows afresh to draw Christian blood, and with impatience awaited their day of deliverance. Treachery, in spite of all their precautions, lurked in their own ranks, and their whole plan of operations became known to the Spaniards. Five days before the revolution was to commence, two Indians of the pueblo of Tezuque visited the Spanish governor at Santa Fé, and divulged to him the conspiracy, and thus he was placed upon his guard.

The Indians were aware, the same day, that their plot was discovered, and, fearing that delay might endanger the whole enterprise, they resolved to take up arms immediately. They commenced the work of death that night, and killed all the Spaniards who had the misfortune to fall into their hands, being particularly hostile against the priests. The Christians were in dismay, but made the best disposition to defend themselves possible. Word was sent to all the settlements of the rebellion, with orders for the inhabitants to prepare themselves for the emergency. In a few days several thousand Indians were in arms, and advanced upon Santa Fé, the capital, which they surrounded and placed in a state of siege. The place was closely invested for some time, and several actions were fought between the opposing parties, when the Spaniards evacuated the town, which the Indians allowed them to do without molestation. The Pueblos immediately entered and took possession of the place. They dismantled the Christian churches, and destroyed the images and sacred vestments; they established, in place of the Catholic religion, which force had compelled them to adopt, their heathen rites in all their relations; they re-opened the estufas, which had been closed for years, and celebrated their success in the *cachina* dance. This course was pursued in all parts of the country, and they endeavored, as far as possible, to obliterate all traces of the Christian religion.

The defeated Spaniards marched to El Paso del Norte, undergoing many hardships on the way. The fugitive troops remained encamped near that place until the autumn of the following year, awaiting re-enforcements and supplies for a reconquest of the country. They arrived in October, and in the month of November Otermin took up the line of march for New Mexico, with an army of several hundred men and a good supply of provisions. He proceeded, in spite of deep snows and cold weather, which he encountered nearly all the way up the valley as far as the pueblo of San Félipe, where he met the enemy in such force that he deemed it advisable to retreat, and so retraced his steps to El Paso. Several subsequent efforts were made to bring the revolted Indians to subjection, but none of the commanders were successful until the Viceroy of Mexico sent Bargas into the country in 1692. He succeeded in reducing all the pueblos to terms, and by the year 1696 peace and quietness were restored to the whole province. He marched throughout the country with his victorious arms, and village after village submitted to the conqueror.   During the contest Santa Fé was taken and retaken several times, and the poor natives exhibited a bravery worthy the cause in which they were fighting.

From the close of the rebellion of 1680 to the year 1837 the two races lived in comparative peace with each other.   The Spaniards abated some of the rigor they had hitherto practiced toward the Indians, and the latter were secured in the enjoyment of privileges they did not before possess.   In the latter year, as has been already mentioned, they again rose in rebellion, and advanced in thousands upon the capital.   The troops were defeated, the governor and leading officials put to death, and the government fell into the hands of the Indians.   They retained it, however, for a few weeks only, when they were overpowered by the Mexican authorities, and again brought to subjection.   Since the close of the war with Mexico they have remained at peace with our government, and seem pleased with the change of masters. They are friendly in their feelings toward the Americans, but have always manifested hostility to the Mexicans. The good-will they manifest toward our people is probably produced, in some degree, by circumstances.   It is said they have always had a tradition among them that a new race of men would come from the east to deliver them from the bondage of the Spaniards and Mexicans, and the Americans, coming from that quarter, may have led them to believe that we were their promised deliverers.   When General Kearney took possession of the country in 1846, the Pueblo Indians were among the first to give in their adherence to the new order of things, and, with the exception of the Taos Indians taking part in the rebellion of 1847, they have never manifested other than the most friendly disposition.   Upon several occa-

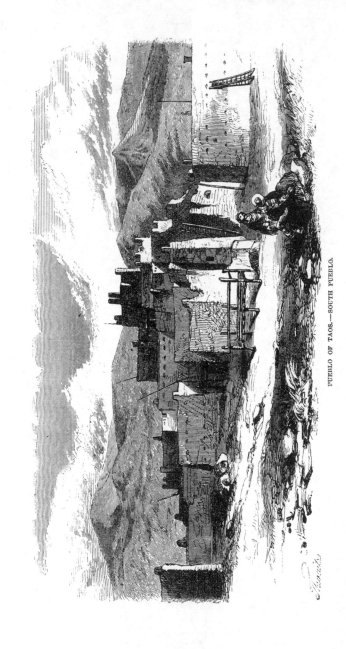

PUEBLO OF TAOS.—SOUTH PUEBLO.

sions they have volunteered to assist our troops in chastising the wild tribes for depredations committed upon
the settlements, and have always fought with a gallantry
hardly second to the United States troops. As guides
and spies in Indian warfare they are invaluable, and they
will follow a hostile trail with the keenness of a blood-
hound, and that, too, even when the most experienced
woodsman can see no signs of footsteps.

The population of the Pueblo Indians at the present
time is not more than ten thousand souls. They yet
live in little communities entirely separate and distinct
from the Mexican population, with their own local customs and laws. Their villages are constructed of adobes,
and in a style peculiar to themselves. In some instances the houses are small, and built around a square
court-yard, while in other cases the village is composed
of two or three large buildings contiguous to each other,
which sometimes accommodate as many as a thousand
or fifteen hundred people. They look much more like
fortresses than dwelling-places, and if properly manned
are capable of making a strong defense against small
arms. The pueblo near the town of Don Fernandez de
Taos, in the northern part of the territory, is the best
sample of the ancient mode of building. Here there are
two large houses three or four hundred feet in length, and
about a hundred and fifty feet wide at the base. They
are situated upon opposite sides of a small creek, and
in ancient times are said to have been connected by a
bridge. They are five and six stories high, each story
receding from the one below it, and thus forming a struc-
ture terraced from top to bottom. Each story is divided
into numerous little compartments, the outer tiers of
rooms being lighted by small windows in the sides, while
those in the interior of the building are dark, and are principally used as store-rooms. One of the most singular

features of these buildings is the absence of any direct communication with the outside on the ground floor. The only means of entrance is through a trap-door in the roof, and you ascend, from story to story, by means of ladders upon the outside, which are drawn up at night, and the population sleep secure from attack from without. This method of gaining access to the inside of the house is common to all the pueblos, and was probably adopted in early times as a means of defense against the wild tribes by which they were surrounded. In the two buildings at Taos about eight hundred men, women, and children live together like one large family, and apparently in much harmony. It is the custom to have a sentinel stationed upon the house-top, whose duty it is to give notice of the approach of danger.

Each pueblo contains an *estufa*, which is used both as a council-chamber and a place of worship, where they practice such of their heathen rites as still exist among them. It is built partly under ground, and is considered a consecrated and holy place. Here they hold all their deliberations upon public affairs, and transact the necessary business of the village. It is said to be their custom, when they return from a successful war expedition, to repair to the *estufa*, where they strip themselves of their clothing, and dance and otherwise celebrate their success; and that, upon some occasions, they remain there two or three days before visiting their families.

The government of the pueblos is purely democratic; and although they are in some instances subject to the laws of the United States and of the Territory, in most respects they are independent communities. Each village is entirely independent of the others, with its own local government and laws; and there is no common bond of union between them. An election is held each year for a governor, alcalde, fiscal or constable, and a war captain, and in all cases the majority of votes decides the contest. The governor is also called the *cacique ;* and immediately after his election he repairs to Santa Fé to the agent for the Pueblo Indians, to receive confirmation of office.

The latter has no power of confirmation, but they come and announce their election as a matter of custom. They formerly presented themselves to the governor of the Territory, but since an agent has been appointed to watch over their interests, this official visitation is made to him. Upon such state occasions, his red excellency brings with him a silver-headed cane, his staff of office, and assumes as much dignity as a bona fide white governor. The process of confirmation simply consists in the agent taking the cane into his hands, and then handing it back to the governor; but under the Mexican government it was the custom, I believe, for the new incumbent to kneel before the governor of the Territory, to whom he presented himself, who confirmed him by some process of laying on of hands. The alcalde is the judiciary of the village, from whose court there is no appeal; and the fiscal serves all legal process, and enforces obedience to their customs and laws. The war captain is their mighty man of Mars—he who sets their squadrons in the field, and leads them on to victory. In the " piping times of peace" he is a mere nobody, and has neither power nor dignity of office wherewith to console himself; but when the "blast of war sounds in his ears," he is clothed with great authority. He then becomes "commander-in-chief of the army and navy" thereof, and is the champion of the tawny warriors both in the council-chamber and in the field.

Besides the officers elected by universal suffrage, the principal chiefs compose a " council of wise men," whose duty it is to manage the internal affairs of the pueblo.

Whenever any business of importance is required to be transacted, the governor assembles the council, his " constitutional advisers," in the *estufa*, where the matter is discussed and afterward decided by a vote of those present, the majority always controlling. Among other regulations is the appointment of a secret watch, whose duty it is to prevent vice and disorder in the village, and particularly to have an eye on the young people, and see that they do not have improper intercourse with each other. If any act of this kind is discovered, the offenders are arraigned before the governor and council to answer, and if the case is clearly established they are compelled to marry forthwith ; but if the girl is of good character, and the man refuses to marry her, there is no force used, but they are sentenced to remain apart, under penalty of being whipped. Their strictness in this particular has done much toward preserving the chastity of their females.

As heretofore mentioned, the Pueblo Indians have embraced the Catholic religion, and at the present time I believe the Moquis are the only ones among whom there are neither transitory nor permanent priests. At an early day there were missionaries among the latter, who were either killed or driven away during the revolution, and their places were never afterward filled. Although nominally Catholics, they still cling to many of their heathen rites, and mingle their pagan ceremonies with the forms of Christian worship. One of their ancient rites is called the *cachina* dance, to which they are much attached, and which they celebrate at certain seasons of the year with great rejoicings. This dance was suppressed by the Spaniards when they first made a conquest of the country and forced their religion upon the natives, which the Indians considered so great a deprivation that it is alleged as one of the main causes of the

rebellion of 1680. Each village has a church, where a
Catholic priest officiates at stated periods, one priest serv-
ing two or three pueblos where they are not a great distance from each other. They pay tithes of all they possess, which is a burdensome tax upon them. They are
punctual in all the outward observances of the Church,
but they scarcely understand more than the mere forms
that are presented to the sight. They are said still to
worship the sun, as was the custom with their heathen
ancestors, and that every morning they turn the face toward the east, whence they look for the coming of Montezuma.

The land belonging to each pueblo is held in common
by the inhabitants, but for purposes of cultivation it is
parceled out to the several families, who raise their own
crops, and dispose of the produce of their labor. Irrigation is necessary, and by careful tillage they can raise
as fine crops as any produced in the Territory. They
grow wheat, corn, beans, and vegetables and fruits.
They have paid considerable attention to the cultivation
of the grape, and some of the pueblos own large and valuable vineyards. They make wine from the grapes, and
also sell them in a ripe state in the neighboring Mexican
towns. They raise stock, and some of the pueblos own
considerable herds of horses, mules, oxen, and sheep.

As a class, the Pueblo Indians are among the most
orderly and useful people in the Territory; they are industrious, frugal, and peaceable, and generally live in
harmony with each other and the surrounding Mexican
population. There are no paupers or drones among them,
because all are obliged to labor and contribute something
to the weal of the community to which they belong.
Their weapons are the bow and arrow, and a few old
guns. They are a brave people, and have oftentimes
shown themselves more than a match for the wild In-

dians. The only defensive armor they use is a rude shield made of raw bull-hide. When a dispute arises among them, it is generally settled in an amicable manner by the governor and his council, and it is very seldom they go into the courts of justice to seek redress. They are in a lamentable state of ignorance, and it is a very rare thing to find one who can either read or write. They are extremely superstitious, and are firm believers in witchcraft in all its variety. A little more than two years ago, the council and governor of the pueblo of Nambé caused two of the inhabitants of that village to be put to death in a most cruel manner, because they were accused of eating up all the little children of the pueblo. They are degenerating as a race, the principal cause being their constant intermarriage in the same pueblo; and it is a very rare thing that any of the young men seek wives among the neighboring villages. In this respect they seem to follow the example of the royal families of Europe, and their blood is losing its strength about as rapidly. As a class they are honest, and are generally free from drunkenness.

They retain, in a great measure, their aboriginal costume, and in but few instances have adopted the dress worn by the Mexicans. The outer garments of the men consist of a jacket and leggins made of deer-skins, tanned; the leggins are worn by all, but many dispense with the jacket, and wrap up in a buffalo robe, which they gird around the waist. Some wear a blanket instead of the buffalo robe, and a few wear cotton shirts. The women wear leggins the same as the men; but instead of the jacket or buffalo robe, they wear a handsome blanket or mantle over the shoulders, in such a manner as to leave both arms free. A shorter blanket, called a *tilma*, is worn in front, falling down as low as the knee; and both the *tilma* and the blanket worn over the shoulders are fastened by a girdle around the waist. They are of a dark ground, and woven in various figures of bright colors, and the leggins are ornamented with beads. Both sexes wear moccasins upon the feet instead of shoes, and go bareheaded. The hair is worn long, and is done up in a great queue that falls down behind. There is a variance in the dress of the different pueblos, some approaching nearer to that of the wild Indians of the prairies. There is a marked difference between the costume of the northern and southern pueblos.

They appear to have lost most of the few arts they possessed when the country was first discovered by the Spaniards. Then they manufactured some fabrics of cotton, and other articles of curious workmanship. They still make a coarse kind of blanket for their own use, but they devote the greater part of their time to the manufacture of earthenware, which they sell in quantities to the Mexicans. It exhibits some skill, and is often adorned with various devices painted upon it before it is burned. This ware is in universal use in the territory, and there is considerable demand for it in the market. They also make vessels of wicker-work tight enough to hold water after they have been once saturated. They are formed of the fibres of some plant ingeniously plaited together, and some of the proper size and shape are used by travelers as canteens.

Their food is simple and wholesome, and is the same found in common use among the Mexican population. It consists principally of *tortillas, frijoles, atole, pinole*, and *chile*, the method of preparing all of which will be described elsewhere. They are probably of aboriginal origin, and were adopted by the first Spanish settlers who came into the country. They make another quality of bread from maize different from the tortilla, the use of which is principally confined to the Indians, which is called *guayave*. The corn is first ground on the *metate*, and then mixed with water into a thin paste, when it is baked before the fire upon flat stones heated for that purpose. The paste is laid on in exceedingly thin layers, and is almost immediately baked and peeled off, when a new supply is placed upon the stone. They are about the thickness of a wafer, and when a large number of them are baked, they are rolled together and form the *guayave*. The natives make great use of them when performing long journeys, and they will subsist for many days upon a few of these simple rolls.

The Pueblo Indians are not recognized as citizens of the United States, or of the Territory of New Mexico, in which respect they are in the same condition as the wild tribes, but in other particulars they are placed in a more favorable position. The laws protect them in their persons and property, and they have the right to sue in courts of justice the same as citizens, for this purpose being created bodies politic by the territorial Legislature. They are also made amenable to the criminal laws of the Territory for offenses committed against one of their own number or against a citizen. An agent is appointed by the President to watch over their interests, and Congress has appropriated twelve thousand dollars to be expended in the purchase of agricultural implements for the various pueblos.

The question as to whether the Pueblo Indians are citizens of the United States has been mooted and discussed upon two occasions, and there are not wanting those who contend that they are entitled to all the political rights of the free white male inhabitants of the Union. This view of the case is manifestly wrong; and where the evidence is so clear to the contrary, this opinion must have been embraced in the absence of a proper examination of the subject. It is maintained by those who hold the affirmative, that inasmuch as these Indians were citizens of the republic of Mexico before the United States acquired the territory, they became, upon the ratification of the treaty of Guadalupe Hidalgo, citizens of the United States. I will examine the question briefly.

While Spain held the country, none but Spaniards or Europeans were recognized as citizens of the monarchy, all the mixed races being excluded. During the revolution which resulted in the independence of Mexico, the revolutionists, in order to attach the masses to their cause, declared all the inhabitants of the country to be citizens, whether Europeans, Africans, or Indians. This doctrine, in words at least, appears to have been recognized in the plan of Iguala, the treaty of Cordova, and two or three subsequent decrees of the Mexican Congress, down as late as the 17th of September, 1822. But after the independence was established, and the federal Constitution formed, I know of no law or act of the government that recognized them as citizens of the republic, but the contrary appears to have been the case. If the Pueblos were entitled to these rights, so were the wild tribes also, as the word " Indians" is used without any qualification as to class ; and if the authorities cited embrace one portion of the race, they embrace all, which would include the Nabajos, Apaches, and Utahs. The truth is, that Mexico, after the revolution, never did consider the Pueblo Indians citizens, but they were always viewed as wards, subject to the control of the government. The land they occupied was only held by the right of possession, and they were expressly forbidden to sell, rent, lease, or in any manner alienate the same ; and as late as the year 1827, the Mexican Congress had to confirm the sale of a rancho belonging to the pueblo of Cochiti before the purchaser could obtain a title. The acts and decrees upon this subject are still in force in

New Mexico, wherein they do not conflict with the Constitution and laws of the United States. Now it is very evident that if these Indians had enjoyed an equality of civil rights with the other inhabitants of Mexico, as is alleged, they would have been allowed to dispose of their lands, as was the case with Mexican citizens.

But, admitting that the Pueblo Indians were citizens of Mexico while under her jurisdiction, it by no means follows that they were made citizens of the United States by the operation of the treaty of Guadalupe Hidalgo. That document is very clear upon this point, and we need not go behind it to determine the question. The ninth article provides as follows, viz. :

" The Mexicans who, in the territory aforesaid, shall not preserve the character of citizens of the Mexican republic conformably with what is stipulated in the preceding article, shall be incorporated into the Union of the United States, and be admitted at the proper time (to be judged of by the Congress of the United States) to the enjoyment of all the rights of citizens of the United States, according to the principles of the Constitution, and in the mean time shall be maintained and protected in the free enjoyment of their liberty and property, and secured in the free exercise of their religion without restriction."

Now no man who has eyes to read and sense to understand can place a wrong construction upon this clause of the treaty without a willful intention to do so. The only class of persons in the acquired territory who can lay any claim to be admitted to the rights of citizens of the United States are those that belong to the race known as " Mexicans," who are specified as a class, without any reference whatever to their citizenship ; and, according to the tenor of the ninth article, their being *citizens* of Mexico at the making of the treaty does not

seem to have been a requisite to entitle them to the ben-
efits of it in this particular, if they were "*Mexicans.*"
If the words Mexican citizens had been used, then a legal question might have arisen as to who were citizens
of that republic at the time the treaty was made; but,
under the present, circumstances, no such question can
arise, because the treaty designates " Mexicans" instead
of Mexican citizens.   This wording excludes every description of persons except those specially named, unless
by some modern political or judicial jugglery a " Mexican" can be changed into an Indian, or an Indian mould-
ed into a " Mexican."   Such transformation would cast
into the shade all the tricks of Herr Alexander or the
Fakir of Ava.   Even the " Mexicans" themselves did
not become citizens of the United States by virtue of
the treaty with Mexico, who were not admitted as such
until Congress judged the "proper time" to have arrived,
being protected, in the mean time, in the enjoyment of
their liberty and property, and the free exercise of their
religion.   There is a condition annexed to this investi-
ture of citizenship which can only be confirmed according to the principles of the Constitution; and our courts
have held long ago that Indians are not citizens in the
meaning of that instrument.   This article of the treaty
was inserted by the Senate of the United States, and it
is not likely that that body meant to confer rights upon
the Indians acquired from Mexico which are denied to
our native Indians.

The Act of Congress, approved September 9th, 1855,
establishing a territorial government in New Mexico,
shows the construction Congress placed upon the treaty
as regards citizenship.   Under this act Indians are excepted in providing for an apportionment of the inhabitants for representatives, and none are allowed to vote
and hold office except " white male inhabitants," citizens

of the United States, including those recognized as citizens by the treaty with Mexico. These authorities seem clearly to settle the question, and deny the rights of citizens to all Indians, the Pueblos as well as the wild tribes; but if Indians are citizens of the United States by virtue of the plan of Iguala, the treaty of Cordova, subsequent decrees, and the treaty of Guadalupe, so are Africans, since whatever political rights these two races have in the territory acquired from Mexico are drawn from the same source and must be equal.

Many curious tales are related of the superstitious customs of the Indians, among which I find the following told of the Pecos pueblo. It is said that in the *estufa* the sacred fire was kept constantly burning, having been originally kindled by Montezuma. It was in a basin of a small altar, and, in order to prevent its becoming extinguished, a watch was kept over it day and night. The tradition runs that Montezuma had enjoined upon their ancestors not to allow the fire to expire until he should return to deliver them from the Spaniards, and hence their watchful care over it. He was expected to appear with the rising sun, and every morning the Indians went upon the house-tops, and, with eyes turned toward the east, looked for the coming of their monarch. Alas for them, he never came; and when the smouldering embers had expired, they gave up all hope of deliverance, and sought new homes in a distant pueblo. The task of watching the sacred fires was assigned to the warriors, who served by turns for a period of two days and two nights at a time, without eating or drinking, while some say that they remained upon duty until death or exhaustion relieved them from their post. The remains of those who died from the effect of watching are said to have been carried to the den of a great serpent, which appears to have lived upon these delicacies alone. Mr. Gregg, in speaking of this circumstance, remarks as follows : " This huge snake (invented, no doubt, by the lovers of the marvelous to account for the constant disappearance of the Indians) was represented as the idol which they worshiped, and as subsisting entirely upon the flesh of his devotees ; live infants, however, seemed to suit his palate best. The story of this wonderful serpent was so firmly believed in by many ignorant people, that on one occasion I heard an honest ranchero assert that, upon entering the village very early upon a winter's morning, he saw the huge trail of the reptile in the snow as large as that of a dragging ox."

The survivors of the Pecos Indians relate another tradition connected with the early history of their people. Upon one occasion, and before the Spaniards had settled in the country, a man and his little son went into the mountains to gather wood. The boy was startled at the sound of a voice, and asked his father who spoke to them, who replied that he did not hear any body, and they continued to pick up wood. In a few moments the voice was heard again, when the father looked up and saw a large eagle perched in the top of a high pine-tree. The bird now told the Indian that the king across the waters was sending people into the country to take care of the Pueblos, and that if he would come back to that spot in eight days, it could tell him when they would arrive. The eagle also directed him to inform his village what he had heard. When the Indian returned to the pueblo, he told the head men he had something to communicate, who assembled in the *estufa* to listen to him, when he related an account of the appearance of the eagle and what it had said to him. At the end of eight days he returned to the mountain, where he found the eagle awaiting him, which informed him that the men from across the waters would arrive in two days, and that all his people must go to meet them, and welcome them to the country, which was accordingly done. This tradition is believed by the remnant of this pueblo, and they relate it with apparent pleasure as an important epoch in their past history. In reference to the legends of the Pueblo Indians, I would remark that they should be received with much allowance, particularly those that ralate to Montezuma. Among these people there exists neither the semblance of music or poetry never so rude, and it is at least questionable whether correct tradition can be preserved among those who have no knowledge of these two arts; and I doubt whether the Pueblo Indians ever heard of Montezuma until they came in contact with the early Spanish priests.

At stated periods they practice various dances in their villages, which have been handed down from their heathen ancestors. Some belong to their religious rites, and others do not. That known as You-pel-lay, or the green corn dance, as performed by the Indians of Jemez, is thus described in the journal of Lieutenant Simpson: " When the performers first appeared, all of whom were men, they came in a line, slowly walking, and bending and stooping as they approached. They were dressed in a kind of blanket, the upper portion of their bodies being naked and painted a dark red. Their legs and arms, which were also bare, were variously striped with red, white, and blue colors, and around their arms, above the elbow, they wore a green band decked with sprigs of *piñon*. A necklace of the same description was worn around the neck. Their heads were decorated with feathers. In one hand they carried a dry gourd containing some grains of corn, with which they produced a rattling kind of music; in the other a string, from which were hung several *tortillas*. At the knee were fastened small shells of the ground turtle and antelopes' feet, and dangling from the back, at the waist, depended a fox-skin. The musicians were habited in the common costume of the village, and made their music in a sitting posture. Their instruments consisted each of half a gourd, placed before them with the convex side up, and upon this they placed with their left hand a smooth stick, and with their right drew forward and backward upon it, in a sawing manner, a notched one. This produced a sound much like that of grinding corn upon a *metate*, a slightly concave stone.

" The party were accompanied by three elders of the town, whose business it was to make a short speech in front of the different houses, and at particular times join in the singing of the rest of the party. Thus they went from house to house singing and dancing, the occupant of each awaiting their arrival in front of their respective dwelling."

In conclusion of this subject, I give a vocabulary of words in the language of most of the pueblos, taken from the journal of Lieutenant Simpson. It will be seen that we differ a little in the classification of the pueblos as regards their nationality. My arrangement is based mainly upon the classification of Cruzate made in 1692, which I have no doubt was correct as then given. He spent a considerable time in the country, visited the various pueblos, and had a good opportunity of becoming acquainted with the Indians and their language. He divides them into four nations, and places Jemez, Zuñi, and Moqui as belonging to the Queres division and speaking the same language. The vocabulary of Lieutenant Simpson makes these pueblos speak different languages, which can not be the case unless Cruzate was in error, or that since his time these people have changed their languages, neither of which is probable. These villages in 1692 spoke the same language as his class marked (1), as also did that of Old Pecos, now classed with Jemez, and I believe he has fallen into an error in separating them.   The first three classes represent the nations of Queres, Piro, and Tegua, and, with the exception of the discrepance I have pointed out, his classification substantially agrees with that of Cruzate.   As to the Indian names of the various objects he gives, I have no means of testing their correctness, as I have not had an opportunity of learning any of the languages mentioned.   I take them, however, to be in the main correct.

A COMPLETE VOCABULARY OF WORDS IN THE LANGUAGES OF THE PUEBLO OR CIVILIZED INDIANS OF NEW MEXICO.

Name of the Object in English.	In the language of the Pueblo Indians of—					
	Santo Domingo, San Felipe, Santa Ana, Silla, Laguna, Acoma, Cochiti. (1.)	San Juan, Santa Clara, S. Ildefonso, Pojnaque, Nambé, Tezuque. (2.)	Taos, Picoris, Sandia, Isleta. (3.)	Jemez and Old Pecos. (4.)	Zuni. (5.)	Moqui. (6.)
God	Dios (Spanish). Montezuma, they say, is synonymous with Dios	Give no other word than the Spanish Dios	Huam-may-ah	Pay (same as for sun)	Ho-ae-wo-nae-we-oh-nah	Toe-kill.
Heavens	....	....	....	....	....	....
Sun	....	Pah	Hoo-len-nah	Pay	Yat-tock-kah	Toke-pay-lah.
Moon	....	Poy-ye	Pan-nah	Pah-ah	....	Tah-wah.
Star	She-cat	A-doy-e-ah	Hah-he-glan-nah	Woon-hah	Mo-yat-chu-way	Moo-yah.
Cloud	....	....	....	....	....	O-mow.
Earth	Hah-ats	Nah	Pah-han-nah	Dock-ah	Ou-lock-nan-nay	Touch-quae.
Man	Hats-see	Say-en	Tah-hah-ne-nah	Shu-o-tish	Oat-se	Se-ke-ah.
Woman	Nai-at-say	Ker	Clay-an-nah	Ste-osh	O-care	....
Wife	Kar-nats-shu	Nah-we-so	Could give no word	Ne-ohoy	Could give no word	....
Boy	O-nue	An-noh	Oy-you-oo-nah	....	Art-se-ke	....
Boy (infant)	Sah-wish-sha	....	....	Ah-cue	....	....
Girl	Koy-yah	An-ugh	Koo-ay-lon-nah	....	Tza-nah	....
Girl (infant)	Sah-wish-sha	....	....	Tond-o-hos-che	We-at-zah-nah	....
Head	Nash-can-ne	Pum-bah	Pi-ne-mah	Chit-chous	O-shuck-quin-nay	Qua-tah.
Forehead	Cop-pay	Sic-co-vah	Pah-hem-nah	Wah-pay	Huck-kin-nay	Col-ler.
Face	Ko-wah	Cha-ay	Cha-gah-neem-may	Tcho-lah	No-pon-ne-nay	....

Name of the Object in English.	Santo Domingo, San Felipe, Santa Ana, Silla, Laguna, Acoma, Cochiti. (1.)	San Juan, Santa Clara, S. Ildefonso, Pojuaque, Nambe, Tezuque. (2.)	Taos, Picoris, Sandia, Isleta. (3.)	Jemez and Old Pecos. (4.)	Zuni. (5.)	Moqui. (6.)
Eye	Kan-nah	Chay	Che-nay	Saech	Too-nah-way	Po-se.
Nose	Kar-wish-she	Shay	Poo-ae-nah	For-saech	No-lin-nay	Ya-kuch.
Mouth	Tsee-kah	Sho	Clah-mo-e-nah	E-ae-quah	Ae-wah-tin-nay	Mo-ah.
Teeth	Har-at-chay-nay	Moo-ah	Moo-en-nah-en-hay	Goo-whan	O-nah-way	Tah-mah.
Tongue	Wah-at-chin	Hah	May-oon-on-en-ah	Ain-lah	Ho-nin-nay	Ling-a.
Chin	Tzars-kah	Sab-boh	Clah-bon-hay	Ah-tish	Klay-which-chin-nay	Ke-at.
Ear	Kah-u-pah	O-ye-o	Tag-lay-o-nay	Wash-chish	Sah-schuck-tin-nay	Nock-a-wuck.
Hair	Har-tran	Poh	Pah-han-nay	Fore-lah	Ti-ah-way	Hay-me.
Neck	Wit-trah-ne	Kah	Gah-ne-may	Toe	Kiss-sin-nay	Qua-pe.
Arm	Kah-u-may	Ko	Hah-en-nay	Hah	Ar-se-way	Mah-at.
Elbow		Mah				Cher-ber.
Hand	Kah-mosh-tay			Mah-tish	Shon-che-way	Mock-tay.
Finger		Pe-ah	Pah-ah-kay-nay-ne-may			Mah-latz.
Breast	Quaist-pah		Pah-nay	Pay-lu	Po-at-tan-nay	Toe-witz-kah.
Leg	Kay-ah-kah			Hong	Sack-que-way	Ho-kah.
Knee		Ah				Tom-me.
Foot	Kar-tay	Pah-ye	E-en-en-nah	Awn-dash	Wake-que-a-way	Her-kuck.
Deer	Ke-ah-ne	Kah	Tah-mean-mah	Pah-ah		
Buffalo	Moo-shats	As in Sp.	Kah-nah-neem-mah	Toss-chach	Too-she-kay-one-na-nay	
Horse	Kah-yai-oh (probably a corruption of the Span. caballo)		Kah-wan-nah (probably a corruption of the Spanish)	Gu-wah	Too-she	As in Spanish.
Serpent	Skers-ker	Could give no word	Hatch-oo-nah	Pay-chu-lah	Che-to-lah	
Rattlesnake	Shrue-o-we	Poy-yoh	Pi-ho-own	Kae-ah-vae-lah		

English						
Dog	Tish	Cher	So-dor-nah	Can-nu	Wat-se-tah	Po-ku.
Cat	Moos	Moo-sah	Moo-se-e-nah	Moon-sah	Moo-sah	......
Fire	Kah-kan-ye	Fah	Pah-an-nah	Fwa-ah	Mack-ke	Day-bor.
Wood	......	Sun	......	......	......	Ser-her-be.
Water	Tseats	Ogh	Poh-ah-oon	Pah	Ke-a-o-way	......
Stone	......	......	......	Ke-ah-ah	......	......
Cactus	Ae-mocch-te	Sow-wah	......	Te-ah	Tze-nan-nay	Kar-uk.
Corn	......	......	......	......	Melah	Se-ka-mo-se.
Bean	......	......	......	......	......	......
Bread	Pah (probably a corruption of the Spanish *pan*)	As in Sp.	Ah-coon-nah	Zo-tane-bae-lah	Moo-lun-nay	......
Flesh	Ish-sha-ne	Pe-we	Toe-an-nay	Gu-nay-wat-si	She-lay	Au-tah.
Bow	......	......	......	......	......	Ho-huck.
Arrow	O-nistz	Pe-quar-re	Tah-we-nah	Tah-lis-tah	Toe-o-an-nan-nay	A-muck-te.
Fusil	......	......	......	......	......	Se-po-wah.
Sword	......	......	......	......	......	Se-pom-uck-ke.
Spurs	......	......	......	......	......	Wo-bock-pe.
Whip	......	......	......	......	......	Chong.
Pipe	......	......	......	......	......	Pa-ta-nock-a.
Hat	......	......	......	......	......	Chee.
Friend	......	Ke-mah	......	......	......	......

CHAPTER VII.

SANTA FÉ, WITH SOME ACCOUNT OF THE MANNERS AND
CUSTOMS OF THE PEOPLE.

Situation.—How built.—Houses.—Public Buildings.—Sight-seeing.—
Legislative Anecdote.—Burro.—Cock-fighting.—Mexican Family.—
Furniture.—Tortillas and Frijoles.—Reception.—Manners.—Smok-
ing.—Leave-taking.—Gambling.—Monte.—Señora Barcelo.

SANTA FÉ, or, as it sometimes is written, *Santa Fé
de San Francisco*, the city of the Holy Faith of Saint
Francis, is the capital of the Territory of New Mexico,
and has been the seat of government of the province
since the Spaniards first settled the country. It is situated in a valley on both sides of the small river of the
same name, and about twenty miles east of the Rio del
Norte, into which the former stream empties to the southwest. The town lies at the western base of a chain of
high mountains, some of which are covered with snow
most of the year, and which extend a long distance to
the north and south. They are part of the great Rocky
chain, and form a barrier that all must pass who enter
the Territory from the east. The valley is mountain-
locked on every side, but is more open toward the southwest, the direction we take to reach the valley of the Del
Norte.

A good deal of uncertainty and doubt hang over the
first settlement of Santa Fé both as to time and persons.
I was informed by an old resident of the place that six
men who belonged to one of the early Spanish expedi-
tions into the Floridas, and which was wrecked and
broken up, wandered, in pursuit of game and adventure,

SANTA FÉ.

through what is now New Mexico, and were the first Europeans who passed near where Santa Fé stands. Thence they pursued their way toward the southwest, and met a body of Spaniards who were coming into the country from Southern Mexico. The six men here referred to must have been Cabeza de Baca and his ship-wrecked companions, the survivors of the unfortunate expedition of Narvaez, as they are the only white men known to have passed through the country previous to the expedition of Coronado in 1540–43. Independent of tradition, we have evidence extant that the country was permanently settled between the years 1580 and 1600, and that Santa Fé was one of the first points at which a settlement was made. It was the capital before the year 1680, as we learn from the journals of the Spanish officers who served in the country, and particularly from that of Don Antonio de Otermin, who was at that time, and had been for some years, the governor and military commandant of the province. The latitude is 35° 41′ north, and the longitude 106° west from Greenwich, and the elevation is more than seven thousand feet above the level of the sea.

The city occupies very nearly the same site as the ancient capital of the Pueblo Indian kingdom. Here upon the surrounding hills these people had constructed several of their quaint-looking buildings, and when the Spaniards first came to the country they found this point the centre of their strength. In the vicinity of the town pieces of painted pottery are still found, and parts of two of the old buildings are standing on the west side of the river, on the road leading to San Miguel. The Indians resided here many years after the Spaniards made a settlement, but in course of time the pueblos fell into decay, the inhabitants seeking new homes in other parts of the country. The modern town of Santa Fé, like its great namesake and prototype, Timbuctoo, is built of mud, and the inhabitants, with great truth, can call their houses "earthly tabernacles." The population, according to the census of 1850, was between four and five thousand, and may be set down about the same at this time, but this number includes all the little settlements along the river up to the foot of the mountains. It is laid out with considerable regularity in the manner of all Spanish-built towns. In the centre is a public square or plaza, some two or three acres in extent, from the four corners of which lead the main streets, at right angles to each other. The streets are of medium width and wholly unpaved; and but for the shelter afforded by the portales (the side-walks) in the rainy season, they would become almost impassable for foot-passengers. In the middle of the Plaza stands a flag-staff, erected by the military authorities some years ago, from the top of which the star-spangled banner daily waves to the breeze.

The houses are built of *adobes*, or mud bricks dried in the sun, and are but one story in height; and there are only two two-story houses in the place, neither of which was erected by the Mexicans. The walls are much thicker than those of a stone or brick house, and, being of a drier material, they are cooler in summer and warmer in winter than the former. The almost universal style of building, both in town and country, is in the form of a square, with a court-yard in the centre. A large door, called a *zaguan*, leads from the street into the *patio* or court-yard, into which the doors of the various rooms open. A portal, or, more properly, according to the American understanding of the same, a porch, runs around this court, and serves as a sheltered communication between different parts of the house. The roof is flat, with a slight parapet running around it, which adds somewhat to the appearance of the building; and the water which collects upon it is carried off by means of wooden spouts that extend into the street, and which look not unlike the guns of a small fortress looking through the embrasures. The only wood used about the roof is the sleepers, and the boards laid across them to hold the earth, because of the high price of timber. They cover the sleepers with a foot or eighteen inches of dirt, which they pack down, and then besmear it with a top coating of mud to make it water proof. In time it becomes hard, and unless there should be a heavy fall of rain, it will turn water very well. Sometimes a single roof will weigh several tons, the load of dirt accumulating from year to year. This seems a very primitive way of roofing a house, but it is the best arrangement that can be made under the circumstances. When a roof begins to leak, it is repaired by putting a few sacks of dirt upon it; and after a heavy dash of rain, it is usual to see every family upon the roof giving it a thorough examination, and carrying up fresh earth to mend the breaches. The greater part of the year being dry, the mud roof answers very well, but it would soon be washed down if as much rain should fall annually as is the case in other parts of the United States.

Along the principal streets the houses have portales in front, after the plan of colonnades in some of the European cities. They are of very rough workmanship, but are an ornament to the place, and a convenience to the inhabitants, as they afford a sheltered promenade around the town in the rainy season. A row of portales extends around the public square. The Plaza is the main thoroughfare, as well as the centre of the business of the city, and fronting upon it are most of the stores and shops of the merchants and traders, and some of the public buildings. The public edifices in Santa Fé are few in number and of rude construction. The government palace, a long, low mud building, extends the entire north side of the Plaza, and is occupied by the officers of the territorial government, and is also made use of for purposes of legislation. Near by, and on the street that leads out at the northeast corner of the square, is the court-house, where the United States, District, and Supreme Courts hold their sessions. On the south side, and opposite the palace, stands the old Mexican Military Chapel, now in the possession of the Catholic Church, and in which the bishop of the diocese officiates. About one square to the east of the Plaza is the parochial church, much improved within two years, and adjoining are convenient buildings for a boarding-school for boys; and on the north bank of the Rio Chiquito is situated the boarding and day school for girls, under the management of the Sisters of Charity. The building is a large two-story house, and was erected a few years ago for a hotel. Both the institutions were established by Bishop Lamy, and are in as flourishing a condition as could be expected. They number forty or fifty pupils each, who are instructed in ancient and modern languages, music, drawing, and other branches of a useful and polite education.

Three years ago the American Baptist Board of Home Missions caused to be erected in Santa Fé a small but neat place of worship. It is a combination of the Gothic and Grecian styles, built of adobes, and is quite an ornament to the part of the town where it is situated. The Odd Fellows have erected a new hall for their order, one square from the Plaza, in the street leading to San Miguel. On a vacant lot north of the palace, and near the American Cemetery, a new state-house is in course of erection, at a cost of near a hundred thousand dollars, which, when completed, will make a handsome and imposing edifice, and of which the Territory stands in great need. Near by, and a little to the northeast, is the site of the new Penitentiary, also in course of erection. Such an institution is badly wanted, and the country abounds with admirable subjects for it. On a hill to the north-east of the town are the ruins of old Fort Marcy, built during the late war with Mexico, but which has not been occupied since the conclusion of peace. In addition to the two churches already mentioned, there is one on the west side of the Rio Chiquito, dedicated to Our Lady of Guadalupe, and a fourth on the street of San Miguel, in both of which service is held upon certain occasions. The city also contains one hotel, one printing-office, some twenty-five stores, numerous grog-shops, two tailoring establishments, two shoe-makers, one apothecary, a ba-kery, and two blacksmith's shops. The present military garrison of the place is one company of the third United States Infantry, whose barracks are just in rear of the palace, and it is also the military head-quarters of the department.

Santa Fé has figured somewhat both in the ancient and modern history of New Mexico. As has already been mentioned, during the governorship of Don Antonio de Otermin in 1680, it was besieged for several days by the Pueblo Indians, who had risen in rebellion against the Spaniards. The garrison and inhabitants, being un-able to defend the town, were obliged to retreat and let it fall into the hands of the Indians. The town was again attacked by the same people in 1837, and a second time they acquired possession of it; but they held it for a few days only, when they abandoned it, doing no other damage than confiscating the goods of some of the Mex-ican officials who were most obnoxious to them. In the war with Mexico the American army directed their march upon Santa Fé, which was the first place they took pos-session of, where head-quarters were established, and whence operations were directed for the entire conquest of the country.

Having thus given the reader a brief general description of Santa Fé, I will, in order to make him better acquainted with the localities of the place, and also the manners and customs of the people, ask him or her to accompany me in a perambulatory visit around the town, and take note of whatever of interest turns up on the way. We will commence our tour of sight-seeing on a clear summer's morning, and will imagine the place of setting out to be opposite the court-house. This building is nearly or quite a hundred feet in length, some twenty-five wide, and one story high. It was formerly used as a store-house of the quarter-master's department, and was fitted up for a court-house after the establishment of the territorial government. We pass through the large double doors that open toward the street into the court room, some sixty feet long, and which is much better fitted up than any other one in the territory. The floor is laid with pine boards, and comfortable seats are provided for the jurors, parties, and witnesses. The many tons of earth that form the roof are supported by a row of square pillars extending through the middle of the room. The platform of the judge, built in the old pulpit style, is about midway of the southern wall, and on the side opposite to the place of entrance. The bar for the attorneys occupies the centre of the room, immediately in front of the "justice seat," with room enough between for the desks of the marshal and clerk. These two officers have their office in the same building, and adjoining the court-room are rooms for the grand and petit juries.

Having seen all the sights in and about the court-house, we turn our backs upon the *casa de justicia*, and continue our voyage of route. We enter the Plaza at the northeast corner, and immediately the eye ranges along the portal of the palace in front of which we are

now standing. It is not far from three hundred and fifty
feet in length, and varies from twenty to seventy-five in
width. The portal or piazza in front is about fifteen feet
wide, and runs the whole length of the building, the roof
being supported by a row of unhewn pine logs. As I
have already mentioned, the building, from the founda-
tion to the pinnacle of the roof, is constructed of mother
earth, and of an age " whereof the memory of man run-
neth not to the contrary." It was standing in 1692, but
when built no one knows. At each end is a small adobe
projection, extending a few feet in front of the main building—that on the east being occupied by the post-office,
while the one on the west was formerly the *calabozo*, but
is now partly in ruins. The first apartments we come
to in going the rounds of the palace are the office of the
secretary of the Territory, which we enter through a
quaint little old-fashioned door. The office is divided
into two rooms : an inner one, in which the books and
records are kept, and where the secretary transacts his
official business, and an outer one, used as an ante-room
and a store-room. The latter is divided by a cotton
curtain, hanging down from the beams above, into two
compartments, one of which is stored with the old manuscript records of the Territory which have been accumulating for nearly three hundred years. The stranger
will be struck with the primitive appearance of these ruins : the roof is supported by a layer of great pine beams,
blackened and stained by age ; the floors are earthen,
and the wood-work is heavy and rough, and in the style
of two centuries ago.

We next visit the chamber of the Legislative Council. Passing along under the portal, we again enter the
palace about midway of the front, and, turning from a
small vestibule to the right, we find ourselves in the
room where a portion of the wisdom of New Mexico an-

nually assembles to make laws.   The room is a comfortable one, with a good hard floor, and just large enough to accommodate the thirteen councilmen and the eight officers.   The pine desks are ranged round the wall facing inward, and the president occupies a raised platform at one end, which is ornamented with a little red muslin drapery.   Figured calico is tacked to the walls to prevent the members carrying away the whitewash on their coats—a thing they have no right to do in their capacity of law-makers.   The executive chamber is on the opposite side of the passage-way, into which we step, and find his excellency hard at work.   This room is in keeping with the republican simplicity that marks the appearance of the whole establishment.   A few chairs, an old sofa and bureau, with a pine centre table, make up the furniture.   Within the last year the luxury of an American-made carpet has been indulged in, but before the advent of which the floor was covered by a domestic article called *gerga*, worth thirty cents per yard.   This change is an evidence of pride in the executive.   Bleached muslin is tacked to the beams overhead for a ceiling, and a strip of flashy calico, about four feet wide, is nailed to the four walls.

Next in order is the House of Representatives — *la Camara de Reperesentantes*, the door of which opens upon the portal.   This room differs in no essential particular from the council-chamber except being about one half larger, and having a small gallery separated from the body of the room by an adobe wall breast high, where the " unwashed" and " unterrified" sit and behold the operation of making laws with wonder and astonishment, but fail to discover whence comes so much wisdom as they imagine presides over the deliberations of this august assembly.   Before we leave the room, it may not be out of place to mention one or two incidents in the history of early legislation in New Mexico.   Upon one occasion, during an election for officers of the House, the vote was being taken for engrossing clerk, when one of the members, when his name was called, came forward to the speaker's chair and said, " *Que quieres usted de mi, señor ?*" (What do you want with me, sir?)   He was told that his name was called that he might vote on the question before the House, when he returned to his seat.   In a few minutes his name was called again, when, as before, he demanded, " *Que quieres usted de mi, señor?*"   He was again instructed as to what was required of him, and a second time took his seat.   His name was now called a third time, when, as before, he came forward and demanded why his name was called so many times.   At this stage of the proceedings, a friend caught the obtuse member by the coat-tail, and directed him for whom to vote.   Upon another occasion, when a vote was being taken *viva voce*, a member, an American, who felt no interest in the question, replied to the call of the clerk, " Blank."   The next member called was a Mexican, who, supposing that his predecessor had voted for a *bona fide* person, and having confidence in his choice, replied, " *Yo voto para Señor Blank tambien*" (I also vote for Mr. Blank).   These circumstances are said to have occurred at the first session of the Legislature, but there has been an improvement since that time in this particular.

Leaving the hall of the House, we enter the territorial library, which opens into a small vestibule leading from the portal.   We find ourselves in a room not more than fifteen feet square, filled with books from the floor to the beams overhead, ranged around the walls on shelves, and numbering some two thousand volumes.   They embrace the standard text-books on the various branches of common and civil law and equity, the reports of the United

States and the state courts, and the codes of the various states and territories, besides a number of congressional documents. The judge, other United States officers, and members of the bar have access to the library, and can take out books to keep a limited time, after they shall have been registered by the librarian, and being responsible for their safe return. Opening into the same vestibule is the office of superintendent of Indian affairs, which, with another room adjoining, used for a storeroom, occupies the west end of the palace building. Near by is a large vacant room, appropriated to the use of the Indians when they come in to see the superintendent on business, at which times they are fed by the government.

In passing under the portal to the western end of the palace, we encounter the market on our way, where the country people sell the meats, fruits, and vegetables they bring to town. The supply is scanty enough, and hardly sufficient to meet the limited demand of Santa Fé. It consists principally of mutton, an occasional porker, red peppers, beans, onions, milk, bread, cheese, and, during the proper season, grapes, wild plums, and wild berries. In the winter, Indians and others bring in, almost daily, fine venison and wild turkeys, and now and then the carcass of a large bear is exposed for sale, all of which are shot in the mountains a few miles from the town. The various articles are brought in on burros, or carried on the backs of the Pueblo Indians; and it is often the case that one of them will come several miles with less than a dollar's worth of marketing. The meats are hung upon a line made fast to two posts of the portal, while the vegetables are put on little mats or pieces of board on the ground, beside which the vender will sit and wait for customers with a patience that seems to rival Job; and if they do not sell out to-day, they are sure to return with the same stock to-morrow. The cultivation of vegetables in New Mexico, except beans, has only been attempted to any extent and variety since the United States acquired the territory. Onions and beets thrive well, and grow to an enormous size, but there is something in the climate or soil adverse to the growth of potatoes, which, at the present time, can only be raised in a few localities. I do not know that Mexicans have yet attempted to cultivate them. They are scarce, and high in price, ranging from four to six dollars per bushel. The hay and grass market, if the traffic in these articles deserves to be thus spoken of, is on a narrow street at the southwest corner of the Plaza. During the summer and fall the rancheros come in from the country every morning with newly-cut grass or hay, each with a bundle of about twelve pounds tied up in a blanket and carried on a burro. The bundles are ranged side by side along the side of the street, and are sold at twelve and a half cents each, cash upon delivery, without the blanket.

Continuing on our round of sight-seeing, we cross the Plaza to visit what was formerly known as the Military Chapel, and on our way we observe a thing or two that arrests our attention. We see before us an uncouth little animal, quite a stranger to an American who has just entered the country, with a large load of wood strapped to his back, and urged along in a slow trot by a sharpened stick. His ears vouch for his relationship with the ass, and the name he bears is *burro*. In every particular he appears to be patience personified, and has been as highly favored with genuine ugliness as any species of the animal kingdom. They are small in stature, with a head wholly disproportioned to the body, with a pair of ears that should belong to a first class mule. But their virtues more than make up for their homeliness ; they are the most useful animals in the country, and their services could not be dispensed with. They carry the marketing of the peasant to the towns to be sold, and bear their master home again; they carry the wife and children to church on Sundays, or whithersoever they desire to go; and if the country belle wishes to ride into Santa Fé on a shopping tour, she mounts her burro without saddle or bridle, and ambles off to town. They are capable of long fasting and much fatigue; they bear the most unkind treatment with the resignation of a martyr, and after a hard day's work will make a comfortable supper on thorn or cedar bushes, and their happiness is complete with a heap of ashes to roll in. They are made to serve innumerable useful purposes, and not only fulfill the duties of horses and mules in other countries, but are used instead of all sorts of wheel carriages, from a coach and four to a wheelbarrow. They are the universal hackney of the country people, who, when they mount the burro, instead of sitting on the back, sit astride the rump abaft the hips, and guide the docile beast at pleasure with a sharpened stick. When New Mexico shall have become a state, the faithful burro should be engraven on the coat of arms as an emblem of all the cardinal virtues.

A few steps farther on our way we encounter a crowd of people who have formed a ring on the Plaza, and appear to be witnessing some amusement. If we take a peep within the circle, we will see that cock-fighting engages their attention. This is a national and favorite amusement with the Mexican people; all classes indulge in it more or less, from the peon in his blanket to the *rico* in his broadcloath, and the priesthood are not entirely free from participating in this *elegant* pastime. The young bloods of the towns train their chickens for the ring with as much care and assiduity as gentlemen of the turf bestow upon their favorite horses; and while in course of training, you will see them tied around the houses by a little cord to one leg, or they will be allowed to walk about with hopples. Sunday is the favorite day for this pastime, when the best chickens are trotted out and pitted in the ring.

We leave the cock-fighters to their amusement and pass on to the chapel, which we enter through a front door opening upon the Plaza. The building is in the form of a cross, about a hundred feet long and nearly as many in width. Two plain towers rise up in front a few feet above the roof, and on the latter are suspended two bells, which are rung by boys ascending the roof and pulling the clappers from side to side. The style of construction differs from the true Gothic cross in that the transept runs north and south instead of east and west. The appearance of the building, inside and out, is primitive and unprepossessing. The altar is in the south transept, and is very plain. The ornaments are few, and not of a costly kind. The wall behind the altar is inlaid with brown stone-work, wrought in the United States, representing scriptural scenes; and a few old Spanish paintings hang upon the walls. The choir is over the north transept, and is reached by ascending an old ladder. A tin chandelier is suspended over the centre of the cross, and engravings of a few saints are seen in various parts of the house. The roof is supported by large, unpainted pine beams, ornamented with a kind of bracket where the ends enter the wall.

We leave the church and pursue our way. We next call upon a Mexican family, in order to obtain some knowledge of the manners and customs of the people in their social intercourse. A few steps bring us to the house of a friend, and we stand before the large door that leads into the *patio*, knocking for admittance. While the old *portero* is coming to inquire who is there and to

let us in, I will say a few words more about the houses
and their mode of construction. It will be borne in
mind that the material is simple earth in its raw state,
and that all, whether in town or country, are built in the
form of a square, with a court-yard in the centre. The
style of building was borrowed from the East, and is as
ancient as the time of Moses, and was essential here in
early time because of the hostility of the Indians. The
roof is called *azotea la puerta del zaguan.* An *adobe*
is about six times the size of an ordinary brick, and they
cost, delivered, from eight to ten dollars the thousand.
Neither skill nor practice are required in order to make
them. A piece of ground is selected for the purpose,
upon which water can be turned from an acequia, and
the earth is dug up and mixed until about the consisten-
cy of mortar. Each adobe maker has a frame the proper size, which he fills with the soft mud, strikes off the
top evenly, when he empties it out upon the ground to
dry in the sun. The adobes are very seldom laid in
lime and sand, but with the same kind of mud they are
made of. In time the walls become quite solid, and
houses are in use, built in this manner, which have stood
for nearly two hundred years ; but they would not last
long in the States, amid the great storms that prevail
there.

By this time the porter has made his appearance at
the door, where we have been standing some two or three
minutes. There is great dread of robbers among the
people, and they will not always admit you before you
are known. The porter, therefore, as a matter of precaution, salutes us in the first place with *Quien es?* (Who
is it?) to which we respond, *Amigos* (friends), when he
opens the door sufficiently wide to see who we are, and
permits us to enter. Being now assured that we are not
robbers, he conducts us across the patio, and ushers us

into the *sala*, or reception-hall, where we remain seated until the family come in to welcome us. While they are making their appearance—which may be some minutes, if the hour is afternoon, and they have not arisen from their *siesta* (afternoon nap)—we will, in imagination, make an excursion around the house to notice the *locus in quo*, as a lawyer would say, or, to speak more familiarly, to observe the manner in which it is furnished and the style thereof. The internal arrangement of a Mexican house is as different from that of an American as the building itself. The style is essentially Spanish, blended with which are observed many traces of the Moors, their early ancestors. As has been remarked before, all the rooms open into the patio, except some which communicate directly with the sala and with each other. It is a very rare thing to see a board floor in a Mexican house, the substitute being earth, cheaper in the first place, and more easily repaired. A coating of soft mud is carefully spread over the earth, which, when dry, makes a firm and comfortable floor. The common covering for the floors, when they are covered at all, is a coarse article of domestic woolen manufacture, called *gerga*, which answers the purpose of a carpet. The inside walls are whitened with calcined *yezo* or gypsum, which is used instead of lime, but it does not adhere to the walls with the same tenacity, and comes off upon every article that touches it. To prevent this, the rooms are lined with calico to the height of four feet, generally of bright colors. The coating of mud and yezo on the inside of the house is generally put on by females, who make use of their hands and a piece of sheep-skin with the wool on for that purpose, instead of brushes and plasterers' tools.

The ceiling is never plastered, but in those of the wealthier classes the beams that support the roof are

planed and painted in various colors, and sometimes an
artificial ceiling is made by tacking bleached muslin to
them. In some sections of the country, small round
sticks are laid from beam to beam in herring-bone style,
and painted red, blue, or green ; but it is only a choice
room that is ornamented in this manner. The fire-place
is built in one corner of the room, and occupies a small
space. The mouth is somewhat in the shape of a horse-
shoe, not generally more than eighteen inches or two
feet in height, and the same in width at the bottom.
The back is slightly concave instead of being a plane
surface, and the little circular hearth in front is raised a
few inches above the level of the floor. The use of and-
irons is unknown, the wood being placed on end against
the back of the fire-place. These small fire-places appear to give out more heat than the larger ones in use
in American houses, and, being in a corner of the apartment, they occupy less space. I do not remember to
have ever seen shovels or tongs in a Mexican house.
When the house becomes dingy, if outside, they besmear
it with a new coating of soft mud ; or if inside, the walls
are again daubed with yezo, followed by a coat of fresh
mud on the floor. This renovation suffices instead of
the semi-annual house-cleaning which causes American
housewives so much annoyance.

The furniture, as well as the manner of arranging the
same, differs materially from the style in the States.
Few chairs or wooden seats of any kind are used, but in
their stead mattresses are folded up and placed around
the room, next to the wall, which, being covered with
blankets, make a pleasant seat and serve the place of
sofas. This is an Eastern custom, and was undoubtedly borrowed from the Moors. At night they are un-
rolled and spread out for beds ; and it is customary for
the whole family to sleep in the same room at night that

they sit in during the day.   Bedsteads are almost unknown, and if the mattress is raised at all above the floor,
it is placed on a low wooden frame.   Bureaus and other
furniture of that description, in such common use in
American houses to contain the clothing of the family,
are seldom seen among the Mexicans, their place being
supplied by an increased number of trunks and anti-
quated chests.   In the houses of the wealthier classes a
few chairs and cumbrous settees are found, generally
made of pine, but among the peasantry such articles of
luxury are unknown.   This economy in articles of furniture was an absolute necessity in early times, caused
by the almost entire absence of mechanics in the country ; and such as they possessed were handed down from
generation to generation as heir-looms in the family.
At the present day, although there are American mechanics, but few of the people have adopted our style of furniture, but cling to that of olden times.   Every article
of this description sells at a price enormously high, and
ordinary pine furniture costs more than that made of
mahogany in the Atlantic States.   The females in particular, prefer the easy *colchon*—folded mattress—to the
straight and stiff-backed chairs and settees ; and frequently they spread a single blanket in the middle of
the floor, upon which they sit at work and receive visitors.

The kitchen utensils are equally meagre in their appointment.   They cook almost universally in earthen
vessels, which bear the general name of *tinaja*, and it is
a rare thing to see any other description of culinary articles.   I have never seen a stove in a Mexican house.
The *sala* is the largest room about the establishment,
and in the colder parts of the country it is only used
during warm weather, when, for the time being, the family literally live there, lounge among the *colchons* during
the day, receive their visitors, sleep at night, and hold

the *baile.* The family room is adorned with a number of rude engravings of saints, among which the Virgin of Guadalupe is always conspicuous.

It has been stated elsewhere that the *tortilla,* a thin cake made of corn, is one of the principal articles of food among all classes of the people. The duty of making them has devolved upon the women from the earliest times, and they pride themselves upon the skill and rapidity with which they can prepare them. While we are in the kitchen, should we extend our adventures in that direction, we will see the manner in which the tortilla is made. The corn is boiled in water with a little lime, to soften the skin so that it can be peeled off, when they grind it into a paste upon an oblong hollowed stone, called a *metate.* The operator kneels down behind it, and takes in both hands another long round stone like an ordinary rolling-pin, between which and the *metate* she mashes the corn. To bake, the *tortilla* is spread upon thin sheets of tin or copper, and in a few minutes they are ready for use. They are quite palatable when warm, but when cold are almost as tasteless as so much shoe-leather. This, with the bean called *frijole,* makes the staff of life of all classes of the population. In Southern Mexico it is the custom for women, with small portable furnaces on their backs or strapped to a burro, to travel the streets of the large towns making and vending *tortillas* and *frijoles* to the passers-by.

By this time the siesta of *La Senora* has come to an end, and she makes her entrance into the sala where we have awaited her coming. The people of all classes receive their friends with much genuine affection, and it is customary to embrace each other when they meet. Our hostess upon this occasion, if perchance I am on intimate terms with herself and family, will encircle me with her fair arms, or, in common parlance, salute me with what is vulgarly called a *hug*, while you, who are a stranger, must be content with a shake of the hand. To make this distinction between a person and his friends is certainly aggravating to him who falls in the vocative, but a short acquaintance will place the outsider upon an equally pleasant footing. If all the family should make their appearance, each one in turn will embrace you, which is by no means an unpleasant performance when the pretty daughters are a party to the operation, but it is much less agreeable to be hugged in the brawny arms of the father and brothers. This custom is universal among all classes, and even the filthy beggars in the streets meet and embrace each other with an affection truly laughable.

The Mexicans are distinguished for their politeness and suavity, and the *lepero*, covered with abominations, often exhibits a refinement of manners and address that would well become a prince, and which they as well practice toward each other as toward strangers. In their houses they are particularly courteous, and in appearance even outdo the most refined code of politeness. It is customary for them to assure you that you are in your own house the moment you cross their threshold, or to place themselves entirely at your disposal. If you admire an article, the owner immediately says to you, "*Tomele Vmd., Señor, es suyo*" (Take it, sir, it is yours). But in these flattering expressions the stranger must bear in mind that the owner has not the most remote idea that he will take him at his word—that he will either command his household, lay his personal services under contribution, or carry off whatever pleases his fancy.

We have already gone through with the hugging and kissing, and are now seated in the presence of our fair hostess. One of the first acts of courtesy of the mistress of the house is to invite you to smoke. She carries about her person a small silver tobacco-box, in which she keeps the noxious weed, and also has at hand a little package of corn-husks, one of which she fills with the fine-cut tobacco, rolls it up into a *cigarrito*, lights it, and hands it to you to smoke. The American cigar is rarely used by the men, and never by the females, both substituting the article here named. The *cigarrito* is made by each person as he requires them, who always has on hand for that purpose his box of tobacco and package of husks. Gregg, in his "Commerce of the Prairies," says upon this subject, "The mounted vaquero will take out his *guagito* (his little tobacco-flask), his packet of *hojas* (or prepared husks), and his flint, steel, etc., make his cigarrito, strike his fire, and commence smoking in a minute's time, all the while at full speed ; and the next minute will perhaps lazo the wildest bull without interrupting his smoke." Smoking is habitual with all classes, not excepting the most lovely and refined females in the country. The habit is bad enough in men, but intolerable in women. The *cigarrito* seems to be an abiding presence, being handed round at the dinner-table as a refreshment, and served up in the ball-room ; and it is common to see ladies smoking while they are engaged in waltzing and dancing, and some even indulge the luxury while they lie in bed. In Southern Mexico the ladies use a pair of golden tongs to hold the *cigarrito* while they light it, and the coal of fire is brought by a servant on a small silver salver.

In the more southern cities of Mexico, next to providing the guest with the means of smoking, chocolate and sweet bread are served up, the former being a delicious article of domestic manufacture, and the latter a superior quality of sponge-cake. During our stay, the mistress of the establishment and her daughters will endeavor to make the time pass as agreeably as possible. They are

great talkers, and we will have enough to do to maintain
the negative side of the question, now and then throwing
in a word, in order to draw out the colloquial powers of
our fair companions.   When we come to take leave, the
same ceremony is used as at the arrival, and you are
passed around the family circle to receive an embrace
from each member.   This custom is as much a matter
of course as that of shaking hands among the Americans,
touching noses among the Chinese, or grunting among
the North American Indians; and the most modest lady
in the land has no scruples about giving and receiving
such salutation.   The whole family accompany us to the
door, and wait there until we have fairly made our exit,
instead of turning us over to an impudent lackey, as has
become the *fashion* in the States.

Among the *élite* of Spanish society, they are more exact in the observance of etiquette and formalities than
the rather primitive people of New Mexico.   In speaking of leave-taking, the Honorable Joel R. Poinsett makes
the following remarks : "Remember, when you take leave
of a Spanish grandee, to bow as you leave the room, at
the head of the stairs, where the host accompanies you;
and, after descending the first flight, turn round, and you
will see him expecting a third salutation, which he returns with great courtesy, and remains until you are out
of sight; so that, as you wind down the stairs, if you
catch a glimpse of him, kiss your hand, and he will think
you a most accomplished cavalier."   This is not an
overdrawn picture of Spanish politeness, and frequently
have I made the same parade in leaving the house of
Mexican gentlemen.   At each stage of the above-de-
scribed leave-taking, it is customary for the host to say
ádios, the last of which is waved to you from the window after you have entered the street.

We are once more in the street, and have resumed our

round of sight-seeing. We next bend our steps to the gaming-houses, as they are part of the social system of the country, or, to use the language of another, gambling "is impregnated with the constitution in man, woman, and child." This vice seems to be a national amusement among the Mexican race, and nearly all indulge in it to a greater or less degree. In Southern it is more prevalent than in New Mexico. There the saintly priest does not deem it in derogation of his holy calling to gamble, and he is a frequent visitor at the monte table. They also indulge in bull-baiting and cock-fighting. So thoroughly is this vice ingrafted into the population, that I have frequently seen children of ten years of age playing cards for pennies with as much apparent interest as professional gamblers. In New Mexico, gambling, in its variety, prevails to an alarming extent among all classes of the people; but within three or four years a reformation has taken place among the priesthood in this particular. It is licensed and protected by the laws of the country, hence no one thinks it disreputable to keep a gambling-house when thus sanctioned and frequented by the most respectable citizens. The principal game is *monte*, played with cards, in which chance has more to do with the winnings and losings than in any other game. In Santa Fé there is always one or more public gambling-houses, where gaming is carried on day and night, and every day in the week.

The modus operandi of gaming is thus described. The proprietor of the house takes out a license, and rents tables to gentlemen of the profession, who set up a bank and commence operations. Sometimes three or four tables will be in full blast in one room at the same time, and in the course of an evening thousands of dollars will change hands. We will enter one of these places, and watch the thing in motion. We see little crowds of men, in various parts of a long room, collected around the tables. If we approach nearer we will observe that one person sits behind the table, who is the banker, and deals the cards. The table is covered with a green or red cover divided into four squares, and as the cards are drawn one is thrown upon each square. The betters place their money upon their favorite cards, in sums according to their will or means. The money being staked, the cards are now drawn, either by the banker or another person, and when the result is announced, each one is paid the amount of his winnings, when the pack is again shuffled for a new game. While the cards are being drawn, it is interesting to watch the parties in interest; each eye and mind is intently fixed upon the game, and often a breathless silence reigns until the result is known, when the fortunate ones rake their gains to them, and the losers depart or prepare to try their luck again.

In former times females were frequent visitors at gambling-houses, and lost and won their doubloons at monte and other games with a *sang froid* truly masculine. A change for the better has taken place in this particular, and the fairer portion of creation are now seldom seen at the gaming-table except at the public fairs, when they indulge a little for amusement's sake. A few years ago, quite a celebrated female, known as Señora Doña Gertrudes Barcelo, led the van in gambling in Santa Fé. She was a Taosite by birth, but extended her adventures to the capital, where she established her headquarters. Here she struck the tide that " leads on to fortune," and for a considerable time was known as the most expert monte dealer in the city. Her wealth leavened the social lump, and gained her admittance into the most fashionable and select circles, and she soon became one of the *upper tendom* of the city. She died about the year 1851, and was buried with the highest honors of the Church, at an expense of upward of sixteen hundred dollars for spiritual services in the burial alone, including the grave. The bill was duly made out by the Bishop of Santa Fé, with his name signed thereto, and was presented to her executors and paid. Among the items were *los deréchos del obispo* (the rights of the bishop), one thousand dollars; *los posos*, each fifty dollars, which means that each time the procession halted on its way to the burial, and the bier was placed upon the ground, the Church made a charge of this amount; and the other charges were in proportion.

In the spring of 1856 a young Mexican gentleman was buried in Santa Fé according to the rites of the Catholic Church, and a friend afterward handed me a copy of the bill the officiating priest presented for the services, which, though considerable in amount, is quite reasonable compared to that previously mentioned. As a matter of curiosity, I append an exact copy of the bill of fees, viz. :

Dobles (tolling the bells)	$10 00
El sepulcro (the grave)	30 00
La cruz alta (the grand cross)	1 00
La capa (high mass vestments)	3 00
La aqua bendita (holy water)	1 00
Los ciriales (candlesticks)	1 00
El incensario (vessel for incense)	1 00
Las mesas (resting-places)	3 00
El entierro (the interment)	30 00
La misa (mass)	20 00
El organo (use of the organ)	15 00
Los cantores (the chanters)	6 00
El responso del oratorio (the response of the oratory)	10 00
Mas al diacono (the deacon's fee, additional)	10 00
	$141 00

It must be borne in mind that these charges are solely the dues of the Church for the religious services of the burial, and the bills are made out in mercantile form and duly presented for payment. From this showing, it is an expensive matter to die and be buried in New Mexico, and appears to cost quite as much as it does to live.   There is no doubt about the right of the Church to charge for the burial service all the people are willing to pay, but we may fairly question the propriety of making such simple and necessary religious rites so expensive, the effect of which must be any thing but beneficial to the parishioners.   It is an abuse in the Church that has grown up in the course of two hundred and fifty years of unlimited sway in the country, but which should not be indulged in in this enlightened age.   Facts of this kind are a strong argument in favor of the abolition of the system of tithing in New Mexico, and in stead giving the priests a fixed salary, as is the case in other parts of the United States.   Religion and the attending rites should not be made a luxury only to be enjoyed by the rich, but all its offices and consolations should be within the reach of the poorest in the land.

We have now finished our tour of sight-seeing, having taken a peep at all the most notable things in Santa Fé.   We will retrace our steps to the point whence we started, where we will part company, at least so far as physical perambulations are concerned, but I will ask you to continue with me mentally to the end of the volume.

CHAPTER VIII.

MANNERS AND CUSTOMS OF THE PEOPLE—*Continued.*

Correr el Gallo.—El Coleo.—Costume.—Mounted Caballero.—Horse Furniture.—Education.—Agriculture.—Soil.—Acequias.—How Water distributed.—Land cultivated.—Mode of Cultivation.—Plow.—Productions.—Pasturage.—Sheep Grazing.—Goats.—Sale of Animals.—Pack Mules.—Arrieros.—Lazo.

AMONG the country people there are various primitive sports, some of which afford much amusement to both the lookers-on and the parties engaged. They are not as much indulged in, however, as formerly, and are gradually going out of use. That known as *Correr el gallo*, running the cock, is thus described by Gregg: "One of the most attractive sports of the rancheros and the peasantry, and that which more than any other calls for the exercise of skill and dexterity, is called *Correr el gallo*, practiced generally on St. John's day. A common cock or hen is tied by the feet to some swinging limb of a tree, so as to be barely within the reach of a man on horseback; or the fowl is buried alive in a small pit in the ground, leaving only the head above the surface. In either case, the racers, passing at full speed, grapple the head of the fowl, which, being well greased, generally slips out of their fingers. As soon as some one more dextrous than the rest has succeeded in tearing it loose, he puts spurs to his steed, and endeavors to escape with the prize. He is hotly pursued, however, by the whole sporting crew, and the first who overtakes him tries to get possession of the fowl, when a strife ensues, during which the poor chicken is torn into atoms. Should the holder of the trophy be able to outstrip his pursuers, he carries it to the crowd of fair spectators and presents it to his mistress, who takes it to the fandango which usually follows as a testimony of the prowess of her lover." This sport is not confined to the rancheros and peasantry, but the young bloods of the capital also indulge in it, and on the afternoon of St. John's day the Plaza is thronged with caballeros riding to and fro, and testing the stretching qualities of the chickens' necks.

The *vaqueros*, or cow-herders, have another sport more amusing, and at the same time more manly.   It is called *el coleo*, or tailing, and is practiced on days of festivity. A wild ox is obtained and turned loose upon a level plain, where the parties are assembled on horseback ready for the fun.   The poor animal sets off at full speed to escape, pursued by the whole crowd, when the foremost horseman, as soon as he comes within reach of the ox, seizes him by the tail, and, by a sudden jerk, lays him sprawling upon the ground.   This sport is not unattended with danger, and not unfrequently the rider finds himself and horse making the topsy-turvy evolutions he intended for the ox, and he is fortunate if he is not mashed into a jelly.   This amusement should rank next in order to that of catching a pig with his tail well greased, both of which are reckoned intellectual performances.

The national costume of the Mexicans is fast disappearing among the better classes, who are learning to adopt the American style of dress.   The females conform themselves to the fashions of Paris and New York with greater facility than the men, but they are so far removed from the world of dress as to be a year or two behind the times.   The bonnet they discard entirely, and wear instead the *rebozo*, which appears to be a fixture in the toilet of a New Mexican lady.   It consists of a long scarf, made of silk or cotton, according to the

taste of the wearer, which is worn over the head, with
one end thrown across the left shoulder. A lady is
never seen in the street without her *rebozo*, and it is
rarely laid aside within doors, when it is drawn loosely
around the person. When promenading, the face is so
much muffled up that not more than one eye is visible,
and it is almost impossible to recognize your most intimate friend in the street. The dress of the peasant-
women seldom consists of more than a chemise and *ena-
guas*, or petticoat of home-made flannel, generally of
bright colors. They usually go barefooted, and wear
the *rebozo* upon the head. The common people have
also improved in their style of dress since the Americans
have had possession of the country. A few years ago
the *serape*, or blanket, was universally worn, and that
which served for a bed at night made a suit of clothes
during the day. The head is thrust through a hole in
the middle, and the whole person is enveloped in its ample folds. This article of clothing is gradually disappearing, and its place is being supplied with shirts and
coats. A large proportion of the peasantry in the country still dress in tanned deer-skin, and wear moccasins
upon the feet. Among all classes, the females are extremely fond of jewelry, and when they appear in public they wear a profusion of ornaments, if they can obtain
them. In dress they like bright colors, and are more
fond of making a show than a neat and genteel appearance; and those who can afford it wear the most expensive articles of dress, but display little or no taste in the
adornment of their persons.

The Spanish costume of the mounted *caballero* is a
dress at once striking and handsome. The head is covered with a *sombrero* with a very wide brim, and a high
or low crown, to suit the fancy of the wearer; a band of
tinsel cord surrounds it, and on each side is an ornament

of silver.   It is made of plaited grass covered with oiled
silk, and is a heavy and homely affair.   At the present
day many are made of felt, and are a more comfortable
covering for the head.   The jacket is of blue or brown
cloth, handsomely embroidered, and adorned with silver
buttons.   The pantaloons, called *calzones*, are the most
stylish article of a *caballero's* wardrobe, and are really a
dashing garment.   They are also made of cloth, and fox-
ed with the same material, of a different color.   The legs
are ornamented with silver buttons on the outer seams
from the hips down, besides two or three silver clasps on
each side near the waistband.   Suspenders are dispensed
with, and in their stead a silk sash or scarf is drawn
tightly around the waist, with the ends hanging down.
A pair of embossed leather leggins, called *botas*, are fastened around the leg below the knee, to protect the pantaloons.   They are often richly embroidered, and are ornamental as well as useful.   The personal costume is complete with a beautiful *serape* thrown over the shoulder
or laid across the saddle-bow.   They are made wholly
of wool, woven in gay colors, and some of them cost a
hundred dollars.   They are always carried when mounted, and afford the wearer good protection from the weather.

The furniture of the horse is in perfect keeping with
the equipments of the rider, and is gotten up in a manner only seen among the Spanish race.   The style of
saddle is peculiar to this people, and some of them cost
several hundred dollars.   The pommel is high, and the
tree deep, which affords a firm and easy seat to the rider.
The stirrups are of wood, at least four inches wide, and
are suspended from the tree by a broad strip of leather,
embossed and ornamented.   They are frequently fanci-
fully carved and ornamented with silver rosettes ; and
hanging down at the sides are two long leathern flaps,

with a piece of stiff leather in front, that affords protection to the foot. A quilted cushion of leather, oftentimes wrought in silver, covers the seat of the tree, and attached to the hind tree is an ornamented housing of leather of deer or wild-cat skin, tanned with the hair on. This is called *cola de pato*, and is made to correspond with the *coraza* or cushion. The saddle is richly trimmed with silver. The head of the pommel is covered with it, as also the hind tree and other parts. The bridle is fairly loaded down with silver ornaments, and sometimes the bit is made of the same material. The latter is an uncouth and barbarous article, and is of such power that the rider can guide the most restive horse with ease, and he can, at any time, bring him upon his knees without exerting half his strength. The spurs are frequently made of silver, but most generally of steel, and are provided with rowels two or three inches long. The equipments of man and horse are complete with the *armas de palo*, which are made of goat-skins tanned with the shaggy hair on. They are drawn over the legs when it rains, and buckled around the waist; they afford complete protection to the lower extremities.

In Southern Mexico the horses are often equipped in a kind of harness made of thick leather, which covers them from the saddle backward, and reaches down as low as the mid-thigh. It is ornamented with silver rosettes, and around the lower edge is a fringe of steel tags, which keep an incessant jingling as the horse moves, and announces the approach of a mounted caballero. It is said by some that this article was used by Cortez at the time of the conquest as a defense for the horse against the arrows of the Aztecs, while others contend that it is worn to give the horse an ambling gate, half pace and half canter. Thus equipped, we behold a Mexican gentleman of the first water, who, mounted upon his gay little steed, presents a gallant appearance; and with all the "sounding brass and tinkling cymbals" that make up his trappings, when in motion he creates quite as great a sensation as the old lady poetized in childrens' story-books, who,

> " With rings on her fingers and bells on her toes,
> She makes music wherever she goes."

The standard of education in New Mexico is at a very low ebb, and there is a larger number of persons who can not read and write than in any other Territory in the Union. The census of 1850 shows a population of 61,547 inhabitants, of whom 25,089 are returned as being unable to read and write. I feel confident that this ratio is too low, and that the number may safely be set down at one half the whole population who can not read their catechisms and write their names. The number attending school is given as 460, which is about one scholar to every one hundred and twenty-five inhabitants. This exhibits a fearful amount of ignorance among the people, and is enough to make us question the propriety of intrusting them with the power to make their own laws. It was always the policy of Spain and Mexico to keep her people in ignorance, and, so far as New Mexico was concerned, they seem to have carried out the system with singular faithfulness; and in no country in the world, that lays the least claim to civilization, has general education and a cultivation of the arts been so entirely neglected. The few who received any education at all, except those destined for the Church, and the sons of some of the *ricos* who were sent into Southern Mexico, had to be content with the simplest rudiments, and if they were able to read and write, and had a smattering of arithmetic, they were considered learned. There is not a native physician in the country, nor am I aware that there has ever been one.

The education of the females has, if any thing, been more neglected than that of the males, and the number of them who can not read and write is greater. Gregg, who wrote ten years ago, in speaking of female education in New Mexico, says, "Indeed, until very recently, to be able to read and write on the part of a woman was considered an indication of very extraordinary talent; and the fair damsel who could pen a billet-doux to her lover was looked upon as almost a prodigy." This picture is a little overdrawn, but, at the same time, except among the few wealthy families, it is a rare thing to see a woman who possesses these useful accomplishments. Those who have received any education at all have been taught in the most superficial manner, and it proves of little benefit to either head or heart.

A slight change for the better has taken place, in an educational point of view, since the country fell into the hands of the United States. The boarding and day schools at Santa Fé, under the care of Bishop Lamy, will, in time, produce a good effect in the Territory. The pupils come from various sections of the country, who, when they shall return to their families and friends, will carry with them enlarged ideas, and be the means of disseminating, to some extent, a knowledge of our country and institutions. They will make a new generation of youth of both sexes, and, if so disposed, can do much toward the regeneration of New Mexico. The American missionaries who have come into the country have also taken an interest in the cause of education, and, wherever stationed, have endeavored to establish schools. In some instances they have been able to gather together a few scholars, but the opposition of the priesthood to the children being educated in Protestant schools is so great that they could not accomplish much. It is to be hoped, however, that the few seeds they have sown will in due season spring up and bring forth good fruit. The Reverend Mr. Gorman has extended his labors into a new vineyard, and established himself in the Indian pueblo of Laguna, some fifty miles west of the Rio del Norte. He has opened a little school which some of the children attend, and a few of the adults seem desirous to be instructed in the knowledge of the white man.*

No branch of industry in New Mexico has been more neglected than that of agriculture, which seems to be in about the same condition as when the Spaniards first settled the country. It has been pursued merely as the means of living, and no effort has been made to add science to culture in the introduction of an improved mode of husbandry. There are causes which must always operate as a serious drawback upon the agricultural advancement of the country, the principal of which is the absence of regular and frequent rains. Except in the rainy season, which extends from August to October, very little rain falls, not enough to be of service to the

* The territorial Legislature, at the session of 1855 and 1856, passed an act establishing a system of common schools, to be supported by a tax levied upon the property of the inhabitants. Four counties were exempted from the general operation of the law, and the citizens thereof were allowed to vote upon its acceptance or non-acceptance. The election was ordered by the proclamation of the governor, and was held on the 31st day of March, 1856, with the following result, viz. :

Counties.	For the law.	Against the law.
Taos	8	2150
Rio Arriba	19	1928
Santa Ana	8	456
Socorro	2	482
	37	5016

The returns show that, in a popular vote of 5053, there were only 37 men to be found in favor of public schools, a fact which exhibits an opposition to the cause of education truly wonderful. This great enmity to schools and intelligence can only be accounted for as follows : that the people are so far sunk in ignorance that they are not really capable of judging of the advantages of education. From this result the cause of education has but little to hope for from the popular will, and the verdict shows that the people love darkness rather than light.

growing crops, and therefore all cultivation is carried on by means of irrigation. From this cause there is comparatively a small quantity of land under tillage; and it has been estimated that, of the whole surface of the Territory, not more than one hundredth part, or eight hundred square miles, is susceptible of irrigation. A large portion of the land thus lying unproductive is naturally as good as any that is cultivated, and, if water could be carried to it, would yield good crops. The valleys of the streams can alone be cultivated, while the upland is used for grazing.

The appearance of the soil indicates barrenness and unfertility, but in reality it is much better than appearances indicate. The dull reddish hue which prevails in most parts is imparted to the earth by the iron with which it is impregnated; and that which looks like pure silicious earth is found to be, upon closer examination, decomposed feldspar, a quality of soil which, if properly cultivated, is highly productive.

The system of *acequias*, or irrigating ditches, is a subject so new to the American farmer, that an explanation at some length of the manner in which the land is cultivated by means of them may not be uninteresting. It must be borne in mind, as we have already remarked, that all the land capable of being farmed lies in the valleys through which runs a river or other stream large enough to supply the necessary quantity of water. Now, supposing the arable land to lie on both sides of the stream, as is the case in the valley of the Del Norte, the first thing for the proprietors to do is to dig a large ditch on each side of the river, called *acequia madre*, or mother ditch, from three to five yards wide, and from two to six feet deep, with strong banks. It is necessary to tap the river sufficiently high up, so that the level of the water in the *acequia* will always be above the land to be irrigated, else it could not be overflowed. The valleys are generally narrow, approached on either side by hills, and it is customary to cut the ditch along their base, when only one is required for a given tract of country, so that after the water shall have been distributed, the surplus can find its way back to the river. The main ditch is sometimes several miles in length, and resembles a miniature Erie Canal; and it is dug by the joint labor of all the proprietors along the line, each one being required to furnish a number of hands in proportion to his land to be irrigated.

The *acequia madre* being completed, in the next place the inferior proprietors dig smaller ditches tapping the main one, for the overflow of their lands that lie adjacent to the point of junction. These are called *contre acequias*, or cross ditches. Still smaller ditches are constructed to convey the water on to the land of the individual owners, being always dug upon the highest part of that intended to be irrigated. The distribution of the water is governed mainly by circumstances. The secondary canals are provided with flood-gates, to regulate the flow of water into them from the mother ditch, so that the quantity can be increased or decreased at pleasure. When the main ditch is full, each proprietor lets upon his land as much water as he wants; but in time of scarcity from drought, or, as is often the case, the supply is limited along the smaller streams, application has to be made to the "overseer of ditches," who grants a permit for the applicant to use the water for a limited time. Under such circumstances, each farmer is allowed to flow the water upon his land for a day or part of a day, but at no other time without license. The land is made ready for irrigation by dividing it into small beds about sixty by forty feet, the earth being heaped up around the edge of the beds, so as to form a series of

water-courses among them.   The minor ditch that con-
veys the water upon the fields of the respective farmers
is now tapped at various points, and the water is let out
upon the beds at the highest point, so that it will overflow the whole.   Thus bed after bed is watered in rotation, until the whole cultivated plat has been served.
The operation is slow and tedious, and one man will not
be able to water more than five acres a day under the
most favorable circumstances.   If the land is uneven, or
water scarce, he can not water much more than one third
the quantity.   Land that is to be planted with corn is
usually watered a week beforehand, to mellow the soil to
receive the grain ; and both corn and wheat are watered
three or four times after the seed is in the ground, according to the season.

That section of the Territory where the system of irrigation is more extensive and perfect, and where the land
is under a higher state of cultivation, is known as the
Rio Abajo (the country down the river).   It lies on both
sides of the Del Norte, and is considered the most productive section of the country.   Here the proprietors
own larger tracts of land, and in some parts of the valley several thousand acres in one body are watered by
the same *acequia madre*.   The original grants under
which most of the land is holden were made to villages
and communities which held as proprietary occupants of
those portions cultivated, and the lapse of time has given
them an individual title.   This rendered the supply of
water necessary for cultivation a matter of public interest ; and as no one individual was likely to procure a
supply for the whole, nor would the community do it ef-
fectually of their own free will, the subject was taken under the control of the town authorities, and has been so
regulated ever since.

The whole management of irrigating ditches is now

governed by a law of the Territory in pretty much the same manner as roads in the States. The several justices of the peace are authorized to call together annually the owners of ditches, and the proprietors of the land watered by them, to elect one or more overseers, whose salary is determined by the landowners interested. It is made the duty of the overseers to superintend the erection and repairs of ditches ; to regulate the number of laborers to be furnished by each proprietor, according to the quantity of land watered; to distribute and apportion the water among the several proprietors, and see that no one gets more than his share ; and to enforce all the regulations upon the subject. If a landowner should refuse to furnish the number of workmen called for by the overseer, he is subject to a fine of ten dollars for the use of the ditch ; and every person who interferes in any manner with a ditch, or obstructs the flow of water in the same, is liable to a like fine. If, in constructing a new ditch, the land of any person is infringed upon, and he demands damages, they shall be assessed and paid by the joint owners of the land. Every person is prohibited by law from erecting mills upon any stream so that it will interfere with the supply of water for the *acequias*, because, in the words of the statute, " the irrigation of the fields should be preferable to all others." In all that devolves upon the overseer of ditches, he has about the same duties to discharge as a supervisor of roads in the several states. Hence it will be seen how much importance is attached to the system of irrigation ; and, inasmuch as the entire cultivation of the country depends upon the ditches and the supply of water they furnish, they are deserving of great attention.

The landowners and overseers watch the *acequias* during the watering season with great care, lest some accident should happen to them, and their crops be injured.

They need frequent repairs besides those required by the ordinary wear and tear of the water. A sudden rise in the stream is likely to overflow the ditch and deluge the fields; or a sudden fall will leave them entirely dry, when the crops will perish for the want of water. In the case of a freshet the people have to be on the alert, or extensive damages will be done to the crops before assistance is rendered. Upon such occasions the overseers summon the people from their beds at night, and from every other occupation during the day; all other kinds of work must cease, and the whole disposable force rushes to the ditches. In some cases the alarm is sounded by the ringing of church bells. The water is shut out of the *acequias* during the winter, and let in again in the spring as early as they can be put in a state of repair, and the ground is ready for irrigation. It sometimes requires fifteen or twenty days' labor, with a full force of hands, to place the *acequia madre* in good order.

The quantity of land cultivated by the respective proprietors is rarely more than a few acres. By the last census, the average to each farmer under cultivation did not much exceed ten acres, and the majority of them did not cultivate half that quantity. The highest return of improved land in a single tract was in the county of Berralillo, which contained seventeen hundred and twenty-one acres. In New Mexico there is no land-measure equivalent to the American acre, and it is the custom to rate the quantity under cultivation by the amount of grain they sow. They will mention growing a *fanega* of corn, which means that the seed they sowed was of that measure, equal to about two bushels and a peck. In buying and selling land, it is generally reckoned at so much per *vara*—a Spanish measure of thirty-three inches and a third—or the square league. The former is the standard measure for cultivated land, and they buy

or sell so many hundred or thousand varas fronting on a
stream and running back to the hills.   The price is regulated by the facility with which it can be irrigated.
Very few of the cultivated fields are inclosed, except a
chance one surrounded by poles or a low adobe wall.
A regular system of fencing or hedging is unknown;
hence, to prevent cattle trespassing upon the cultivated
fields, the owners are obliged to have herdsmen with
them constantly, and if they chance to do any injury to
the crops, the owners are compelled to make good all
damage.

The manner of cultivation is exceedingly rude and
primitive.   Until within a very few years all their agricultural implements were wooden, and the use of iron
for this purpose was hardly known.   At the present
day many of the peasantry cultivate with the hoe only,
and plows are alone seen among the larger proprietors.
The native plow is a unique affair, and appears to be
identical with the homely implement used in the time of
Moses to turn up the soil of Palestine.   The following
description of one of them is a true picture to the very
life.   "The Mexican plow is an implement of a very
primitive pattern, such as perhaps was used by Cincin-
natus or Cato; in fact, it is probably a ruder instrument
than the plow used by these great ancients.   It is not
seldom the swell *crotch* or knee timber of a tree, one
branch of which serves as the *body* or *sale* of the plow,
and the other as the handle; or, still more frequently, it
is made out of two sticks of timber.   The body is bev-
eled at the point, which is shod with a piece of sharp
iron, which answers for a share.   It has also, mortised
into its upper surface about midway of its length, an
upright shaft, called a *tranca*, which plays vertically
through the plow-beam.   This beam, which is a ponder-
ous piece of timber not unlike a wagon-tongue, is fast-

ened to the plow at the junction of the handle with the body, and, being raised or lowered at pleasure upon the *tranca*, serves to regulate the dip of the share-point. To this beam is attached a yoke of oxen, no other plow-beasts being known here." The above implement is in general use where the hoe has been laid aside, except with the wealthy proprietors, who have purchased more modern plows from the United States, but not of the latest pattern. In some instances as many as twelve or fifteen of these homely affairs, drawn by as many yoke of oxen, will be in use at the same time in a single field. Two men are required to each plow, one to hold up the handle and guide the machine, while the other is employed in goading up the oxen with a long pole shod with a piece of sharp iron. Such is plowing in New Mexico.

The staple grains are corn and wheat, which are raised in considerable abundance. The corn is a species of the flint, is very hard, and, when shelled, will weigh about fifty-six pounds to the bushel. The grains are yellow, or a bluish black and red, and very frequently a variety of colors is blended upon the same cob. The stalk does not grow so high as in the States, and, as it is not planted and cultivated with the same care, the yield per acre is less. The wheat resembles the red and white flint wheat of the Northern States, and is very hard and firm. The grain is large and plump, and, when well ground and bolted, the flour makes excellent bread and very white. The wheat is cut down with the sickle, and allowed to remain on the ground until it is well dried before gathering, and when gathered the grain shatters but little, owing to the manner in which it adheres to the chaff. In the northern section of the Territory frost comes very early in the fall, on which account the farmers are in some instances obliged to cut their corn before it is ripe. There are no barns among the rancheros, and the grain is stacked out, or housed under a kind of barrack built of poles, and covered with brush and grass. Flails and thrashing-machines are unknown, and all the grain is trod out by mules upon the ground. Sometimes a thrashing-floor is constructed of lime and sand, but it is most generally made in the field where the grain is gathered, by treading or pounding down the earth to make it solid. When the crop is thrashed out, it is carried on burros or mules to the nearest trader, each animal carrying a leathern or buckskin sack across his back. Beans are also raised in large quantities, and with some farmers they are the principal crop. A little tobacco and sugar are cultivated, and in times past some cotton was grown, all of which would thrive well in the southern part of the Territory if proper attention was paid to their cultivation.

The pasturage of New Mexico excels every other branch of agriculture. While the scarcity of water renders the great plains entirely useless for ordinary farming purposes, they afford good grazing, probably among the finest in the world. They are covered with a species of grass exceedingly nutritious, and which grows with a very limited amount of moisture. During the rainy season it springs up to some height, and after being frost-bitten it withers down and cures upon the ground. Cattle are seldom housed in the winter season, or fed on grain, but are turned loose upon the plains, and subsist upon the dry pasturage furnished by the withered grass. Greater attention has been paid to sheep-grazing than any other branch of husbandry, and they may be considered the grand staple production of the country. In former years this occupation was in a much more prosperous condition than at the present time, being greatly retarded by the hostile incursions of

the numerous bands of Indians who live in and around
the Territory. Many farmers have had their entire
flocks run off, and in but few instances have they received any remuneration from the government, although
there is a law to that effect. When this business was
in its prime some fifteen or twenty years ago, it is said
that half a million of sheep were annually driven to the
markets of Southern Mexico, and a single proprietor has
been known to own as many as three hundred thousand
head at one time.

A flock of several thousand sheep are placed under
the care of a single shepherd, who is accompanied by
three or four large dogs trained for the purpose. They
are driven out upon the plains, and when no immediate
apprehension is felt from the Indians, they venture a considerable distance from the settlements. They wander
several miles from water, and are driven to a pond or
stream every two or three days, the shepherds supplying
themselves in the mean time with water from gourds or
kegs which are carried upon a burro. The shepherds,
with their sheep and dogs, pass the night upon the plains,
some suitable place being selected for the temporary
sheepfold, and thus for weeks they traverse the country seeking the best pasturage. The dogs which accompany the flocks render important services, and it
would be impossible for a single person to manage so
large a number without their assistance. They exhibit
an intelligence and sagacity truly astonishing. At times
two or three will be sent out alone with a large flock,
which they conduct for miles in as orderly a manner as
the shepherd could do himself. They tend them while
they graze during the day, and drive them back home
again at night. When the flock passes the night upon
the plains, the dogs stand sentinel over them, and are
good protection against the attack of wolves and other

,nimals of prey.   In all these particulars the shepherd-
dogs render invaluable service.   The sheep of New Mexico are of a smaller breed than those raised in the States,
and are somewhat remarkable for their large horns; the
flesh is finely flavored, and is the principal article of food
of the inhabitants.   Notwithstanding the great number
of sheep in the country, wool has never yet become a
staple article in trade.   That produced is a very coarse,
inferior article, and at the ranchos does not sell for more
than four or five cents per pound, and but a small quantity has found its way to the United States market.

The farmers have retained the original stock of sheep,
and have made no effort to improve the breed.   There
has never been enough encouragement at home to warrant the importation of a better class of sheep, and to the
present day they have been raised for their flesh alone.
Since the settlement of California, a considerable trade
in sheep has sprung up between the two countries.
Large flocks have been annually driven across the deserts from New Mexico, and which have commanded in
California a price that remunerates the owners for the
risk, trouble, and expense of driving them thither.   They
cost from two to three dollars a head at home, and bring
from six to eight in the market of San Francisco and
other places.   By reason of the fine climate and the good
pasturage that most generally abounds upon the table-
lands, New Mexico is probably better adapted to the
raising of sheep than any other portion of our country.
The expense is merely nominal.   The year round they
can feed upon the natural grass of the plains, and four
or five shepherds, with as many dogs, can manage several thousand.   When New Mexico shall have become
connected with the States by rail-road, the woolen man-
ufacturers will find it to be to their interest to raise their
own wool there instead of importing so much from abroad.

They can pasture their flocks at a very small expense; in shearing season drive them near the line of rail-road, where they can be sheared and the wool shipped to their mills, and all at less cost than they can import it or raise it at home.   This subject is worthy of consideration.

Goats are also numerous in the country, but they are not raised in such numbers as sheep. ˙Their milk, which is sweeter and richer than that of the cow, is in very common use among the inhabitants.   In one respect they are a very desirable domestic animal, inasmuch as they can live upon the most sparse pasturage, where a cow could hardly subsist, at least to be worth much. The flesh is also in quite common use; it is cheaper than mutton, but is not so well flavored.   The horses of New Mexico are small, but hardy and serviceable animals, and are seldom used for any other purpose than the saddle. Mules and burros are the beasts of burden, and the former are used for draught.   Oxen are also much used for draught, and the greater part of the heavy teams that annually cross the extensive plains that lie between the United States and New Mexico are drawn by them.

In all Spanish countries there is a peculiar custom in relation to the buying and selling of domestic animals. Each person has his own brand, with which he marks all his mules, horses, and other animals as soon as they come into his possession, and they are rebranded as soon as they change hands.   This is called the *fierro*, or buying brand, and when an animal is sold the old marks are obliterated with another brand called the *venta*, and in the absence of this the sale is not a valid one.   When a man loses an animal, in order to claim him, under the Mexican law, he is only required to show a *fierro* that corresponds with the marks upon him, without any other evidence of property.   Since New Mexico was erected into a Territory, the law has been altered in this respect, and now ownership of this description of property is proved in the usual manner.

The Legislative Assembly, at their session of 1851, passed an act upon this subject which modifies the old law in several particulars. All persons are required to have their horses, mules, cattle, sheep, goats, and hogs branded with their respective brands, which they are obliged to have registered in the office of the clerk of the Probate Court in the county in which they reside. When a branded animal changes hands, the late owner is required to give the purchaser a certificate of sale in the presence of two witnesses, stating the price and describing the animal, and also to rebrand it with the brand reversed. Fine and imprisonment is fixed by the act as the punishment for counterfeiting a brand. If a person has in his possession an animal thus marked, and has neither a brand nor a bill of sale, he will be obliged to prove his ownership if it should be claimed by a third person. Under the old Mexican law, a great deal of imposition was practiced upon strangers in case the *venta* or sale-brand had not been put upon animals when they changed owners. It is not an uncommon thing in Southern Mexico, when a fine horse is seen without the *venta* upon it, for some one to hunt up a branding-iron that will match the old marks, and then lay claim to the animal; and, in such cases, they most generally succeed in making their claim valid.

I have remarked elsewhere that the greater part of the transportation in the country is carried on by means of pack-mules, on account of the badness of the roads and the absence of wheeled carriages. The mule and the burro are of as much service to the people of New Mexico as the camel to the Arab. The pack-mules, with their loads of near three hundred pounds each, travel in droves of several hundred, and sometimes thousands; and their hardy endurance enables them to cross rugged mountains and sandy deserts, where it would be almost impossible for horses to convey burdens. The loads are carried on pack-saddles of a peculiar shape, made for the purpose, and, in the language of the country, are called *caparejo*. They consist of a wide leather pad, stuffed with hay or grass, which fits across the back of the animal, and extends some distance down the sides. They are secured with a wide bandage of sea-grass or leather, and are drawn as tight around the mule as can be borne. The packages, sometimes one and at others two upon each animal, are bound upon the pack-saddle with ropes of grass or raw-hide. Each load is called a *carga*. When there is but one package it is fastened on the top of the saddle, but when there are two they are secured one upon each side. The train of pack-mules is generally led by a steady old animal with a bell around the neck, and is called the *mulera ;* the train is called an *atajo*, and those who conduct it and take care of the animals are called *arrieros* or muleteers. There is generally one man to about every ten mules ; the train is conducted with much order and system, each *arriero* having his particular place and a specified duty to perform.

During the march all the muleteers are busily employed. The packs constantly require adjusting, the bandages which secure them becoming loosened; and very frequently the animals become fatigued and lie down, when they have to be helped up, as they can not rise with the load on without assistance. A usual day's travel of an *atajo* is twelve or fifteen miles, and the mules are not unloaded until they stop for the night. The *arrieros* load and unload the mules with great dexterity, and one who is master of his business can adjust the pack in a few minutes. When they have finished the day's travel a convenient camping-place is selected, when the mules are relieved of their burdens, and turned out to graze under the care of the *subanero*, always being accompanied by the old mulera, which keeps them from wandering away. The packs and saddles are piled up in a row upon the ground, and, when required, are so arranged as to form a kind of inclosed camp, to afford protection against the Indians. If it should rain, they are covered with a grass-cloth, carried along for that purpose. This mode of transportation is less expensive, and nearly as rapid as upon wheels. The muleteers are generally mounted upon good horses, which enables them the more easily to manage a large mule-train.

The people of New Mexico are fine horsemen, as the most usual way of traveling is mounted, and boys are taught to ride from their infancy. The *arrieros* and *vaqueros* can be classed among the most accomplished horsemen in the world, and can not be excelled by the Tartars and Cossacks of the Don. The inhabitants of Southern Mexico are also exceedingly fine riders. When riding at full speed, they will stoop from the saddle and pick a pocket-handkerchief from the ground without checking the horse; and they will also, in the twinkling of an eye, turn their horse upon his haunches when going at full speed, and ride off at the same gait in an opposite direction. The muleteers and cow-herds are remarkably skillful in throwing the *lazo*. This consists of a long rope, made of horse-hair or raw-hide, with a running noose at one end, and the other made fast to the pommel of the saddle. With this is their favorite mode of catching the animals that stray away from the herd, and when one of them makes chase after a truant beast, with his unerring *lazo* he is sure to be made captive. The noose is thrown over the horns or neck, and so certain is the aim that they rarely miss, even when both animals are going at full speed.   As soon as the noose has dropped, the horseman gives the *lazo* two or three turns around the pommel of the saddle, and stops his horse suddenly, which seldom fails to throw the captive.   In this manner they capture the wildest horses upon the plains, and make prisoner and subdue the fiercest bulls.

The *lazo* is more or less in use among all classes of the country people, and practice with it grows up with them from childhood.   The little boys take to it as readily as American children incline to the gun, and begin to use it at a much more tender age.   I have frequently been amused to see the boys trying their " prentice hand" on the geese, chickens, and turkeys that live around the house ; and many a time have I seen an old gobbler, strutting with all his state and pride, suddenly brought to a dead halt by the *lazo* of some mischievous little urchin catching him around the legs.   The pigs, ducks, and other domestic creatures come under their annoyance as legitimate and appropriate prey.   The people sometimes employ it as a weapon of attack in their encounter with their enemies.   They have been known to noose Indians around the neck or body, and afterward drag them at full speed over the rough ground until so much stunned that they could dispatch them at pleasure.   In their fights with bears and other wild beasts they often make the *lazo* do good service, and many a fierce inhabitant of their mountains and plains have thus been made prisoner and dispatched without the aid of powder or ball.

CHAPTER IX.

MANNERS AND CUSTOMS OF THE PEOPLE—*Concluded.*

Mechanic Arts.—Carts.—Silversmiths.—Domestic Manufactures.—Se-
rapes.—Gerga.—Tinajas.—Mexican People.—Intermarriage with Indians.—Character.—Courage.—Morals.—Vice.—Cause of Prostitution.—Carrying Weapons.—Beggars.—The Beggar and Bull.—Religion. — Superstition. — Saints. — Diezmos. — Marriage Fees, etc.—
Revenue of the Bishop.—Priests.—Corruptions of Church.—Peonism.
—Law upon the subject.

THE state of the mechanic arts among the New Mexicans is very low, and apparently without improvement
since the earliest times. There are a few carpenters,
blacksmiths, and jewelers among the natives, but, if ever
so well skilled, it would be impossible for them to accomplish much with the rough tools they use. The gold
and silver smiths excel all the other workmen, and some
of their specimens, in point of ingenuity and skill, would
do credit to the craft in any part of the world. Nearly
all the lumber used for cabinet-making and building is
sawed by hand, and carried to market on burros, two or
three sticks or boards at a time, and sold by the piece.
The heavier scantling is dressed with an axe, and sold in
the same manner. Before the Americans occupied the
Territory saw-mills were unknown, and their place was
entirely supplied by hand-labor; but since that time two
or three mills have been erected, which do a good business. A few flour-mills have also been built, and the
grain is better ground than formerly. In building they
have no idea of architectural taste, but they construct
their houses in the same style as their ancestors—rather comfortable, but very homely affairs.

All the implements used in husbandry are of the rudest description, and until within a few years the hoes and spades were made of wood.   I do not recollect to have ever seen a wagon of Mexican manufacture.   The vehicles in common use for farm purposes, and for hauling produce to market when burros and pack-mules are dispensed with, are called *carretas*, a rude cart, made in the style of two centuries ago among the first settlers.   If exhibited in the States they would attract as much attention as the hairy horse or the sea-serpent.   They are generally made without iron, being fastened together with strips of raw-hide or wooden pegs.   The wheels are frequently solid pieces of wood, being a section of a large cottonwood-tree, with a hole through the centre for the axle.   Sometimes they consist of three parts, the middle one with a hole through it, and the two sides, segments of a circle pegged on to the first.   An undressed pole of the proper length is fastened to the axle for a tongue.   The body of the *carreta* consists of a frame-work of poles, much like a crockery-ware crate, which is made fast by being tied to the tongue and axle.   The machine has no bottom, and, when necessary to prevent the load falling out, a bull-hide is spread down.   These carts are universally drawn by oxen, and sometimes three or four yoke are hitched to one at the same time.   The ox-yoke is in keeping with the vehicle, and consists of a straight piece of wood laid across the head of the oxen behind the horns, lashed fast with raw-hide, and is secured to the tongue in the same manner.   For the peasantry of the country these primitive carts answer every purpose, and on feast and holy days you will often see the whole family pleasuring in them, or driving to the nearest town to attend mass.   The wheels are never greased, and as they are driven along they make an unearthly sound, which echoes through the mountains far and near, being

a respectable tenor for a double-bass horse-fiddle. Some
of the wealthiest proprietors have purchased American-
made wagons of late years, and only use the clumsy
cart for ordinary purposes around the farms. Among
the *ricos* there are a few old-fashioned Spanish carriages,
cumbrous and uncouth vehicles, which are drawn by four
or six mules, with outriders and postillions. When a
Mexican travels he carries with him both bed and board,
and encamps on mountain or plain where night overtakes
him. He and all his attendants go armed, which is a
precaution highly necessary in whatever part of the country you travel. In New Mexico there are no public
houses by the wayside in which the traveler can find rest
and food for the night, and unless he is able to reach
some village where there are friends, he is obliged to encamp out. In some of the towns Americans have opened places of " entertainment for man and beast," where
a few can find tolerable accommodations at New York
prices. Before the public house in Albuquerque hangs
a sign-board, on which is painted, in large letters, " Pacific and Atlantic Hotel," being considered the half-way
house between the two oceans.

There is no capital invested in domestic manufactures,
which do not exist as a separate branch of industry. The
few articles that are made are of a coarse texture, and are
manufactured in families. The leading fabric is a coarse
woolen blanket called *serape*, which is made to some extent for domestic use and sale. At times a considerable
trade is carried on in it with the neighboring Mexican
States and the Indian tribes. It forms an important
article of clothing among the peasantry, and many of the
better classes use it instead of cloaks and overcoats. A
few of a finer texture, in imitation of the *serape saltil-
lero*, are also manufactured, some of which sell for forty
and fifty dollars each. They are woven in bright and

handsome colors, and are quite beautiful.   The serape is a leading article of domestic manufacture in Southern Mexico, and the costume of a *caballero* is hardly considered complete without one.   Mier, on the Rio del Norte, in the State of Tamaulipas, is famous for this article, whence they are sold into all parts of the country.   The New Mexicans also make an article of wool, called *gerga*, a stout and coarse twilled stuff; it is woven in checkers and stripes, and is much used for carpeting, and also for clothing among the common people.   This has become quite an article of traffic between the merchants and peasantry, and as it is made with little expense, the latter derive considerable profit from the trade.   It is retailed in the stores at from twenty-five to forty cents per *vara*, and is manufactured for less than half that sum. The few articles of domestic manufacture are made wholly of wool, or nearly so, very little cotton being used, and neither flax nor hemp having yet been introduced into the country.   Their spinning and weaving apparatus is exceedingly rude, and illy suited to the purpose.   A machine, if it can be so called, known as a *huso* or *malacate*, is in common use; the spindle is kept whirling in a bowl with great dexterity, while the operator draws the thread and weaves the fabric.   The peasantry also make earthenware for domestic use, and carry considerable quantities of it to the towns to be sold.   It consists principally of jars—*tinajas*—which are light and porous, and well adapted for refrigerators for cooling water.

In some respects the New Mexicans are a peculiar and interesting people.   They are of Eastern origin, and in general possess all the vices of those whose homes are washed by the blue waters of the Mediterranean Sea, whence a branch of their ancestors originally came. When the Moors were expelled from Spain, they left behind them, as a legacy to the people by whom they had been conquered, many of their manners and customs, which, during their residence in the country, had become firmly ingrafted into society. They had intermarried with the Spaniards, and thus formed a mixed race, in whose veins flowed the blood of both ancestors. Among the early adventurers who came in quest of gold and fame into Mexico were many who had sprung from this union of the Moor and Spaniard, and whose manners and customs assimilated, to a considerable degree, with those of their Moslem ancestors. A portion of that gallant band of men who assisted Hernando Cortez in the subjection of the Aztec empire, or those who followed in his footsteps, in the course of time found their way into New Mexico. A thirst for further conquest, coupled with religious zeal, invited them thither, a distance of two thousand miles from the seat of Spanish power in America. They streamed up the valley of the Del Norte, and formed settlements upon the banks at the most favorable points that presented themselves, where they also established missions to convert the native heathen, and military posts for defense, and became themselves permanent settlers. The Good Book as well as Nature taught them that "it is not good for man to be alone," and so they considered the propriety of taking partners to share their exile and hardships. In this domestic emergency there was but one alternative; their own fair countrywomen, "the dark-eyed maids of Castile," were thousands of miles away, and could not be obtained for wives, and they were therefore compelled, by force of circumstances, to look to the daughters of their Indian neighbors for help-meets. This course was adopted, and all the settlers and gay cavaliers who were in want of the gentler sex to smooth the pathway of life and keep their houses in order took to their bed and board Indian maidens. Here was a second blending of blood and a new union of races; the Spaniard, Moor, and the aboriginal were united in one and made a new race, the Mexicans.

The new people who sprung from this intermarriage between the conquerors and the conquered were dark and swarthy in appearance, and so have remained, through the change of generations, for nearly three hundred years. Among the present population there is found every shade of color, from the nut-brown, which exhibits a strong preponderance of the aboriginal blood, to the pure Castilian, who is as light and fair as the sons and daughters of the Anglo-Saxon race. Of the latter there are only a few families among the *ricos* who pride themselves upon not having Indian blood in their veins. The great mass of the population are very dark, and can not claim to be more than one fourth or one eighth part Spanish. The intermixture between the peasantry and the native tribes of Indians is yet carried on, and there is no present hope of the people improving in color. The system of Indian slavery which exists in the country conduces to this state of things. The people obtain possession of their children by purchase or otherwise, whom they rear in their families as servants, and who perform a life-time servitude to hard task masters and mistresses. When they grow up to man's and woman's estate, many of them marry with the lower class of Mexicans, and thus a new stream of dark blood is constantly added to the current. Tawny skins are seen in all ranks in society, and some of the most intelligent and wealthy of the native population exhibit the most enduring traces of their Indian origin. From these causes there exists an amalgamation in color that is found in no quarter of the world except in the Spanish portions of the American continent.

In stature they are below the medium height, both male and female, but are well made, with sound constitutions, and are graceful and athletic. They have, with

but few exceptions, black hair and dark eyes. The females exhibit, in some instances, the features of the Indian, high cheek-bones and thick lips, and many of them
possess considerable personal beauty. Their fine eyes,
small hands and feet, and graceful carriage, are distinguishing traits. The males have generally finely-devel-
oped chests, and possess much more personal strength
than is generally conceded to them. As would naturally be the case, a people so various in their origin as the
Mexicans, and in whose veins flows the blood of three
distinct races, would present a corresponding diversity
of character. They possess the cunning and deceit of
the Indian, the politeness and spirit of revenge of the
Spaniard, and the imaginative temperament and fiery impulses of the Moor. They have a great deal of what the
world calls smartness and quickness of perception, but
lack the stability of character and soundness of intellect
that give such vast superiority to the Anglo-Saxon race
over every other people. They have inherited a portion
of the cruelty, bigotry, and superstition that have marked the character of the Spaniards from the earliest times.
These traits seem constitutional and innate in the race,
and the more generous and enlightened sentiments that
characterize the present age appear not to have penetrated the veil that shuts from the human heart the no-
blest impulses of our nature. The fault, no doubt, lies
in some measure with their spiritual teachers, who have
never instructed them in that beautiful doctrine which
teaches us to love our neighbors as ourselves. Their
want of tolerance and their cruelty may also be excused
to a degree, because of their impulsive nature, and the
easy sway their superiors have always exercised over
them, and to whom they have ever yielded the most im-
plicit obedience.

I believe the Mexicans have been unjustly accused of

cowardice as a race, and denied the attributes of personal courage that belong to every other people.   In looking at the source whence they sprung, we see no reason why they should not possess all the physical virtues that belong to the human race.   In former times the Spaniard was justly celebrated for his gallantry and courage, for proof of which we need only cite his conquest of a large portion of the two Americas, in which he encountered every hardship that falls to the lot of a soldier.   In those days the Spanish infantry was among the best soldiery in the world.   The history of the Moorish battle-fields establishes the courage of that race beyond a doubt; and the manner in which the American Indians have ever resisted the approach of white settlers settles the question as to them.   Hence we find the blood of three brave races uniting in their veins, and there is every reason why they should possess the ordinary amount of courage.

In the late war between the United States and Mexico, the rank and file of the Mexican army, in many instances, exhibited a bravery that would have done honor to any troops in the world; and upon the frontiers of New Mexico, in their conflicts with the Indians, the peasantry have frequently behaved in the most gallant manner.   That which has given the appearance in the field of cowardice has been a lack of confidence in their officers, which begat a want of reliance in themselves. The great body of the population have ever been an oppressed and down-trodden people, and have never received from their superiors that kind of treatment which fosters courage.   At home, their manhood has been almost crushed out of them; and when led to the field, they had no interest in the contest, and nothing to fight for.   They had been so long taught to believe themselves an inferior race, and destitute of manly attributes, that they came to believe this their condition, and ceased to have confidence in themselves. With American officers to lead them, they will make excellent troops ; and they possess a power of endurance under fatigue which excels most other people.

An evidence both of their patriotism and courage came under my observation. In the month of January, 1855, the governor of the Territory called for a battalion of mounted volunteers to assist the regulars in chastising the Indian tribes who were in hostile array, and in a very few days more companies offered their services than could be accepted. They served for a period of six months ; and it is the unanimous testimony of the United States officers who were on duty with them, that in all the conflicts with the enemy they exhibited a courage equal to, and power of endurance greater than, the troops of the line. They were ever among the foremost in the fight, and were noted for their good order and discipline ; and I am justified in saying that a desire to serve the country sent them into the field, since the greater part of them had nothing to lose from Indian depredations.

The composition of the Mexican army is such that, under the most favorable view of the case, the conduct of the soldiers should not be made a criterion of their valor. The ranks are filled up by what Kendall calls the "involuntary volunteer system," which is pretty much the same as the impressment system in England. Recruiting officers are sent out into the country, who seize the peasantry, take them by force from their homes, and march them under a strong guard to the rendezvous. They are enlisted by force, kept in service by force, have nothing to fight for, receive little or no pay, and, of course, there is no inducement to exhibit bravery. Such was the mode of recruiting for the Mexican army a few years ago, and I presume no change has taken place in this particular. The officers are inferior to the men, being the creatures of those in power, who in a great number of instances receive their commission as a reward for having pampered to the vice and peculations of their superiors. Officers of this class can not possess an elevated standard of honor, and have no reputation to make. With such leaders, the rank and file can not be expected to make good soldiers.

While the Mexicans lack the courage and enterprise of our own people, they neither possess their turbulent and uneasy spirit. They are a peaceful and quiet race of people, and in their general disposition are rather mild and amiable. They are prone to order, and riots and kindred disturbances are almost unknown among them. They are temperate in their habits, and it is seldom that one becomes an habitual drunkard. When their passions are not aroused by anger they are universally kind, and in an intercourse of some years with them I have never received other than the most polite treatment from all classes. They bear a deadly hatred toward their enemy, and will manifest it whenever the opportunity offers. If they obtain an advantage over an enemy, they will oppress him beyond measure, and deem it a virtue; and, in return, they look for the same treatment when they are brought under in the wheel of fortune. They possess great talent for intrigue and chicanery, but lack stability and firmness of purpose. With all their faults, they are easily governed if they are treated with kindness and justice.

I regret that I am not able to speak more favorably of the morals of New Mexico, but in this particular the truth must be told. Probably there is no other country in the world, claiming to be civilized, where vice is more prevalent among all classes of the inhabitants. Their ancestors were governed in this matter by the standard of morality that prevailed in Southern Europe and along the shores of the Mediterranean, where morals were never deemed an essential to respectability and good standing in society, and laches in this respect had no visible effect upon their social position. The people of New Mexico have inherited all the vices of their ancestors, which they have continued to practice to this day. They have never received any moral training, in the American sense of the word, and have been allowed to grow up from infancy to manhood without being taught that it is wrong to indulge in vicious habits. The standard of female chastity is deplorably low, and the virtuous are far outnumbered by the vicious. Prostitution is carried to a fearful extent; and it is quite common for parents to sell their own daughters for money to gratify the lust of the purchaser, thus making a profit from their own and their children's shame. It is almost a universal practice for men and women to live together as husband and wife, and rear a family of children, without having been married. One thing which has greatly conduced to this condition of life in times gone by was the high price of the marriage fee. The peasantry could not afford to be married according to the rites of the Church, and as no other ceremony was legal, they were, in a measure, driven into this unlawful and sinful intercourse. This irregular mode of life is also encouraged by the matrimonial system practiced, which results in illy-advised matches, which, in a large number of instances, drives the parties to a separation, when one or both assume an illicit connection.

It is the custom for married men to support a wife and mistress at the same time, and but too frequently the wife also has her male friend. A gentleman of many years' residence in the country, and who has a thorough acquaintance with the people, assured me that such practices are indulged in by three fourths of the married population. The marriage vow is held sacred by a very few, and the ceremony is more a matter of convenience than any thing else. The custom of keeping mistresses appears to be part of the social system, and the feelings of society are in no manner outraged by it, because the public opinion of the country sanctions it; and what seems to argue an exceedingly liberal code of morals is the fact that the standing of neither party is injured in the community in which they live, but they seem to maintain the same degree of respectability as though they did not thus violate the rules of propriety and decency. This mode of life is practiced openly and without shame. The parties keep up a regular domestic establishment, receive their friends, and appear together in public, as though their union was sanctioned by the holy rites of marriage, and blessed by the laws of God and man.

There are two or three causes for the almost universal looseness of morals among the native population, the principal of which is the entire absence of that necessary moral training which children receive in the States. In times gone by the Church conduced much to this state of things; a majority of the priests themselves lived in open prostitution, and the most abandoned characters retained their standing in the Church, if they were regular at the confessional, and paid the customary dues without fail. The organization of society is such that a large number are driven into this mode of life by sheer poverty. There are no employments to which indigent females can resort to make a respectable living, as in the States. All domestic labor is performed by Indian slaves, and women can find no occupation in housework for their own maintenance. Thus, when their parents die, and they are thrown upon their own resources for support, they have but the alternative of starving or

adopting this degraded mode of life, which, not being considered in the least disreputable, neither driving them
from society nor injuring their prospect of a subsequent
marriage, is most generally embraced.   In other respects
society is not as refined as would be desirable.   I have
already mentioned that gambling is almost universal, and
is considered a gentlemanly and respectable calling.   The
practice of carrying deadly weapons is nearly as common, and most of the inhabitants go armed at all times:
they wear knives or pistols girded around them during
the day, and sleep with them under the head at night.
The merchant behind the counter waits upon his cus-
tomer with a six-shooter or a big knife at his side; and
when the lawyer goes into court to try a cause, he too is
armed to the teeth.   These "peace-makers" also accompany the owner to the ball-room and the evening party;
and even when they enter the house of God on the Sabbath they go better prepared to resist assassins than to
worship their Maker.   There is some necessity to wear
arms, but not to the extent practiced, and the consequence is that many unfortunate affrays take place.

In all Spanish countries beggars abound in large numbers, who appear to form an estate of the social system.
They are quite numerous in New Mexico, but much more
so in Southern Mexico, where they swarm in crowds in
all the large towns and cities, and beset your steps with
appeals for alms whithersoever you turn.   The mendicant race are known by the name of *Limosneros*, who
are the most wretched and repulsive people imaginable.
They are covered with abominations from head to foot,
and their whole appearance indicates the most abject
poverty.   In some parts of Mexico Saturday is set apart
by custom as the day for almsgiving, when you will see
the profession out in full strength.   There is a deal of
system in their begging, and they exhibit a perseverance

that could not fail to bring them great success in any honest pursuit. Each one has his favorite set of orisons, which he sings at the top of his voice, and which call down untold blessings upon the heads of those who contribute to them. Begging is not always adopted and pursued from necessity, as the last resort before starvation, but in many instances is followed as a regular profession. Children from their earliest infancy are trained up to this way of life, and duly initiated into all the arts and mystery that belong to the calling. Instances have been known of parents maiming their children in order that they might be more able to move the feelings of almsgivers; and these poor little mendicants are sent into the world to beg a living for the lazy parents who remain at home.

In the city of Mexico, where they abound in thousands, I have frequently seen a whole family upon the same street corner. Some have customary stands, where they may be seen year after year, with sightless eyes and outstretched hands, imploring alms of the passer-by in the name of God, until death relieves them; and then, when the father is gone, the son is ready to take his place. Sometimes they feign decrepitude, and other infirmities which incapacitate them for labor, and on hands and knees drag themselves from door to door during the day, and at night they enjoy the fruits of their labor in some quiet corner. Such rascals now and then get picked up handsomely. Gregg tells an amusing story of a fellow of this character in Chihuahua, who experienced a remarkable recovery of the use of his limbs after being an apparent cripple for many years. He was in the daily habit of sliding around the town on a begging tour, and had, to all appearances, entirely lost the use of his lower extremities, but was otherwise a hale, hearty man. He was looked upon by the citizens as an object of pity, and many a dime found its way into his supplicating hand. One day, when on his customary rounds, he was sitting in the street imploring alms in the most piteous manner, when a furious bull came tearing down the street in the direction where he sat, and without the least disposition to pay any respect to the mendicant, who must either beat a retreat or be run over. He resolved upon the former, and, forgetting his decrepitude, he sprang to his feet and took to his heels in a manner that would have done honor to Gildersleeve. This closed his professional adventures in that locality. In Mexico the law makes no provision for paupers, hence all the aid they receive is from the generosity of the public.

As a race, the people of New Mexico are extremely superstitious, and which prevails to a greater or less degree among all classes, the intelligent as well as the most ignorant. They have an abiding faith in saints and images, and with the mass of the inhabitants their worship appears no more than a blind adoration of these insensible objects. Some of the most intelligent of the better class look upon these bits of wood as all-powerful in every emergency; and upon the occasion of a fire in Santa Fé a few years ago, a prominent Mexican gentleman was anxious that one of the wooden saints should be brought from the church to quench the flames. The second summer of my residence there, there was a severe hail-storm in the month of June, when the people, in order to protect their crops, stuck up crosses in their fields; and it is no uncommon thing for them to have their fields blessed by a priest after the seed is put into the ground, in order that they may bring forth good crops. Upon one occasion, when visiting a family, a member of which was quite ill, a number of friends came in with a small image of a favorite saint, altar, and other necessary apparatus. They were placed in the middle of the room, when a few coals of fire were brought from the kitchen and put in the vessel that contained the incense, which ignited and filled the room with its odor, the whole party the while performing some ceremony that I did not understand. I left them in the midst of their semi-heathen incantations, neither being able to appreciate the service nor being willing longer to witness what I looked upon as a senseless and unmeaning performance. The sick person recovered, and I have no doubt another miraculous cure was placed to the credit of the dingy little image. The number of saints in the religious calendar makes up a long array, and to all the leading ones particular days are devoted, and observed with appropriate ceremonies. The Virgin of Guadalupe, who heads the list, appears to be the key-stone of the whole system of worship in Mexico.

As another evidence of the superstition of the people, I need only mention their general belief in witchcraft and every other kind of sorcery, which is not confined alone to the most ignorant portion of the community. In the year 1853 a man was arrested in Taos for this imagined offense, and bound over by an alcalde to answer at the next term of the United States District Court. When the cause came up for trial it was at once dismissed, and the prosecutor was made to understand that there were no such offenses under our laws. Subsequently two Indians of Nambé were put to death for a similar offense. These facts exhibit a fearful amount of superstition in the middle of the nineteenth century, when knowledge, in every department of learning, is making such rapid strides toward universal intelligence.

The religion of New Mexico is that of the Roman Catholic creed, which was introduced into the country at the time of the first conquest by the Spaniards, and has prevailed up to the present time, without opposition from other sects, except by a few Protestant missionaries, who have been located there since the Territory came into the possession of the United States.   When first establish-ed, it was with all the rigor practiced in Old Spain, and the Indians were forced " to come quietly to the ac-knowledgment of the true Christian faith, and listen to the evangelical word" at the point of the bayonet and under blows from the halberd.   Under the Spanish and Mexican governments no other religion was tolerated, and the rites of the Church were administered with a de-gree of bigotry and fanaticism almost incredible.   The natural consequence of this undisputed sway for near three centuries was the growth of many and serious abuses, some of which have remained to this day, and call loudly for redress.   I have nothing to say about the peculiar tenets of Catholicism, whether the belief of those who profess this religion is right or wrong, the creed true or false, because this is a matter which lies wholly between the professor and his Maker, and with which I have nothing to do.   Every man is responsible for his own religious belief, and it would be exceedingly unjust for me to arraign others before the bar of public opinion for what I might consider heresy.   But, while I have nothing to do with the religion itself, I deem the abuses that have grown up under it, and are still practiced, just and rightful subjects of animadversion.

One of the greatest abuses that belongs to the Church is the system of tithes, which still remains, and to the Church is contributed one tenth of the worldly increase of the people for the maintenance of the priests, repairs of the buildings, etc.   There is no legal enactment to sustain the system and compel payment, and, as far as the law is concerned, the contributions are voluntary ; but, nevertheless, it exists in full force.   It falls heavily upon the poor people, who are obliged to give a tenth of all the yearly increase of their flocks, and herds, and whatever else they raise, while the rich compound their tithes, and are let off by paying a comparatively small sum of money.   The people are beginning to understand that the Church can not collect these *diezmos* by law, and in some instances they have refused payment.   This is the first step toward à reformation in this particular, and, in the course of time, an entire change will be made in the mode of paying the priests, and each person will be allowed to give such an amount as he can afford and feels disposed to contribute.   I was informed by a former *mayor domo* of the Bishop of Santa Fé that the tithes of the whole Territory which come to his hands amount to about eighteen thousand dollars annually. He receives one half, the other half being divided into two parts, one of which goes to the various parish priests, while the balance is appropriated to the repair of the churches.   In the county of Santa Fé, in which the bishop resides, he receives his tithes in kind, but in other counties his half is sold and the money paid him.   They are collected by an authorized agent, who receives about fifteen per cent. for collection.   Notwithstanding the large revenue the bishop receives, he does not spend it in sumptuous and extravagant living, but appropriates a large portion in repairing the churches and other religious buildings in Santa Fé.   His establishment is modest in its appointments, and by no means in keeping with his income.

Another abuse that should be remedied is the high price of marriage, baptismal, and burial fees that the Church exacts from the people.   In the case of marriage the high rates have heretofore prevented lawful wedlock, and driven a large portion of the population into licentiousness.   They were not able to pay the fees demanded by the priest, and no civil officer had power to unite people in matrimony. In former years it was more expensive to die than to live; and poor parents have been known to abandon their dead children because they could not afford to pay the cost of interment by the Church. The regular fees for marriage and burial service have in some instances been known to be as high as four and five hundred dollars, the price always being regulated by the length and kind of ceremony; and, in the case of burial, by the number of masses said for the repose of the soul. It sometimes costs the poor peasant the greater part of his worldly store to have his children baptized. This ceremony becomes a matter of great solicitude with the mother, since those who are not baptized are supposed to dwell in *Limbo* when they die, while those who receive this rite of the Church are placed in the regions of eternal happiness. The fees for these respective rites have been decreased somewhat, but are yet too high for the public good; and a further reduction, particularly as regards marriage, would have a tendency to lessen illicit intercourse between the sexes.

In no country have the evils of celibacy in the clergy been so clearly made manifest, and such great harm done to the cause of religion. Until within a recent period, the priests of New Mexico were noted for their corruption and profligacy, and instead of being teachers in morals they were leaders in vice. Their lascivious pleasures were quite as public and notorious as their priestly duties, and there was hardly a priest in the country who did not rear a family of illegitimate children, in direct violation of his holy vows and the laws of religion and morality. I am pleased to mention that a reformation has taken place in this particular since Bishop Lamy has been at the head of the Church in New Mexico. One of his first acts in assuming the duties of the bishopric was to dismiss those who had been the most notorious in their transgressions, and to replace them with better men. I am personally acquainted with several of the new incumbents, and believe them to be men of spotless reputations and blameless lives. Notwithstanding this improvement in the morals of the priesthood, there is a margin left for further reformation, which must be made before the Church can be at all purified. Among other practices that have been abolished is the procession of the Host, at least with the parade and show that accompany it in Southern Mexico; and when the holy sacrament is carried to be administered to a sick or dying person, it is done in a quiet manner.

Of late, an important step has been taken toward a further reformation in the Church, and which, in time, will have a good effect. The bishop has directed that the confessional and communion be denied to all females who are known to lead immoral lives; and such are not buried according to the rites of the Church if they die while in sin and before confession. Still, many of the old corruptions of the Church remain in full force, and either no attempt has been made to cure them, or the remedy, if applied, has failed to have the desired effect. The vice of prostitution has become so prevalent that the whole moral frame-work of society is rotten and undermined, and a great revolution of feeling must take place before the evil can be remedied. The priesthood have an important work before them, and they should join with one voice and mind, and teach their parishioners that such practices are contrary to the precepts of their religion and the doctrines of Christianity. Even to this day, in the sacred processions of the Church upon feast and saint days, the most abandoned characters are allowed to unite and bear a leading part, and the " ten virgins" have been personated by the most vicious females in the city. While vice is thus openly smiled upon, we can not expect that much reformation will be made in the morals and religion of a people.

In speaking of the vice and immorality of New Mexico, I must not be understood as including the whole population in the same category. Amid so much that is corrupt, there are some as pure in mind and morals as can be found in any country, and who are as much alive to all the amenities and proprieties of life. Many of the mothers and daughters are as virtuous as can be found in any section of our extended and happy land, and the fathers, sons, and brothers as high-minded and honorable men. The vices that prevail are constitutional and national—more the result of habit, example, and education—or, rather, the want of it—than from natural depravity. We should bear in mind that such have been the habits of the Spanish race from time immemorial, and charity should induce us to make a reasonable allowance for their infirmities. They should be compassionated rather than shunned because of their degraded condition, and an efficient effort should be made to raise them to the standard of enlightenment that is found in other sections of our land; and they should be none the less kindly welcomed to our great political brotherhood because they do not bring with them all the virtues and wisdom possessed by our own people, who have been reared under a purer code of morals and a wiser system of laws. We claim that our free institutions make men better, wiser, and happier; then let us endeavor, through their agency, to work out the regeneration of the people of New Mexico, morally, socially, and religiously, and the triumph will be a greater one than any we can achieve upon the field or in the cabinet.

Another peculiar feature of New Mexico is the system of domestic servitude called peonism, that has existed, and still exists, in all the Spanish American colonies.

It seems to have been an institution of the civil law, and in New Mexico is yet recognized by statute.   The only practical difference between it and negro slavery is, that the peones are not bought and sold in the market as chattels ; but in other respects I believe the difference is in favor of the negro.   The average of intelligence among the peones is lower than that among the slaves of the Southern States ; they are not so well cared for, nor do they enjoy so many of the blessings and comforts of domestic life.   In truth, peonism is but a more charming name for a species of slavery as abject and oppressive as any found upon the American continent.

The statutory law recognizing its existence in the Territory is dignified with the title of " Law regulating contracts between masters and servants."   This is all well enough on paper, as far as it goes, but the statute is found to be all upon the side of the master.   The wages paid is the nominal sum of about five dollars per month, out of which the peon has to support himself and family. The act provides, among other things, that if the servant does not wish to continue in the service of the master, he may leave him upon paying all that he owes him ; this the poor peon is not able to do, and the consequence is that he and his family remain in servitude all their lives.   Among the proprietors in the country, the master generally keeps a store, where the servant is obliged to purchase every article he wants, and thus it is an easy matter to keep him always in debt.   The master is required to furnish the peon with goods at the market value, and may advance him two thirds the amount of his monthly wages.   But these provisions, made for the benefit of the peon, are in most instances disregarded, and he is obliged to pay an enormous price for every thing he buys, and is allowed to run in debt beyond the amount of his wages, in order to prevent him leaving his master. When parents are, as the statute terms it, "driven into a state of slavery," they have the right to bind their children out as peones, and with this beginning they become slaves for life. When a servant runs away from his master, the latter goes before a justice of the peace, or some other civil magistrate, and takes out a "warrant of the debt," which authorizes the arrest of the peon in any part of the Territory. One of the most objectionable features in the system is, that the master is not obliged to maintain the peon in sickness or old age. When he becomes too old to work any longer, like an old horse who is turned out to die, he can be cast adrift to provide for himself. These are the leading features of peonism, and, in spite of the new name it bears, the impartial reader will not be able to make any thing else out of it than slavery.

CHAPTER X.

ARRIVAL IN SANTA FÉ.

First Sight of Santa Fé. — Fonda. — Home-sick. — Rev. L. Smith. — Warm Welcome. — Toilet. — Secretary of Territory. — Governor Meriwether. — His Adventures. — Prisoner in Santa Fé. — Discharge. — Trip to Rendezvous. — Winter Quarters. — Strange Indians. — Great Medicine. — The Indians see him. — Fright. — Encounter with Indians. — Prison fell down. — Sworn into Office. — Mr. Cardenas. — Mrs. Wilson. — Indian Outrages. — How Indians should be governed. — Meeting of Legislature. — Log-rolling, etc. — Organization of the Houses. — The two Houses in Session. — Former political Condition, etc.

THE first sight of Santa Fé is by no means prepossessing. Viewed from the adjacent hills as you descend into the valley, whence it falls the first time under your glance, it has more the appearance of a colony of brick-kilns than a collection of human habitations. You see stretching before you, on both sides of the little river of the same name, a cluster of flat-roofed mud houses, which, in the distance, you can hardly distinguish from the earth itself. But a traveler just off the Plains generally leaves the wire-edge of his fastidiousness behind, and feels rejoiced at the prospect of finding quarters even in a mud house, which he soon pronounces quite a comfortable affair; so true it is,

> " How many things by season seasoned are,
>   To their right praise and true perfection."

The wagons drove in front of the fonda, and the passengers, with bag and baggage, were turned over to the custody of " mine host," who stood at his threshold, in the best possible humor, to receive us. 'Tis true, the

FORT THORN.

establishment was not of the first order—hardly equal to the "Astor" or "St. Nicholas"—but, withal, it seemed an admirable change to us who, for nearly a month, had been exposed to the discomforts of the Plains. We had hardly been shown to our rooms before dinner was announced, when we were conducted to the dining-room, where we found a table spread with all the necessaries and some of the luxuries of life. I can speak for myself, and say that I did full justice to the repast, and in good earnest broke the fast that half rations had imposed upon us the latter part of the way.

On being set down, "a stranger in a strange land," I do not deny that I had the feeling common to all in a similar situation, and for a time that heart-malady called home-sickness made a lodgment in an unoccupied corner of my heart. To a greater or less degree, this feeling will seize upon all comers from the United States when they place foot in Santa Fé for the first time. The whole aspect of things is so entirely different from what they have been accustomed to: a foreign language salutes their ears; a strange race of men gape at them without a particle of sympathy, and the mud city, with its dirty streets and no less dirty population—all presents such an uninviting picture to the stranger, that, in spite of all he can do, he will feel a little "down in the mouth." But reaching this place under the circumstances, after a trip of nearly a thousand miles across an inhospitable and almost barren region, has a tendency to remove many of the unfavorable impressions a traveler receives upon his first arrival. The change from constant exposure and danger to comparative comfort and security is so sudden, and, withal, so much to one's mind, that it begets a favorable opinion of this modern Timbuctoo, and in a short time he finds himself reasonably well reconciled to his new home. But if it was not for the circumstances under which the traveler first enters Santa Fé, he would be tempted to leave again in disgust ere the sound of his footfall had died away in the streets.

As good fortune would have it—and it is always good fortune to know somebody in a strange place—I had an old friend in Santa Fé in the person of the Rev. Louis Smith, stationed there as a Baptist missionary. He had been sent out by the Baptist Board of Home Missions nearly three years before, and during this time he had been laboring faithfully in this new field, but with little success. The tares seemed to choke down all the wheat that was disposed to spring up under the new and improved culture, and thus far he and the other husbandmen who had labored in the field had scarce been able to gather a single sheaf into the garner. As soon after dinner as possible, I wended my way to the house of Mr. Smith, all unshaven and unshorn, hoping to be able to announce my own arrival. In this dilapidated condition, I presented myself at his threshold and knocked for admittance. A servant answered the summons, and in a moment I was in the presence of Mrs. Smith, her husband not being in at the time. At first she could hardly realize that the person who stood before her was a genuine old friend instead of some apparition who had dropped down from—she knew not whence. But it took but little trouble to satisfy her upon this point, when she gave me a welcome to her house and home that was full of meaning, and which went in a straight line to the heart, driving away at once all the legions of home-sickness that had dared to gather there. Her greeting was far from being of the modern school of salutation, so stiff and formal as to fairly drive the milk of human kindness from one's bosom, for such new-fangled notions had not yet penetrated into that distant region. While we were seated, chatting of the days of "old lang syne," her husband came in, who received me no less kindly and warm-heartedly, and which fully came up to that beautiful faith he professes and makes his daily walk and practice. He extended his welcome fully to meet the requirements of Christian hospitality, and invited my companion and myself to partake of his bed and board until we should be able to arrange our own quarters. This was something tangible and real, the substance instead of the shadow, and like sensible persons, and without the least circumlocution, we availed ourselves of the kind offer.

The first and most urgent duty, after the greetings and a few moments' conversation with my old friends, was that of getting rid of the dust of travel, and appearing once more in civilized habiliments, for which purpose we wended our way back to the fonda. After roughing it so long upon the Plains, it is no easy task to make one's toilet, as every gentleman knows who has taken off a crop of beard that has ripened and gone to seed. With a due degree of perseverance, this duty was finally accomplished, and your humble servant was once more metamorphosed into a respectable-looking individual. The whole performance was much more a matter of necessity than pleasure, as every one is aware who has been obliged to undergo the same operation. We now removed ourselves and baggage to the hospitable house of Mr. Smith, where we made our home for the present.

In the afternoon Mr. Smith chaperoned me out into the town to see the sights and make the acquaintance of some of the good people. On our way up the street we halted at the counting-room of the Honorable W. S. Messerve, the Secretary of the Territory, to whom I was introduced. At that time Mr. Messerve was a leading merchant in Santa Fé, where he had been established in business for some years, and made a large fortune. He

is a Massachusetts man by birth, but spent many years
in Mexico.   He is a man of fine talents, and possesses
a fund of wit and humor that never becomes exhausted.
In comparing notes, we found we had met before, and by
mutual consent dated our first acquaintance back to the
month of June, 1847, during the war with Mexico, when
we encountered each other upon the banks of the River
San Juan.   Crossing the Plaza, we wended our way to
the government palace, where I was presented to his
excellency, David Meriwether, Governor of the Territory,
by whom I was received with all the kindness and frankness to be looked for in a Kentuckian.   Governor Meriwether is a Virginian by birth, but, with his father's family, removed to Kentucky in 1805, since which time he
has made that state his permanent home.   He was appointed Governor of New Mexico by President Pierce in
1853, and entered upon the discharge of his duties in
August of the same year.   It is not my intention to
write a biography of this gentleman, but I can not refrain from giving a few of the incidents of his early life,
which, coupled as they are with adventure, can not be
otherwise than interesting to the reader.

Having the desire of adventure so common to the
youth of our country, in the year 1818 he entered the
American Fur Company, and in their employ spent three
years in hunting and trapping upon the plains and waters of the Far West.   His life was a continued scene of
adventure and hardship, in which practical school he finished his education and graduated for the pursuits of
life.   In the year 1819 he was sent with a party of Pawnee Indians to endeavor to open a trade with New Mexico, in order to exchange their furs and other goods for
bullion, and to obtain permission to hunt and trap upon
the streams.   They had advanced as far west as the
Canadian fork of the River Arkansas, when they were at-

tacked by a party of Mexican troops, most of the Indians killed, and himself and negro boy made prisoners. They were conducted to Santa Fé, about a hundred and twenty miles farther west, the then capital of the province, and brought before the Spanish governor, by whom he was accused of being a spy of the United States, and was thrown into prison. At that time there was some difficulty between our government and that of Spain in reference to the Floridas, and the authorities looked upon Americans with great jealousy. He was repeatedly brought before the governor and closely questioned as to his motives in coming into the country, with the design, as it appeared, of entrapping him into some hostile admission, in the absence of any evidence against him. The only medium of communication was a Catholic priest who spoke French, which language young Meriwether partly understood. He was confined in a filthy prison adjoining the palace, while the negro boy was secured in some other part of the town. He was kept in confinement about a month, when one day he was sent for by the governor, who told him that the difficulties between the United States and Spain were adjusted, and that he had permission to return home.

To be thus turned loose upon the world at the approach of winter, in a strange land, and separated a thousand miles from the nearest American settlement, was being placed in a worse condition than while in prison. When arrested, he and his servant were both well armed, and mounted upon fine horses, but their captors had stripped them of every thing but the clothes upon their bodies. Young Meriwether sought an interview with the governor, and represented to him their condition: that to be driven into the mountains without any arms to kill game was certain death, and he had better kill them at once and shorten their misery. This appeal had some effect; and although their own property was not restored to them, he gave each one a mule, an old gun, and a few charges of powder and lead. They were not permitted to leave the country by the same route they had entered it, but were sent by the way of Don Fernandez de Taos in charge of a corporal and two men. The escort accompanied them some little distance above that place, when they suddenly left them and returned to Santa Fé.

Our adventurers were now in no very enviable position. The weather was cold, the mountains covered with snow, and they found themselves turned adrift in an unknown country. They had many hundred miles of inhospitable plains and mountains to traverse, and had two almost useless guns and a small supply of ammunition to kill game and defend themselves from hostile Indians. But there was no time to be lost in contemplating their unfortunate situation. Before taken prisoner, he had appointed a place of rendezvous, where such of the Indians as might be able to make their escape were directed to go and await his coming. He now took a direction for that point, as well as he was able to do without a guide or a knowledge of the country, being guided by the sun during the day and the stars at night— killing game as they went, at the risk of bringing hostile Indians upon them by the report of their guns. After traveling several days across the mountains that lie on the eastern confines of New Mexico, in constant fear of being attacked, and suffering from the cold, they reached the place of rendezvous, and found three Pawnee Indians waiting for them. The meeting was a pleasant one to all parties, and they remained there a few days making the necessary preparations for the continuance of their journey. They resolved to seek some good location upon the head-waters of the Arkansas, where they would remain until spring, and then return to the settlements.

They took up the line of march from the rendezvous, and, after traveling in a northerly direction for several days, they came to a cave, upon the head-waters of the Arkansas, that promised to answer their purpose of a winter residence. It was a large cavern in the side of a hill, and the rocks from above projected over somewhat in the shape of a portico. They set to work, and made the place as comfortable as possible. They divided it into two compartments by suspending before the entrance to the rear a buffalo robe, and they placed poles against the projecting ledge, which, covering with brush and dried grass, made another comfortable room. In the inner room they stored all their most valuable articles, and the outer served them as a place to build their fire and do their cooking. They killed their mules, which, with the buffaloes they occasionally shot, kept them in a supply of meat. Their greatest fear was in being discovered by hostile Indians, and they took constant precaution to prevent their whereabouts being known. Time hung heavily upon their hands, as they were afraid to venture away from the mouth of the cave unless they were compelled to do so in search of food. Among other expedients to kill time, young Meriwether amused himself in fashioning a stone to resemble a man's face, and upon which he stretched a piece of skin. When the skin was dried, he took it off, cut holes for the eyes, nose, and mouth, and thus had a respectable-looking mask. When finished, he laid it away in the cave, without imagining the valuable service it would be able to render him before the winter was past.

One day nine strange Indians came to the cave, whom they suspected very strongly of some hostile intentions, and were therefore uneasy while they remained. They were anxious to look at every thing in and about the premises, and, after having seen all there was in the outer apartment, one of them desired to know what there was behind the curtain. It was very desirable to preserve the inner part of the cave from the eyes of the strangers, and, as they were not able to do so by force, they had to resort to stratagem. Young Meriwether now bethought him of his mask, and, feeling certain that he would be able to make it serve him a good purpose in the emergency, replied to the inquiry of the Indians that they kept their *Great Medicine* behind the curtain. This excited the curiosity of the visitors the more, and they demanded to see him right away, as they wanted to know whether he looked like their medicine-man. He endeavored to satisfy their curiosity in various ways, but nothing would do but a sight of him. Finally, he told the Indians that he would go in and consult the *Great Medicine*, and if he should be willing to be seen by strangers, he would return and admit them. Once behind the screen, he arranged his plans to give the Indians a good fright. He fixed the skin mask upon the point of a rock, and, putting a lighted candle within it, returned to the outer apartment. He told them that if they should see fire and smoke coming out of his eyes, nose, and mouth, it was a sure sign that the *Great Medicine* was very angry, and they must look out for themselves. They were to be admitted one at a time. The skin screen was carefully drawn aside to let one in, who entered; but, seeing the fire and smoke streaming out of the holes in the mask, he took for granted that the Great Spirit was in a towering rage, and about to devour the whole of them, and therefore took to his heels, yelling like a demon, followed by all his companions. Thus they rid themselves of these ugly visitors, and probably this little stroke of ingenuity was the means of saving their lives. They were afraid, however, that the Indians might return with others to see the white man's medicine, and to whom the harmless mask might not appear so terrific, and therefore resolved to break up their camp and seek a more secure location. They took up their march that evening through deep snow, with their packs upon their backs, and traveled all night and the next day before they halted to encamp. Before they laid down to sleep, the mask, with a candle inside, was placed on the point of a high rock, so that, in case the strange Indians should follow upon their trail, they would first be saluted by the *Great Medicine* they so much feared. Thence they continued their journey, and reached a trading-post in safety, at which they spent the remainder of the winter.

After this adventure the governor and a party of trappers had a more serious encounter with some Indians of the Plains. Upon one occasion, when returning from a trapping expedition loaded with packs of furs, they espied in the distance a number of mounted Indians coming toward them. He and his men made for a grove of timber near at hand, where they tied their animals, and, taking off their packs, formed with them a kind of breastwork, in order to make a good defense if it should become necessary. These arrangements being made, and the little garrison having received instructions to hold the camp at every hazard, Meriwether, with a few horsemen, set out to meet the Indians. Both parties approached at full speed, the respective leaders being some distance in advance of their men. The Indian chief came up with his lance at a rest, while Meriwether rode tomahawk in hand; and when within proper distance, the former made a lunge with his lance, which the latter struck down with his hatchet, but not with sufficient force to prevent it piercing his thigh and giving him a severe wound. The shock jostled the Indian, and, before he could recover his position, the negro boy rode up to him, and, with a single stroke of his hatchet on the head, killed him. The chief having fallen, the other Indians turned and fled. As soon as Meriwether was wounded he fainted and fell to the ground, from loss of blood, and when he came to he found himself lying beside his dead foe. The trappers resumed their march in a few days, and reached their trading-post without further molestation. For this gallant act of the negro boy in saving the life of his master he was set free as soon as they returned to Kentucky.

When Governor M. was a prisoner in Santa Fé, he was confined in a room at the west end of the palace; and the same evening he arrived there to assume the executive duties of the Territory, the roof of the room fell in. This the people, with their superstitious notions, interpreted into a favorable omen. It is worthy of note to say, in conclusion, that he who was a poor and unknown boy, and a prisoner in a foreign land, should, in the course of years, return with the power of the United States at his back to rule over the same people who had held him in captivity, and to administer laws in the very building in which he had been confined. Such incidents are not unfrequent in the vicissitudes that mark the life of the public men of our country.

I was sworn into office on Monday, the 28th instant, and held myself in readiness to look after the interests of the government, if perchance it should have any need of my services. My predecessor had taken his leave before my arrival, and upon entering on the duties of the office of United States Attorney I found neither books nor papers to take charge of, and, before I was done with it, was satisfied that it was about as barren of emoluments. It is a sinecure barring the riding the circuit, and consists in the name, which sounds well, and a commission bearing the signature of the President, and the great seal of the United States attached.

A few days after I arrived I made the acquaintance of the Rev. Benigno Cardenas, formerly a Catholic priest in the Territory, but within a few years a proselyte to Protestantism. He is a man of learning and abilities, and at one time occupied a high position in the Church. He now belongs to the Methodist denomination, and is laboring in the southern part of the Territory, where he has gathered a small flock. Some years ago he became involved in a religious difficulty with Bishop Zubiria, who, for a real or pretended cause, suspended him from the discharge of his spiritual functions, and placed him beyond the pale of the Church. Feeling that justice had not been done him in the decision of the bishop, Mr. Cardenas was determined to seek redress from the supreme head of the Church, and for that purpose he made a pilgrimage to Rome, and laid his complaint before the Pope. After his case had undergone the necessary examination by the pontiff and his advisers, he was reinstated in the Church, and was furnished with the necessary documentary evidence to establish the fact upon his return home. He exhibited proof of his justification when he returned, but declined to enter the Church again, because, in the mean time, his religious views had undergone a change. His object in going to Rome was to recover his standing in his own Church before asking to be received into another, which being established, he immediately renounced the faith of his fathers, and began to teach the more liberal doctrine of Protestantism.*

* Since the above was written, Mr. Cardenas has dissolved his connection with the Methodist denomination, and made application to be received back again into the Catholic Church. The ceremony of reception into the Church, and a recantation of his Protestant heresies, took place at Albuquerque the 24th day of February, 1856. He was compelled to submit to the humiliation of receiving lashes upon the back, covered only with his shirt, which were laid on by the hands of the *Vicario*. After this he was fully pardoned and restored to the communion.

About this time there arrived in Santa Fé an American woman, Mrs. Jane Adeline Wilson, lately rescued from the Camanche Indians, with whom she had been captive about one month. She was taken some distance to the east of El Paso, Texas, on her return to her friends from an unsuccessful attempt to go to California with her husband and father-in-law. She succeeded in making her escape, and after wandering about the Plains for some time, was found by a party of Mexican traders, who brought her into the settlements. She mainly owed her safety to a Pueblo Indian of the village of San Yldefonso, whose conduct was such as to entitle him to all praise. She was young, modest in appearance and conduct, and quite intelligent. She remained in Santa Fé until the next spring, when she was sent to her friends.

The narrative of her sufferings, written down at the time from her own lips, made one of the most affecting recitals I have ever read, and the fortitude she displayed, for one of her tender years, under so many trying circumstances, was quite sublime. Imagine a young and delicate female for the period of about a month in the hands of one of the most savage of our North American tribes of Indians, and compelled to submit to the most cruel treatment ever inflicted upon a human being. They made her their absolute slave; and, not satisfied with compelling her to perform the most menial offices, they would cruelly beat her if her overtasked strength failed her. And then, at other times, as if to make her degradation more complete and her sufferings more acute, they would set upon her a human fiend of her own sex, who delighted in tormenting her with a refined cruelty that can not be surpassed. Conceive a woman placed upon the back of a wild mule without saddle or bridle, and because she can not manage the restive beast, to have her head stamped into the ground by an infernal savage;

behold her almost naked, marching under a burning sun, over mountains and across prairies, amid briers and thorns which tear her flesh at every step; and then, after she had eluded her fiendish captors and made her escape, we see her wandering alone for many days without food and without shelter, every moment in danger of being recaptured, with the wolves following her footsteps when she ventured to a spring to drink, and scratching around her place of concealment at night. Let the reader call to mind these bodily sufferings, and add to them the terrible anguish of mind she must have endured, and yet but a faint idea of the hardships she was compelled to undergo can be imagined. For a strong man to bear up under such trials seems almost incredible; but when we know the sufferer was a young and tender female, and about to become a mother, her escape seems miraculous indeed.

Such outrages are of much too frequent occurrence in the distant land of New Mexico. But a few pages back the reader will call to mind the case of poor Mrs. White, who was taken in a somewhat similar manner; but she was not so fortunate as to make her escape, and both herself and child suffered death at their hands. She was treated with equal cruelty, no doubt, but the grave has closed over her sufferings, and they must remain unknown to the world. When Governor Meriwether was on his way to New Mexico, two young Spanish girls made their escape from the Kiowah Indians and joined the train he was traveling with, whom he afterward forwarded to their homes in Chihuahua, whence they had been stolen nearly two years before. They made their escape in the following manner: One day they were sent out by the Indians to herd the animals, when, on ascending a hill, they espied in the distance an American train winding across the prairies just west of the Arkansas. They immediately mounted horses and started for the wagons. Before they reached the train they turned the animals loose and drove them back, and continued their way to the camp on foot, where they arrived soon after dark. They reported themselves to Mr. M'Carty, the conductor of the train, and from whom they received the kindest treatment. The next day some thirty or forty Indians overtook the train and demanded the girls, but Mr. M'Carty denied all knowledge of them, having previously concealed them in the wagons so they could not be seen. The Indians seemed determined not to give them up, and even made an attempt to search the wagons, when the teamsters took down their arms and showed fight. One old squaw, whose slave one of the girls had been, was in the act of getting into a wagon, when Mr. M'Carty laid her sprawling with a stroke from the butt end of his whip. The following day the train of General Garland was overtaken, and the rescued captives delivered to the governor.

They related about the same account of suffering as that narrated by Mrs. Wilson. They mentioned an American woman with a small child whom they had seen in captivity, and who was obliged to submit to the same kind of inhuman treatment. They said that one day, while traveling, one of the Indians seized the child, threw it up into the air, and caught it upon the point of his lance as it came down. The rest of the band amused themselves in the same manner, and thus they passed the child around among them upon their lance-heads until the dead body was pierced like a sieve. Yet, with such abundance of evidence before our eyes of the savage cruelty of these Western Indians, there is a class of people in the United States whose hearts are constantly overflowing with sympathy for these inhuman fiends. This mawkish feeling of pity for the " poor Indian" has existed long enough, and it is quite time the people should come to view them in their proper light. They are the Ishmaelites of the Plains, whose hands are turned against every white man, woman, and child, and they should be chastised in the severest manner instead of receiving pity from their crack-brained sympathizers. The government at Washington has been a little remiss in chastising them for their numerous outrages, and they have learned to despise instead of fear our power. The only mode of governing these savages is by fear of punishment—the "moral suasion" of powder and lead, as their flinty hearts are not capable of appreciating kinder treatment. At this time there are hundreds of captives among the Indians of the Plains and those that inhabit the mountains of New Mexico, principally women and children. They make slaves of the former, and train the latter for warriors. Now and then a captive escapes, but the great majority spend a lifetime with them, and drag out a most miserable existence.

Monday, December the fifth, was the day fixed by law for the meeting of the Legislative Assembly of the Territory, and for a week before that time the members had been coming in from the various counties, and arranging themselves in quarters for the session. Those who were candidates for office in either House and their friends began the system of electioneering so prevalent in other sections of the Union; and the few days that intervened between the arrival of the members and the meeting of the Assembly were spent in wire-pulling, log-rolling, and all the other strategic movements known in modern politics. Juntas were held in the four quarters of the city of the Holy Faith, and the merits of the various candidates for place in the two honorable bodies were discussed and canvassed with as much apparent gravity as though the fate of the Republic depended upon the selection they should make. It was early determined that the weal of the Territory would be eternally sapped should a single Whig obtain place in either branch of the august assemblage about to convene; and it was therefore resolved, *pro bono publico*, that none of that kidney should be allowed to lap up a drop of the pap that was likely to drop from the Democratic table. This once resolved upon, the patriots breathed deeper and freer, and unanimously pronounced the country saved.

In the second place, it was a matter quite difficult to determine who should be the lucky Democratic aspirants. As is usual, each member had his man, and some of them half a score, who *must* be served—good loyal Democrats they were—with their success was closely allied the future well-being of the party—at least they all said so, and some of them ought to be believed. Not only did men urge the claims of respective candidates, but the various sections of the Territory made demands that must be satisfied, and that without delay. Rio Ariba (the country up the river) laid claim to the lion's share in the distribution of patronage, because this region professed to be the strongest in the Democratic faith. At this the Rio Abajo (the country down the river) bristled up wonderfully, and was quite shocked at the exorbitant demands of the Rio Aribaites. Thus the contest waxed and waned, and the whole middle region of the continent appeared to be immeasurably interested in the decision of these *important* questions. As neither party would give ground an inch—what bravery was there!—it was finally concluded that, in the scramble for place, there should be a " free fight," with the full understanding that not a single Whig should be allowed to poke his nose within the sanctuary of either House in an official shape; this was Democratic ground entirely, and these political " heathens" had no business to be intruding therein.

The eventful morning of the fifth—a day big with the

ate of many a new aspirant after legislative honors—at
length dawned, and slowly the time of meeting drew
nigh. At the hour of 10 A.M. the American flag was
run up on the staff in the middle of the Plaza, and at
the same time the two branches of the Legislative Assembly came together in their respective chambers in the
government palace. They were temporarily organized by,
the election of *pro tem.* chairmen, when the members presented their credentials, and were afterward duly sworn
in by the Honorable John S. Watts, associate justice of
the Supreme Court of the Territory, and took their seats.
In the afternoon they proceeded to an election of officers, and completed a permanent organization of the two
houses. Each chamber selected an American as speaker, and the balance of the offices were equally divided
between the two races.

The following day the members of the two Houses assembled in the Hall of Representatives to listen to the
reading of the governor's message. A joint committee
proceeded to the executive chamber, and escorted his excellency to the hall of the House, where he was received
by the members rising and saluting him as he entered.
When silence was restored, the governor read the message in English, after which the chief clerk read it in
Spanish. It was a plain and business-like document,
and contained many suggestions of vital interest to the
Territory.

The spectacle here presented, in the fourth session
of the Legislative Assembly of New Mexico, was rather
pleasing, and furnished food for some interesting reflec-
tions. This was a new people in the art and mystery
of legislation, who, in a great measure, had yet to learn
their duties in the *modus operandi* of making laws. Before the country came into the possession of the United
States the people were ruled with a rod of iron, without

government and laws except in the shape of arbitrary decrees that emanated from a single individual. They possessed no political rights in our sense of the word, and were governed more like a flock of sheep than men. The so-called parent government at the city of Mexico had a semblance of written laws and political institutions for the control of the states and provinces; but, when the same came to be reduced to practical operation, they were generally confined to the breast of the fortunate individual who chanced to fill the executive chair for the time being. For many years General Manuel Armijo governed New Mexico pretty much in accordance with his own individual predilections; he was the Legislature as well as the executive—the judge and jury in all cases whatsoever—and united the whole government within himself. The form was certainly extremely simple, and, while he administered it, equally forcible. The people were robbed of their earnings under this one-man system, and were also kept in ignorance and superstition, because in such condition they made more willing slaves.

Under the circumstances, it is not strange, then, that when they first came to enjoy the privileges of freemen, and began to make laws for themselves, they should feel to a degree embarrassed, and find themselves lacking that kind of knowledge essentially necessary for the discharge of these high functions. But, for beginners in the science of legislation, these representatives cut quite a respectable figure, and played their part with considerable credit to themselves and their constituents. They conducted the business of the two Houses with decorum and regularity, and at times it occurred to me that the dignity with which their proceedings were marked might with great propriety be held up as an example to Congress. The business is transacted in the Spanish language, and each House is entitled to an interpreter and

translator for the convenience of those who are not con-
versant with both languages.   In their discussions they
appeal to the Constitution and laws of the United States
as their political landmarks, and in all their proceedings
manifested a disposition to keep within proper limits
and be loyal to the federal government.   There is one
feature seen in either house that strikes a stranger as
exceedingly modern and out of place, which is the smoking of the members during business hours.   They sit in
their seats and puff away at their cigarritos while the
House is in session with as much nonchalance as though
they were in the Plaza.   The practice is looked upon as
a personal privilege, and, since all indulge, no notice is
taken of it.

CHAPTER XI.

WINTER IN SANTA FÉ.

IN New Mexico, as is the custom in all Catholic
countries, feast and saint days in the Church are observed with strictness and proper religious rejoicings.
The celebration of such anniversaries appears to be a
leading article of their faith, without which their Christianity goes for naught, and their prospect of future happiness slim indeed.

On the twelfth day of December the good people of
Santa Fé ceased from their labors, and went up to their
churches to do honor to the Virgin of Guadalupe, the
patron saint of the country. It was made the occasion
of festivities by all classes of the population. This day
is the anniversary of her appearance, which, according to
the tradition of the Church, took place more than three
hundred years ago, and, by their showing, in the most
miraculous manner. The legend of her advent runs as
follows: In the year 1531, an Indian named Juan Diego
was passing by the mountain of Tapeyac, near the city
of Mexico, when the most holy Virgin appeared to him,
and directed him to return to the city and tell the bishop
to come out there and worship her. The Indian went

as he was directed, but the bishop refused to admit him to his presence, not having faith in the miracle. In passing by the same spot a few days afterward, she appeared to the Indian a second time, and commanded him to return again to the bishop, and say to him that "Mary, the mother of God," had sent him. The bishop still refused to admit the messenger to his presence, being incredulous as before, but directed him to bring some token of the annunciation. The Virgin made her appearance the third time two days afterward, and directed the Indian to ascend the mountain and pluck roses therefrom, which he should present to the bishop. Now the mountain is a great mass of rock, without a particle of vegetation upon it; nevertheless, when he ascended it, he found beautiful flowers growing there, which he gathered and threw into his *tilma*, a kind of apron worn by the inhabitants of the country. He returned to the city and presented himself before the bishop, when, upon opening his *tilma*, instead of finding the roses he had plucked from Tapeyac, he beheld upon it an image of the holy Virgin. The bishop was struck with astonishment, and no longer doubted the miracle; and it is said that the identical *tilma* is preserved to this day in the church which bears her name.

She took the name of the town near which she appeared to the Indian, and was canonized as the Virgin of Guadalupe. The Church made her the patron saint of the country, which position she has ever maintained, and it is as bad as rank heresy in a Catholic to disbelieve in her miraculous appearance. With the Mexicans she is all important, and they believe she exercises a great influence over all the affairs of life. With the mass of the population she appears to be the only identity in religion—the Alpha and the Omega—the beginning and the end of all their faith and practice. She is appealed to upon all occasions, and her name is given to nearly a fourth of the females in the country. Her image is conspicuous in all the churches, and is also quite as common in the drinking and gambling saloons as are those of General Jackson and Tom Thumb in American bar-rooms.

Upon this occasion the festivities commenced the evening of the seventh instant, and lasted through the week until the twelfth, which time was very generally observed as a holiday. At dark a row of bonfires were kindled on the south side of the Plaza, in front of the church, and along the middle of some of the principal streets. The wood was dry and resinous, and the flames sent a bright illumination throughout the town. Crowds of people collected around the fires and amused themselves in various ways until the bells tolled for vespers, when they repaired to the Military Chapel, where appropriate religious services were performed by the bishop, assisted by all the attending clergy. Similar ceremonies were observed on the evening of the twelfth, which closed the festivities.

While the American army occupied the city of Mexico in the winter of 1847, I witnessed a grand annual celebration in honor of this saint at the place where she is said to have made her appearance. In order that the reader may have a knowledge of the manner in which such an affair is conducted, I make a few extracts from my military journal of that period.

" On Sunday, the twelfth of December, I rode out to the town of Guadalupe de Hidalgo to witness the ceremonies in honor of the patron saint of the country. I mounted my horse at an early hour and set out alone, but by the time I had reached the garita and turned upon the causeway I found myself in the midst of a crowd tending the same way. The morning was as pleasant

as ever broke over that lovely valley, and had a semblance of spring-time or early summer. The air had
that balmy softness peculiar to the season of opening
flowers, and the gentle zephyrs wafted from the shining
bosom of Lake Tezcuco were freighted with a delightful
odor. The trees, and bushes, and grass were dressed in
their garb of living green, and the merry-hearted song-
sters were singing their sweetest melodies in honor of
the opening day.

"The throng which poured out of the city was dense,
and as checkered in appearance as ever made pilgrimage
to the shrine of a saint. There were all sorts and con-
ditions of persons, and every rank in life had a representative. Here was seen an elegant carriage drawn by
sleek-looking mules, whose smiling inmates appeared the
very personification of luxury and ease; there came a
rude country cart lined with bull-hide, and filled with the
family of a poor ranchero, and drawn by a pair of raw-
boned oxen made fast by thongs around his horns; here
ambled by a squadron of donkey cavalry, urged forward
in hot haste to the scene of festivities, the legs of the
riders almost trailing on the ground; then thousands
came on foot, some carrying children strapped to the
back, and others bending under a load of knick-knacks
for sale. Men, women and children, mules, donkeys and
dogs, saint and sinner, the greasy and the well-clad, were
all mingled in one crowd, and the noise and confused
sounds that arose reminded one of a modern Babel. On
each side of the causeway, up to the very gates of Guadalupe, booths were erected for the sale of cakes, drinks,
and sweetmeats, and where all kinds of buffoonery were
being carried on. Gambling-tables were numerous, and
here and there were pits for cock-fighting, with anxious
crowds assembled around to witness the cruel sport, and
bets were running high on their favorite chickens. Dan-

cers were collected under the wide-spreading trees, where, to the music of the harp, guitar, and violin, they performed their national dances, dressed in the romantic costume of the country.

"When I arrived at the entrance to the inclosure around the church, the procession of the Host was passing. The image of the Virgin, borne aloft on a pole, was followed by a number of priests in their stove-pipe hats and sacred vestments; then came a platoon of filthy-looking soldiers, with a band of musicians playing upon cracked wind-instruments, the whole being brought up in the rear by a crowd of 'red spirits and white, blue spirits and gray,' shooting squibs, and hallooing at the top of their voices. The whole scene reminded me much more of a Fourth of July celebration or a militia training in the United States than a religious festival.

*   *   *   *   *   *   *   *   *

"On nearly the highest point of the rock of Tapeyac, and near where the Indian is said to have gathered the roses, a small church has been erected, which, tradition says, sprung up out of the rock in a single night. It is a dark stone building, constructed in the style of three centuries ago. It is reached from below by a winding stairway cut in the solid stone, considerably crumbled by time, and worn by the footsteps of thousands of pilgrims who have passed up to worship at the shrine of their favorite saint. I entered the little church, and found it thronged with worshipers, mostly half-naked Indians, who had come from the mountains and valleys beyond on this their annual pilgrimage to the Mecca of their hopes, and who, like the devout Moslem who yearly kneels at the tomb of the Prophet, having finished their mission, were ready to lie down and die. They jostled and pushed each other in their anxiety to approach the altar and touch the garments of the Virgin, and deposit their mite-offering in the little dish that stood ready to receive it. Parents, anxious that their little ones should behold the great saint, lifted them over the heads of the multitude that they might enjoy an uninterrupted view. A benevolent-looking old priest ministered at the altar, and at a given signal the whole assemblage prostrated themselves upon the floor to receive his blessing. The poor Indians gazed in mute astonishment at all they saw and heard; but for them there was no solution of the riddle—they were taught to believe, not to inquire. When they had deposited their mite and received a blessing, they turned away to make room for others who were continually pressing on.

" Turning from this scene of blind faith and humiliation, we led our horses down the stone stairway into the inclosure below, when, giving them to a Mexican to hold, we entered the sacred edifice dedicated to the Virgin of Guadalupe. The building was yet crowded with people, and the high dignitaries of the Church were celebrating some solemn ceremony commemorative of the occasion. In point of beauty and richness of decoration this church far excels all others in Mexico. It appeared almost one blaze of gold and silver in the bright sunlight that streamed through the windows and played upon the dazzling ornaments. The whole ceiling, and particularly the dome, is painted in the most beautiful fresco, and so life-like are the figures that they seem about to speak from the panels. Above the altar, in a frame-work of solid silver, is an image of the Virgin as large as life. Her dress is spangled with precious stones, and inside the frame are strips of gold running the whole length, thickly studded with diamonds, pearls, and emeralds; golden rays beam from either side, and suspended overhead is a silver dove as large as an eagle. The altar is of finely-polished marble, highly ornamented, and in front runs a railing of silver. On both sides of the middle aisle, extending from the altar to the choir—some sixty feet—is a wooden railing, covered with silver a quarter of an inch in thickness. There are several silver lamps suspended in different parts of the house, silver candlesticks around the altar, and some of the sacred desks are beautifully wrought in the precious metals. The choir is made of a beautiful dark wood, richly carved and ornamented, and the ceiling is supported by several marble pillars, highly polished and of great beauty. As we crossed the threshold, the deep, rich tone of the organ, accompanied by many voices chanting a hymn of praise, swelled beneath the lofty dome, and impressed the listeners with feelings of reverence and thanksgiving. The building was odorous with the perfumes of scattered incense, and several priests in gorgeous apparel were ministering at the altar.

" Not far from the church is a holy well, over which a small chapel has been erected, and thither we next bent our steps. The well is supposed, by the ignorant, to be sacred, and to possess the power of healing disease and preserving all who are touched by it. A large crowd were gathered around it, some dipping in the tips of their fingers and crossing themselves, others applying a handful to the face, while the more anxious mothers plunged their dirty children in, head, neck, and heels, in order that the holy water might penetrate through all parts of the system, if the coating of dirt would allow it to do so. With us this closed the scene, and, turning away from the dirty crowd, we mounted our horses and galloped down the causeway toward Mexico."

Such is a brief history of the great patron saint of all Mexico, and the manner in which her miraculous appearance is celebrated. It appears quite incomprehensible how an intelligent person, in the middle of the nineteenth century, can believe in any such nonsense as the pretended appearance of Guadalupe; and yet we find the whole corps of priesthood, great and small, sustaining this glaring cheat, and encouraging the people to bow down and worship this graven image instead of their Maker.

Soon after I arrived in Santa Fé I received an invitation to attend a *baile* (ball), and as the ticket was drawn up in the most approved style, I presumed it would be a very *recherché* affair, and that all the upper crust would be present. I determined to be there as a quiet "looker-on in Venice," in order to see what was done and how they did it. The entertainment was given at the house of a citizen in the western part of the city, and at the hour mentioned in the invitation I wended my way thither in company with two friends. Don Tomas met us at his threshold with open arms, and welcomed us with a cordiality that seemed to have no bounds. The room into which we first entered had been fitted up for a bar-room for the occasion, and upon the ample shelves were paraded all kinds of fluid refreshments, said to be good for both body and soul, which I concluded must be the case from the manner in which those present were imbibing. We were urged to take a little something to keep out the cold such a raw night; but, declining the kind offer, we passed on, and were ushered into the *sala* (hall), where a large number of both sexes were assembled. We were provided with comfortable seats, whence we had a good opportunity of seeing every thing that was going on. Dancing had not yet commenced, and I had a few moments to cast my eyes about to see how things were arranged.

The room was about forty feet long and half as many wide, with seats arranged around the wall in amphitheatre style, leaving the middle of the room unobstructed for dancing. The walls were ornamented with at least twenty small looking-glasses, all of the same size, a few sorry-looking wood-cuts, and the usual number of saints, conspicuous among which was the miraculous Guadalupe. The good lady appeared to smile down upon the evening's entertainment, and I have no doubt the company considered themselves safe from all harm while she was present in their midst. The company was mainly composed of Mexicans, the ladies entirely so, and among them all I did not observe a single national costume. All wore the American style of dress, and some were arranged with considerable taste. In point of color it may be said to have been made up of a wholesome sprinkling of all shades, from those who were as fair in complexion as their Anglo-Saxon brothers and sisters, to others who looked dark enough to be two thirds Indian. In one corner of the room, and perched upon the topmost seat, were the musicians—one harpist and two with violins.

I had not much more than time to make these observations of the room and those within it before the musicians struck up a lively waltz, and the campaign of amusement opened in right good earnest. The floor was filled with willing dancers in a trice, and off they went in double-quick time. The Mexicans, as a race, are much given to this amusement, and they both dance and waltz with exceeding grace; and I could but admire the beauty of their motion as they wound through the figures. The etiquette of the baile-room in New Mexico is quite accommodating, and there is no barrier against a person selecting whom he may desire for a partner. It is not necessary to go through the ordeal of an introduction before you can secure a lady for the dance, but you need only place your eye upon the fair damsel with whom you desire to "trip upon the light fantastic toe," and ask the simple question, when she is yours for the set.

Or, if you are not able to speak her language, a sign answers every purpose, and you have but to take her by the hand and point to the floor, when she allows you to lead her out, a willing captive. After the dancing had once commenced it did not flag the whole evening, for no sooner were one set through than another stood ready to take their places. Considerable attention was paid to the little room where the " creature comforts" were vended, and there was a constant stream of visitors setting to and from it. The gentlemen, as a general thing, took their partners out at the conclusion of each cotillon or waltz ; and it was not unfrequent that the lady escorted the gentleman out and treated him. The latter part of the practice was rather new to me, but, as it is one of the customs of the ball-room, every due allowance should be made.

New Mexico, being situated in the middle of the continent, has communication with both seaboards, the Atlantic and the Pacific—with the former by regular monthly mails and private trains. The communication with the Pacific is less frequent and more dangerous ; the distance, though not so great, is much more difficult to travel, and the trip is only occasionally made. Now and then a party of returned Californians come home the overland route, and take Santa Fé in the way.

On the twenty-fifth of December a small party of Americans arrived in town from California, in a journey of sixty days across the continent from Los Angelos, whence they started in October. They were headed by Kit Carson and Lucien Maxwell, both old mountainmen, and were on their return from driving sheep to California. The trip was made without accident, and they saw but two Indians upon the whole route. From Los Angelos they struck the Rio Colorado of the West at Fort Zuma, near the mouth of the Gila, where they crossed and followed up the latter river to the San Pedro, and thence up the San Pedro until they struck Aubrey's trail. They continued on this trail several hundred miles until they reached the Los Menibres River, some twenty miles below Fort Webster, thence by the ordinary route to the Del Norte, which they struck about midway of the *Jornado del Muerte*, thence they pursued the wagon-road to Fort Conrad, and so up the valley of the river to Santa Fé. They met near a hundred thousand sheep on the road to California, the greater number of which were from New Mexico, and were in flocks of from ten to twenty-five thousand each.

The Supreme Court of the Territory began its annual session in the court-house at Santa Fé, and continued its sitting for the argument of causes about three weeks from the first Monday in January. The judiciary system of New Mexico was established by the organic law, which provides that one session of the Supreme Court shall be held in each year. The Legislative Assembly divided the Territory into three judicial districts, known as the northern, middle, and southern. Each of the three judges presides over a district, who is obliged by law to live within the limits of the same, the chief justice being assigned to the middle district. The middle district is composed of the counties of Santa Fé, San Miguel, and Santa Ana; the northern, of Taos and Rio Ariba; and the southern, of the counties of Bernalillo, Valencia, Socorro, and Doña Ana. Two terms are held in each district annually—in the spring and fall. The time of holding the courts begins in the north, and runs through the different counties to the south in rotation, by which arrangement they do not interfere with each other, and the attorneys have an opportunity of making the circuit of the Territory, which is their usual custom.

The American mode of administering justice is yet something of a novelty to the Mexican people, being so entirely different from what they had heretofore been accustomed to. Under the Mexican government courts of justice were almost unknown, and the governor for the time being took it upon himself to redress all wrongs, civil and criminal. It was some time before the people could come to understand our method of doing these things, and even at the present time a man occasionally presents himself before the executive with his grievances, and asks that justice may be done in the premises. Such applicants are always turned over to the courts, but they can not comprehend how or why it is that the governor can not, as in olden times, try the cause and render justice between the parties. As they gradually become familiarized with our system they begin to appreciate it, and can see in it far greater security to person and property than they enjoyed under the old system, where the same person both made and executed the laws. They are becoming sensible of the fact that the trial by jury is the great attribute of a free government, and in time they will appreciate it as highly as those who have grown up under the system.

On the evening of the 12th of January the dullness of Santa Fé was somewhat broken in upon by an entertainment given in the vestry-rooms of the parish church to Bishop Lamy, on the eve of his departure for Rome. The affair was gotten up by the Catholic clergymen of the city and the boys of the boarding-school, and in all its appointments was well arranged. Cards of invitation had been issued some days before, and the hour of five in the afternoon was fixed upon for the entertainment to come off. A little before the appointed time a goodly company were assembled awaiting the announcement of the feast, consisting of the governor and other civil and military officers of the United States then in the city, the leading merchants and citizens of the place, and a number of the members of the two houses of the Legislative Assembly. The invited guests being assembled, a committee was named to wait upon the bishop and escort him to the vestry, which was accordingly done. The company arose at his entrance, and received him with the respect due to his personal and official character. An hour was then passed in an interchange of the compliments of the season and other pleasant conversation, and which, although not of a very profound nature, served the sensible purpose of killing time, and during which occasional glances were cast toward the door whence it was supposed the summons for supper would come. Appetites grew stronger and faces more anxious as the hands of the clock verged upon the seventh hour.

In due season the master of ceremonies announced supper, and led the way to the saloon. We were conducted across a small court-yard into a detached building, where we found tables spread with an abundance of the necessaries and luxuries of life, including various kinds of wines. It was such a supper as I had not expected to see in New Mexico, and the tables would have compared favorably with a similar entertainment in the States. The bishop having invoked a blessing, we took our seats and began the agreeable duty of disposing of the eatables placed before us, and I am sustained in saying that greater justice was never done upon a similar occasion. While we were discussing the viands the scholars served in a little harmony in the shape of vocal and instrumental music.

After the board had been cleared—but of nothing else than the victuals—a deputation of the lads of the school came forward and read the following farewell address to the bishop in English, French, and Spanish:

" MOST ILLUSTRIOUS SIR,—Upon the eve of your lordship's departure, we have the honor to present ourselves before your worship in the name of a great number of friends, to express to you our respect and sympathy, and the sentiment of high consideration we feel toward your worship. Words are but the faint echo of the feelings of our hearts ; but in looking upon this concourse, you can perceive what our lips are unable to express.

" A grand motive carries you to Europe, to represent the interests of your flock : its rights and interests we are convinced you will defend with dignity, and that the smallest shade of an eclipse will never darken the brightness of your character.

" From the depths of our hearts fervent prayers will go up to the Almighty for the happiness of your journey upon the ocean, and that you may be successful in every attempt of your career, surrounded as you will be by numerous cares, and the troubles in which you will be placed at every step in the discharge of your high duties.

" Remember, illustrious sir, that you leave here in your country, your true country, souls innumerable, who seek your personal happiness in the good result of your enterprise and your destination. God grant that the same hand of Omnipotence which conducts the bark that carries you over the boundless seas, in your return to these shores may cause to shine on your noble brow the rays of a new star on its appearance in the heavens."

I am not disposed to criticise the address of the boys to their spiritual guardian, but it must be admitted that it would have been in much better taste had the tone been less bombastic. To say the least, it sounds strangely in republican ears to hear a minister of the Gospel called " lordship" and " worship," and, had such appellations been used by men, they *might* have been accused of toadyism. Upon the whole, the production was on the "*hifaluten*" order of eloquence, and maybe was manufactured by a machine that runs at random. After the boys had retired other sentiments were pledged in ruby wine, accompanied by a few songs, when the company separated at an early hour, each person being able to walk home without the friendly assistance of his neighbor.

The new Baptist church in Santa Fé was finished about the first of the year, and on the fifteenth instant it was dedicated to the worship of God with appropriate services. This is the first and only Protestant meeting-house erected in the Territory of New Mexico, and was built partly by contributions from the United States and partly with money raised in Santa Fé. It is a neat and comfortable adobe building, forty-one feet long—exclusive of a vestibule ten feet square—and thirty-one feet wide. The finish is plain and substantial, with pews sufficient to accommodate about one hundred and fifty persons. The ceiling is supported by four square pillars, and the pulpit, in the modern platform style, is at the north end, with a little plain drapery in front, and also in rear against the wall, as ornament. In a semicircle over the speaker's stand is painted against the wall the inscription, "*Holiness belongeth unto thy house, O Lord, forever.*"

During the ceremony of dedication there were three Baptist ministers in attendance, the Revs. Samuel Gorman, a missionary among the Pueblo Indians at Laguna, Henry W. Reed, of Albuquerque, and Louis Smith, stationed in Santa Fé. The exercises commenced at eleven o'clock A.M. by singing the following appropriate hymn, written for the occasion by a lady of New York City:

DEDICATION HYMN.

"O Lord, the happy hour has come,
Which we have longed to see,
And now within this sacred dome
Our praise ascends to Thee.

Jesus, how charming is the place,
The courts of thine abode!
Come show us now thy smiling face,
And here thy name record.

Oh! may the desert plains rejoice,
And bless the happy day
That bids us elevate the cross,
And Jesus' love display.

Dear Savior, may that precious word
In all its beauties shine,
And sinners haste to meet the Lord,
And own His power divine.

Breathe, Holy Spirit, light of love,
O'er this benighted land,
Till Christ his majesty shall prove,
And king of nations stand."

After the singing of the hymn, the Rev. Mr. Gorman preached a sermon from the fifth chapter of Matthew, from the thirteenth to the sixteenth verses. Not the least interesting part of the morning's exercises was the presentation of an elegantly-bound Bible and Hymn-book, on behalf of the ladies of Dr. Cone's church, New York, which they had purchased and sent out to Santa Fé. In the afternoon Mr. Reed preached a sermon in Spanish from the text, "*For now have we chosen and sanctified this house, that my name may be there forever; and mine eyes and my heart shalt be there perpetually.*" The exercises of the day were concluded by a sermon by the Rev. Mr. Gorman in English. The congregation was respectable in point of numbers, and very attentive, being composed of American residents in Santa Fé, some soldiers from the garrison, and a few Mexicans.

In the erection of the building much praise is due to the Hon. Joab Houghton, of Santa Fé, who took a lively interest in it from the beginning, and seconded all the efforts of the Rev. Louis Smith to have it completed. The entire cost was about four thousand dollars, being increased about one third by the cupola falling down and damaging other parts of the building.

The position of New Mexico, with the distance from the States, as well as the difficulty of reaching this remote possession, greatly abridges the mail facilities that might otherwise be enjoyed. The mail arrives once a month from Independence, Missouri, and the dates from the Atlantic seaboard are about six weeks old when they are received, and it requires three months to receive an answer to a communication from Saint Louis or any place east of that point. There is also a monthly mail from San Antonio, Texas, but the dates received by it are not so late as those received by the eastern route. The first mail from the States after I had taken up my residence in Santa Fé arrived on the twenty-fourth of December. We had been anxiously awaiting its coming, and many a heart beat once more with renewed gladness when the mule-teams drove into the Plaza, and the conductor deposited the leathern bags of love and news down at the door of the post-office. None but those exiled a long distance from home and friends, and living among a strange people, can fully appreciate the arrival of the mail, and more especially when it arrives but once in a month. How quickly a crowd assemble around the office door, waiting for the "open sesame," when they can enter and receive their letters! While standing there, anxious thoughts chase each other through the head and heart, and you are not wholly at ease until you shall have read every line and syllable addressed to you. You can not help imagining the intelligence you may receive; several weeks have elapsed since the last advices, and in that time sad changes may have taken place among the loved ones at home. Perhaps death has invaded the sacred circle of friends and taken away the one most prized, for the grim monster invariably seeks the dearest first; they may be lying upon a bed of sickness, and suffering some of the many ills that flesh is heir to, or perhaps the mail has miscarried, and you will be disappointed in receiving the letters you are expecting. As the thought of death and sickness at home fills the mind—for it is impossible to repress such thoughts —a feverish heat diffuses itself through the system, and a touch of genuine home-sickness takes hold on a person. Let me ask any one who has been a long time absent and distant from home if these are not the feelings of the heart upon the arrival of the mail, and before the letters shall have been distributed and perused?

Thus, half in hope and half in fear, we stand before the post-office, and await the summons to enter.   Presently the door is thrown open, and in we rush, helter skelter, each one making a dive for the letter-boxes, and demanding to be served first, entirely forgetful that our neighbor has equal claims upon the services of Uncle Sam's agent.   In a little while you receive your letters and leave the office—a happier man than when you entered.   In your own gladness, you pass without pity the poor fellow who walks away sad because there was nothing for him.   You perhaps feel a kind of inward sympathy for his disappointment, but at that time you can not manifest any thing of the kind, being too much occupied with your own new-found joy, and, besides, another time will do just as well.   You hurry away to your own quiet room to read over, in silence and alone, the letters you have received, for it will never do to open such treasures within the ken of stranger-eyes.   You close the door, seat yourself, and spread the letters upon the table. Your anxiety has only been partially removed by their reception, and a new one now awaits you as to their contents. In the first place, you look at the seals, one by one, to see that none are black—the precursor of sorrowful intelligence; being satisfied upon this point, the thermometer of your hopes rises a few degrees, and you next examine carefully the address upon each letter, to see from whom they come. The mind at ease in this particular, you now proceed to separate your letters, placing those of a business appearance, or from passing acquaintance merely, in one pile, and those from the "loved ones at home" in another pile by themselves.

Thus far all things have proceeded satisfactorily; but now comes the most interesting part of the episode—that of reading the letters. If you chance to have a sweetheart, as is sometimes the case, you first select her letter from the pile, examine the superscription again to be quite sure that it is from *her*, and perhaps give the mute messenger a silent kiss—first casting a glance around the room to be sure that no intruding eye is overlooking the operation—before you break the seal. With fingers slightly nervous, you open the envelope, and take therefrom the precious epistle, which, in the first place, you read over rather hurriedly, merely to learn whether she is well. You next take up the others in order, and read those from father, mother, brothers, and sisters, each of which you likewise peruse in rather a hurried manner, reserving a more critical reading until evening, when, in dressing-gown and slippers, and perhaps the feet placed upon the table, you carefully read and re-read each one, even taking pleasure in spelling out some of the expressions of endearment. The poor business-letters are reserved until the last, and are then read more as a matter of duty than because of any interest you feel in the con-

tents. Then comes the answering these numerous epis-
tles, which, in accordance with the doctrine that "it is
more blessed to give than to receive," ought to be a pleasure even greater than was experienced at their reception.
With this the drama closes, and the curtain falls upon
your hopes and fears until the arrival of the next mail.

CHAPTER XII.

WINTER IN SANTA FÉ—*Concluded.*

Marriage in New Mexico.—Fees.—Courtship.—Spanish Custom.—Advantages of the System.—Mexican Wedding.—Our Arrival.—Ceremony.—Music.—Tamouche.—Appearance.—His Squaw.—Medal.—Indian Doctors.—Failure of Chief to go to Washington.—Legislature adjourns.—Difficulty.—Legislation.—Anecdotes.—Saint Valentine's Day.—All Fools' Day.—Twenty-second of February.—Spring.—Climate.—Weather at Santa Fé.—Dryness of Atmosphere.—Rain.—Inhabitants drenched.—Author drowned out.

IN New Mexico, the *modus operandi* of winning and wooing in the court of Cupid is widely different from that practiced in the United States; and if a Yankee sets out for the hymeneal altar, he finds himself traveling in a new and untried road. In that country, the institution of marriage, at best, is little more than a mere matter of convenience, and very few enter into this relation from affection, and a desire to make each other happy. It always serves as a cloak to hide numerous irregularities that many of the married females are prone to indulge in, which can be practiced with more facility in the wedded than in the single state. One great obstacle in the way of marriage, and more especially among the poorer classes, is the high rate of fees the priests charge for tying the knot, which renders legal marriage almost entirely a luxury, only to be indulged in by the rich. It is said the charges in this respect have been somewhat lessened within a few years, but they are yet much too high, and drive hundreds annually into illicit intercourse. In some instances several hundred dollars have been paid for performing the ceremony, being the regular fees of the curate, and not the voluntary gift of the party. The lowest price paid, where the parties are married in church and the simplest rites performed, is about twenty dollars. This exaction is an oppression upon the humbler classes, and injurious to that wise institution, which tends, more than any other, to humanize mankind, and to make the world better, wiser, and happier.

The social system of the country plays hob with the old adage that

"The happiest life that ever was led,
Is always to court and never to wed;"

for such a thing as an out-and-out courtship is almost unknown. There the young people have no moonlight walks and sentimental talks along the bank of a pleasant stream in summer; no strolls in the fields, in springtime, to gather early flowers to present to each other as emblems of their own budding affection; no pleasant drives through shady groves, when the horse goes *so* slow, and the afternoon is *so* warm that it is impossible to return home before night, when the moon will be up to light the road. There, there are no pleasant evenings passed in each other's society, to study character and disposition, and when the eyes often speak volumes though the tongue is silent; no sweet good-bys at the door-step, away from ma's searching eyes, when a sly and gentle pressure of the hand is given and received in token of that affection which is as deep as it is silent. These little manœuvrings and heart-episodes are strangers in all the land of New Mexico in connection with the business of marrying and giving in marriage. The young people have none of these matters to attend to for themselves, their *very* accommodating fathers and mothers relieving them of all such trouble; and a young girl can hardly put her nose outside the door without an old dueña tagging after her to stand guard over her heart.

The old Spanish custom of wooing and winning is still adhered to, and, in the first place, all proposals of marriage are made to the father, or, if he be dead, to the mother, who are supposed to be the rightful keepers of their daughter's affection. In brief, the mode of procedure is simply this : If a lad becomes enamored of a lass, and desires to make her his wife, he unbosoms his troubled soul to his father, who thereupon writes a very business kind of an epistle to the father of the young lady, and, without more ado, asks the hand of his daughter in marriage for his son. The matter is then duly considered by the parents of the young lady, and if the match is viewed as an advantageous one, in nine cases out of ten the proposal is accepted without consulting the wishes of the daughter, who, as a dutiful child, is presumed, as a matter of course, to do just as pa wishes. It is beneath the pride of a Spaniard to regard the inclination or preference of the child in such matters, and if *he* is pleased with the proposed alliance, that is deemed all-sufficient. The length of time given the parents to sit in council over the proposal is generally one month, at the end of which the affair is concluded, and an answer is given in due form. It is very seldom that a young lady thinks seriously of matrimony unless it is proposed by the father, and it sometimes happens that the parties have never met until the day of marriage. This is the general custom in affairs of the heart, but there are some exceptions to the rule, and now and then love is made after our own manner of doing such things.

Here is certainly a mode very different, compared with that in which Anglo-Saxon lovers are in the habit of arranging such delicate matters, but, like most innovations, it is not wholly without its advantages. The young lady is saved a deal of trouble and anxiety, to say nothing of the jealousy which, under our system, in spite of all she can do, will now and then creep into the heart. She is relieved of the necessity of always being "fixed up," in order to be in proper trim to receive her knight, should he come at an unexpected hour. And then, under the Spanish *régime*, there are none of the heart-burnings and uncertainties as to whether her love is returned, as is often experienced under our system, and to which species of disquietude the ladies are more or less given. There is no time lost in rides and walks, nor sleep destroyed by troubled dreams, not to mention an occasional case of bona fide heart-breaking, with suit for damages. This paternal arrangement even presents more advantages for the lad than the lass: it is an immense saving of both time and money, economizes breath, otherwise expended in long-drawn sighs, and last, though not least, is a positive blessing to hired horses. This mode of procedure removes the greatest bugbear in the line matrimonial, and under it a wife can be had without the necessity of passing through the fiery ordeal of "popping the question," which is said to require more nerve than to lead a forlorn hope on the field of battle. Such is the working of the Spanish system, and the manner in which the fair sex are led willing captives in Cupid's net; but, after giving it a careful consideration, I am much inclined to the opinion that "the old way is the best, after all."

Soon after my arrival in Santa Fé, a case in point came under my observation, and I had an opportunity of witnessing the practical workings of this new matrimonial arrangement. In a family in which I was an habitual visitor there was a pretty and agreeable daughter, who had inspired a *caballero* with the tender passion. He made the matter known in due season to his father, who in turn addressed a sort of diplomatic note to the mother of the young lady, proposing that the two young people should become "bone of one bone and flesh of one flesh." I chanced to call at the house the same evening the letter had been received, and the mother, feeling unusually happy in view of the proposed alliance, handed it to me to read, at the same time descanting with considerable eloquence upon the advantages to arise from such a match—that the young man was *mui rico* (very rich) and *mui buen* (very good), with many other words of praise. The letter was an ordinary business document, and couched in about the same language as would be used in the purchase of a mule or the hire of a burro. The mother was quite anxious for the alliance to take place, but told me, in a semi-confidential manner, that her daughter was opposed to the arrangement—a perverseness that the old lady could not understand. The young lady sat close by, a listener to the conversation between her mother and myself, now and then giving us a meaning look from under her long eyelashes, as much as to say, "No you don't, old lady." I determined to know how the matter stood with the daughter, and at the first opportunity asked her a few leading questions touching the matter under consideration, and pretty soon found out the cause of trouble in the camp. She told me, with great frankness, that she did not love her suitor, and would not marry him. Here was the whole question in a nutshell. I counseled treason in the premises, and advised her to have her own way in a matter which was of more importance to her than any one else. She took this course, and the unromantic and unwooing swain was obliged to look elsewhere for a housekeeper. A few evenings afterward I saw the father of the young man at the house, who had come to talk the matter over with the mother; but it did no good, for the young lady had a mind of her own, and neither persuasion nor parental threats could induce her to accede to their wishes.

Notwithstanding the high rate of matrimonial fees, and the artificial restrictions placed upon love-making, people do sometimes marry in New Mexico, after all. The first winter I spent in Santa Fé I had the pleasure of attending a *bona fide* Mexican wedding, both parties being considered as belonging to the *élite* of the city. The father of the bride, Don Antonio, was a *rico*, and the happy groom was an officer of the Legislative Assembly. The ceremony took place on a Sunday evening, at the house of the bride's father, where a large number of guests were in attendance. The young lady was a comely lass, without being beautiful. The invitations specified eight o'clock as the hour when the performance was to come off, and, a short time before, in company with some friends, I wended my way to the scene of the festivities. A carriage had been provided to convey us to the house, which we found in waiting at the door of the Honorable Secretary of the Territory. Duly seated in the rickety old machine, away we rattled, and, after a drive of a few minutes, were safely deposited at the threshold.

The master of the establishment met us at the door, welcomed us in the most friendly manner, and conducted us across the court-yard into the house, passing through the sala into a smaller room beyond. Here were assembled some twenty ladies of all ages, and, in order to be a correct chronicler of events, I must add of all colors, from the fair skin of the pure Spanish blood to a good wholesome Indian brown. They were seated, some on benches and others upon the floor, quite after the manner of a Turk, and nearly every one of them had cigarritos in their mouths, which they smoked with the nonchalance of the same number of men. Upon our entrance they maintained their dignity and silence, nor presumed to salute us even with a *buenas noches*. We seated ourselves, and, in obedience to the command of

Don Antonio, made ourselves as much at home as the circumstances of the case would permit. Several other ladies came in, one at a time, until the room was quite well filled. Some of them were pretty and intelligent-looking, and dressed with considerable taste, but the wreaths of smoke which now and then came from the mouth and nostrils detracted considerably from their good looks, according to the American idea. In the centre of the room stood a table filled with numerous bottles of liquor, both mild and strong, supported on each side by plates of cakes and sweetmeats, which fairly formed a breastwork around the spiritual comforters. As there were no other gentlemen invited to take a seat in the room with the ladies, we considered ourselves more highly honored than the rest of the company—so much for being governor, secretary, and Uncle Sam's attorney.

We had been seated some half an hour, when we were invited to walk into the sala, where the ceremony was about to come off. Here we found a large number of persons arranged around the room, each one holding a lighted candle. Upon our entrance candles were thrust into our hands, and we were conducted to the head of the room, where the altar was erected, and which appeared to be the post of honor. We took our position just to the left of the officiating priest, who, duly robed and book in hand, stood ready to read the service. Immediately behind us were the musicians, two with violins and the third with a harp, who were charged to discourse music upon the occasion. In a few minutes the bridal party, four in number, entered the room, and advanced in front of and near the priest. The service was performed according to the rites of the Roman Catholic Church, and in a very few minutes the affianced couple were pronounced husband and wife. When the ceremony was about half concluded, the musicians commenced their discord, which they kept up until it was finished, the leader accompanying the instruments with his voice, which sounded about as melodious as a dinner-horn out of tune. After the benediction was pronounced the ladies retired, and we saw no more of them ; but the gentlemen were invited to the refreshment-room to partake of a few of the good things of life. In a short time the company bade adieu to the host and bent their steps homeward, and thus was celebrated a Mexican wedding.

Upon entering the executive office one morning about the first of February, I found there a delegation of Utah Indians, who had come from the mountains to the North to have an audience with the governor. They were but two in number : Tamouche, a chief, and his wife — the former somewhat celebrated. He was rather a handsome man, with an intellectual cast of countenance, and indicative of great firmness and courage. His eyes were black and piercing, and, with that habitual quickness that belongs to the wild Indian, they seemed to take in every thing at a single glance. In person he was about medium size, but his figure was developed in beautiful proportions, and he exhibited in his manners as much natural grace and dignity as I have ever seen in any person. His features were regular and classic, and appeared fashioned in Nature's finest mould. He was dressed in a suit of buckskin, the coat being highly wrought with beads, and his arms were the bow and arrow, which, however, he laid aside before appearing in the presence of the governor. Take him all in all, he was the finest specimen of a wild, untutored Indian I have ever met, and in personal appearance would compare favorably with his civilized white brethren. His wife, who sat by his side, was a small and delicate-looking woman, and far inferior to her lord in appearance. She, too, was dressed in buckskin, with the addition of a blanket thrown over her shoulders. As she sat in the presence of the executive, she appeared shy and coy as the belles who figure in civilized life, and, like a sensible woman, allowed her husband to do the talking.

When I entered the room, the governor introduced me to the chief as an officer of the government, whereupon he took me in his arms and gave me an old-fashioned hug, and, through the medium of an interpreter, we mutually pledged each other friendship in the future. He failed to present me to his squaw, which I excused on the ground that such was Indian custom. After the governor and he had finished their talk, the former presented the chief with a large silver medal, in the name of his Great Father at Washington, as an earnest of the friendship that existed between them. He was also told the medal made him a captain in the service of the governor, and that, so long as he carried it and behaved himself well, the whites would do him no harm. The medal was attached to a piece of ribbon, and suspended about his neck; and I doubt whether cavalier ever felt prouder when dubbed a knight than did this untutored savage as he gazed upon his new present. The chief and his wife took their leave in an excellent humor with themselves and their Great Father, and in bidding adieu he favored each one of us with a friendly hug.

Tamouche is a war-chief among the Utahs—one of the most powerful of our Indian tribes, and, as such, he exercises a great influence over them in time of war. He is not of much account during peace, for then his "occupation is gone," and it is only when he comes to lead his warriors to battle that he is a great man among them. He is said to watch over his better half with peculiar jealousy, and his present wife is the third one of his dusky countrywomen whom he has taken to his bed and board. It is said of him, and believed, that he killed two

Indian doctors who failed to cure his former wives. Their skill was at fault, and the squaws died under their treatment, which so much outraged the feelings of Tamouche that he put both the medicine-men to death, and sent them to look after their patients. If this Indian custom was generally adopted there would be fewer physicians in the land, and there might, possibly, be better health among the inhabitants.

The chief promised to go with the governor to Washington the coming spring, and have a talk with his Great Father face to face. He and his wife left their lodge about the middle of March to come down to Santa Fé, whence they were to take their departure; but they were overtaken on the way by a deputation of the friends and relatives of the wife, who came to persuade them to return. Finding their arguments and entreaties of no avail, they seized upon Mrs. Tamouche and carried her home by force, being afraid to trust her so far away in the land of the pale faces. This, as a matter of course, broke up the trip of the chief, because he could never think of making a journey across the Plains without having his wife along to catch and saddle his horse and cook his victuals. To an Indian, a wife is really and emphatically a help-meet; and not only does the labor of the household devolve upon her, but she is also obliged to perform all the out-door work besides. I would recommend the Indian tribes of New Mexico as an admirable field for the labors of the advocates of the modern doctrine of Woman's Rights. Here they would find a wide scope for the exercise of their philanthropic genius, and in the effort to better the condition of their red sisters they would receive much more praise than they are now entitled to.

The two houses of the Legislative Assembly adjourned *sine die* on Thursday, the 3d of February, having concluded their session of sixty days.   In some respects the session was an interesting one, and mainly so because most of the members were untried in the art of law-making.   It must be borne in mind, while criticising the actions of the two Houses, that the members did not spring full-fledged and initiated in the business of legislation, as has been generally the case with the other new territories heretofore organized in the Union.   These are a new people, speaking a strange language, and whose whole method of thinking and acting, in all things political, had been widely different from that of the American people.   Thus far the representative system in New Mexico is somewhat a matter of experiment, it being the first Spanish country in which universal suffrage has been fairly tested.   Although the republican system of the United States is beautiful in its simplicity, and easily understood by those who have breathed its atmosphere and been trained in its ways from early youth, yet a strange people, who have been reared in ignorance of its precepts, and deprived of all political training, must necessarily require time before they can work with ease and facility in the new harness.   All things considered, the people of New Mexico seem to have been as apt scholars in the science of government as could be expected under the circumstances.   During the session just closed some useful laws were enacted, but much was left undone that was required for the well-being of the Territory, and I have no doubt that experience will remedy past errors.

The Assembly came near breaking up in a row, and for a time things wore the appearance of a second edition, on a small scale, of the " buckshot and ball war" that took place in Pennsylvania a few years ago.   At the election for delegate to Congress the previous September, much bitterness of feeling was engendered.   Party lines were tightly drawn, without having a reference wholly to political creeds, and at the meeting of the Legislature old animosities were renewed, which led to a fierce struggle in the two Houses. Members seemed to lose sight of the object for which they had been elected, and forgot how much the public business would suffer by these petty strifes; and, from the beginning of the session, a few weary spirits in each House appeared disposed to control legislation, if possible, even at the expense of the public interest. These hostilities festered and grew as the session wore away, until it reached such a height, three days before the time of adjournment, that an effort was made to break up the session of the House altogether.

The great bone of contention between the respective interests in the two Houses was the question of public printing, which was the subject of much angry discussion, and the immediate cause of the difficulty that took place. The allotment of the work is in the hands of the Secretary of the Territory, who pays for the same with funds appropriated by Congress and put in his hands for that purpose, the prices being fixed at the Treasury Department; but he can not have more work done than the laws of the session, unless the two Houses order the same by a joint resolution. In the early part of the session the secretary made a contract with a printing-office in Santa Fé to do all the printing that might be ordered by the Assembly at their then present session. This contract did not meet the approbation of the House, which endeavored to thwart the same by refusing to concur with the council in a joint resolution ordering the journals to be printed. At various times, to this effect, an effort had been made, but the opposition had voted the measure down, and now the session was drawing to a close without any thing having been done in the premises. The office with which the secretary had contracted had become obnoxious to the majority of the House because

of the course the paper had taken in the late congressional election, and the object of the opposition was to prevent the parties contracted with getting the public work,
which was reckoned a pretty good job.   They could not
obtain it for their own friends, and determined to prevent
any body else getting it.

On the evening of the thirtieth of January, and but
three days before the session would terminate by virtue
of the act of Congress, a joint resolution authorizing the
journals to be printed was introduced into the House.
It met with a fierce opposition, but passed to a second
reading, and would have finally passed had not an adjournment been voted until the next day.   The opposition saw the resolution would certainly pass the next
day unless means were taken to prevent another vote being had upon it, and it is said they held a caucus that
evening to determine upon the course they should pursue, and we have the right to suppose that they resolved
to do just what they afterward did do.   The next morning, eleven members, less than a quorum, met in the hall
of the House twenty minutes before the regular time of
meeting, organized by calling one of their own number
to the chair, caused the journal of the day before to be
read and adopted, when they adjourned until Thursday
evening, the third instant, at nine o'clock, only three
hours before the time at which the session would come
to a close.   They then retired, supposing they had accomplished their object, which was to postpone any further action upon the printing resolution ; but their plans
were completely frustrated.   At the usual hour of meeting a quorum of members assembled, the speaker in the
chair, when the House was duly organized and proceeded to business.   The printing resolution was passed
without a dissenting voice, and also many bills which
party feeling hitherto had kept upon the speaker's table ;

and during the remaining three days more business was done than had been transacted all the previous part of the session.

These rather high-handed proceedings caused considerable excitement in Santa Fé, and a number of persons collected under the portals of the palace to watch passing events; but no further disturbance took place, and the business of legislation proceeded smoothly to the end of the session. Before the adjournment, most of those who had participated in the "Rump Parliament" returned to the House and took part in the proceedings. The same evening of the adjournment, and about nine o'clock at night, four or five of those who had acted with the Rumpites went to the door of the House and tried to enter, but finding it locked, one of the number waited upon the Secretary of the Territory and demanded the key, which he refused to deliver to him. Thus prevented from entering the House, they went to the residence of one of the party, where it is said they held a mock session and adjourned. To say the least, these proceedings were unfortunate, and might be made use of as evidence that the people of New Mexico are incapable of self-government. The actors themselves probably did not realize the full force of the measures they were taking, and I have no doubt the injudicious advice of third parties had much to do in bringing about this state of affairs. This episode in legislation should serve as a lesson, and deter the representatives of the people from engaging in any thing of the kind in future.

At the next session of the Legislature matters were conducted with more regularity, and no attempt was made to interrupt public business. One incident took place that somewhat surprised me, and which shows something at fault in that people. The previous summer two Mexican boys had been purchased from the Indians of the Arkansas by General Whitfield, the agent, and were thus rescued from bondage.   During the session a bill was introduced into the House, making an appropriation to refund the amount to General Whitfield which he had paid for the boys, together with other necessary expenses attending their liberation, the whole not amounting to more than one hundred dollars.   The bill hardly received a vote ; and the reason given by those who opposed it was, that it was the duty of the United States to redeem their children from Indian captivity, and that it was no business of theirs.   Such a course would disgrace any State Legislature in the Union.   At the same session the two Houses refused to appropriate a few dollars to pay freight on books the general government had sent out for the territorial library, and which were allowed to remain in the hands of the freighter, to be sold or destroyed.   If this fact was known to Congress, it might deter that body from donating any more books to the library of New Mexico.

A few days before the eighth day of January, a member arose in his seat in the House and stated that, inasmuch as the eighth instant is the anniversary of the birth of the illustrious Jackson, he would move that the House do adjourn over that day.   This announcement was received with some degree of amusement ; but some member, better posted in the history of the United States, corrected the patriotic mover, and explained that the eighth of January was the anniversary of the battle of New Orleans, when the House adjourned accordingly. At the previous session a member of the Council introduced a resolution requesting the Secretary of the Territory to purchase " an engraving of Washington, the Father of his Country and all the other presidents."   Now it will not be doubted that Washington was the father of his country, but it will hardly be admitted that he stood in this relation to all the other presidents; which, if the case, would give to him the most distinguished progeny that ever fell to the lot of one person. But the most amusing incident in New Mexican legislation is said to have occurred during the first session of the Assembly. One of the members had repeatedly asked a waggish young American to draw him up something to present to the council, saying the other members had all presented papers but himself. So one day he called the member aside, and told him, in an earnest manner, that the Constitution of the United States was not at all applicable to the wants of the people of New Mexico, and should be repealed so far as that Territory was concerned, and concluded by telling him that he would draw up and give him a resolution to that effect if he (the member) would present it. The member took with the proposition, and, at the next meeting of the Council, he arose in his seat and offered the resolution, to the effect that the Constitution of the United States should and ought to be repealed so far as it related to the Territory of New Mexico. It was received with a shout of laughter, and at once laid upon the table.

From some cause or other, Saint Valentine is not known among the list of saints that belong to the country, and his anniversary is allowed to come and go without the least observance in Santa Fé. In Southern Mexico the day is somewhat observed, but in New Mexico it seems to have been entirely lost sight of. In the States, the Fourth of July or militia trainings could as well be dispensed with as Valentine's Day, which would not be half the deprivation to the young people. This day affords a *carte blanche* for those who are that way inclined to give and receive tokens of love from under the watchful eyes of mammas, and all the damage that may be done is laid at the door of the good old saint who sits

upon the throne. In place of Saint Valentine's, " All
Fools' Day" is in vogue and properly observed. It falls,
however, upon the twenty-eighth of December instead of
the first of April, as in the States, and is known as *el
dia de inocente*—the day of the innocent. The custom
of the day is peculiar. People go among their friends
and borrow whatever they can, but which they will never return unless the articles are redeemed by a present.
Under this system greenhorns often part with their most
valuable trinkets, and sometimes they are obliged to pay
a heavy tribute before they recover them. All strangers
should have their eyes open, and their purses shut tight,
if they chance to be in a Spanish country on the twenty-
eighth of December.

As is becoming too common in many parts of the
United States, the twenty-second day of February, the
birth-day of the immortal Washington, was allowed to
pass by with no other demonstration than the firing of
a national salute at sundown, and the burning of a few
fire-crackers in the evening. It is a source of deep regret that a proper observance of such days is falling so
much into disuse of late years, which seems to argue that
our people are degenerating in point of patriotism. Our
national days can not be too sacredly observed, and should
be kept all over the Union by the people and constituted
authorities as national holidays ; when all should cease
from labor, and from hill and valley, town and country,
the whole population should go up to the temple of God,
and most devoutly return thanks for the many blessings
that rest upon us as a nation. It should be made a fitting occasion to teach the youth of our country the great
price our fathers paid for our institutions, and to impress
upon them the necessity of always appreciating and being ready to defend them. It seems evident that, whenever a people cease to observe the national days in their

history, they are fast forgetting the events that made them national ; such neglect marks the first apparent decay of patriotism, and thence the downward road is gradual, but sure.

Toward the close of the month I chanced to meet in Santa Fé the notorious Captain Salazar, the same who figures, in not a very enviable position, in Kendall's " Santa Fé Expedition." He is the man who had charge of the Texan prisoners while marching through New Mexico, and treated them with such savage cruelty, cutting off their ears, and inflicting other unheard-of barbarities upon them. He is a dark and swarthy-looking individual, and by no means prepossessing in his appearance. Upon this occasion he had come in to see the governor, in order to claim damages for his son, who had been killed by the Indians a few days before, out upon the Plains, while hunting buffalo. He laid a valuation of five thousand dollars upon his life, because, he said, it had cost a good deal of money to rear and educate him, and he now wished the United States to pay for his loss. But, as the Indian Intercourse Act does not recognize such claims, the governor declined either to make him any remuneration or refer his demand to the government.

The mail that arrived from San Antonio, Texas, in the month of February, brought me intelligence of the death of a dear friend, Lieutenant Hugh E. Dungan, of the fourth regiment United States Artillery. He died at Fort Brown, opposite Matamoras, on the eleventh day of the previous November, of that terrible scourge, the yellow fever. Lieutenant Dungan was a native of Pennsylvania, and was born almost within rifle-shot of my own home. He entered the Military Academy at West Point in June, 1846, and graduated in 1850 with a high reputation for ability and scholarship. The same fall he joined his company at Fort Brown, where he was sta-

tioned up to the day of his death. In the death of
Lieutenant Dungan I lost a valued friend. Our inti-
macy commenced when we were boys attending the same
school, and as we grew up to manhood our friendship
ripened and strengthened. A nobler and better man I
hardly ever knew, and in all the relations of life, such as
son, brother, and friend, it might be said of him, "*Sans
peur et sans reproche.*" At home, where he was best
known and most loved, he has left a void that no time
can fill up; and his early death has robbed his country
of a gallant officer, in whose service he promised an honorable and useful career. Thus the friends of our youth
glide away one by one, and leave us behind to fight the
great battle of life; and as they pass from time to eter-
nity, we are forcibly reminded that we will soon have
more friends in heaven than on earth. I make no apol-
ogy to the reader for thus noticing the death of my
friend; he was one to whom I had been long and truly
attached, and this slight tribute to his memory is the
least that his worth and virtues merit.

"He sleeps his last sleep, he has fought his last battle,
    No sound can awake him to glory again."

After a somewhat tedious and cold winter, spring
made its appearance the beginning of March, and which,
in whatever land we live or roam, we find the most
pleasant of the four seasons. Summer, autumn, and
winter, each in its turn, has its own peculiar charms, but
spring carries off the palm, and all the others give way
to the season of opening flowers. Now every bud bursts
forth into newness of life; the birds return again to their
old familiar haunts, and make the air vocal with their
sweet songs; the grass grows fresh and green beneath
our feet, and valley, hill, and mountain-side once more
clothe themselves in their pleasant garb. The flowers
spring up on every side, and perfume the air with their

sweet odor far and near, and you again welcome in your path the primrose, the modest violet, and the blushing rose as old acquaintances, and pay court to them as the most lovely of Flora's family group.

Man also feels the change from winter to spring almost as sensibly as the fields and flowers, and both body and mind rejoice in the return of this pleasant season. He experiences a newness of life, and a genial influence apparently pervades the whole system as he breathes the new atmosphere which comes freighted with its quickening influence. The reason we have a higher appreciation of spring than autumn or summer is probably because it follows immediately upon winter, and the contrast between the two seasons is so marked; and this sudden transition from the cold and ice of winter to the mild and more pleasant weather of spring may cause us to award charms to the latter season that exceed the reality.

Spring, in the seasons, has been likened to the period of youth in the life of man, in which there is at the same time a similitude and a wide difference. Spring returns in its course with each rolling year, but youth, once passed, is gone forever; the flowers of life have faded, and so wither away until they are gathered into the grave. In youth, all is beautiful and pleasant; we look on life and the world through a charmed mirror, which tinges and perfumes all things with the color and odor of the rose; and then, when years have come upon us, and the rose-leaves have become seared and fallen, we cast a "longing, lingering look behind" down the vista of time, and, while "distance lends enchantment to the view," we often indulge in bitter and painful regrets that the spring-time of life is lost to us forever.

That which most adds to the enjoyment of the season in New Mexico is the climate, which, in point of salubrity, is not excelled in any part of the world. No country can boast a purer, brighter, and healthier sky, equal in all respects to that which bends over the vine-clad hills of Italy. The atmosphere is dry, pure, and clear, and seldom rains, but when it does, then look to the roof of your house. Fresh meat is preserved by hanging it up in the open air, and salt is seldom used among the Mexican population for this purpose. There is but little decay of vegetable matter, owing to the scarcity of rain and the scanty growth of bushes, grass, and trees upon the mountains and in the valleys. There is comparatively little sickness in the country, and fever or fever and ague are diseases almost unknown. Health seems to be the natural condition of man instead of disease, and a larger number of persons live to a great old age than in any other part of our country, and before they die some assume almost the appearance of Egyptian mummies. During the latter part of summer and the beginning of autumn, in what is called the rainy season, more or less water falls, but there are no periodical rains at other seasons of the year. The soil being sandy and porous, the water soon sinks away, and leaves the surface dry after the hardest dash of rain.

The winters at Santa Fé are quite severe, and the thermometer has been known to sink as many as twelve degrees below zero, and to remain at nearly the same temperature for several days together. Snow sometimes falls to the depth of eighteen inches or two feet, but seldom remains long on the ground in the valleys; but during the severest weather of winter the cold is not felt so sensibly as the same temperature in the States, because of the great dryness of the atmosphere. In the dampest weather moisture is seldom seen upon the walls or windows of the houses, and it is equally rare to see ice or frost on the window-glass in the coldest weather

of winter.   In the summer the heat is greatly tempered
by the elevation of the region, so that in the middle and
northern sections of the country it is never uncomforta-
bly warm, and at Santa Fé it is not too warm to sleep
under a pair of blankets.   In all that part of the Territory south of Albuquerque the climate is much warmer,
and in some sections tropical fruits are raised.   Here the
summers are long and hot, and the winters generally
short and mild.   Spring opens in February, and in the
most southern part vegetation is green most of the year.
In this region there prevail high winds in the spring of
the year, while the atmosphere is filled with fine particles of sand, which seek an entrance into every nook and
corner of the houses, and cover every thing with a coating of dust.   These winds prevail in other sections of
the Territory, but they neither last so long nor blow so
fiercely.   They come periodically from the south and
southwest, and the cause of their prevalence appears
never to have been satisfactorily explained.

The dryness of the climate is owing mainly to the
great elevation of the plains that lie around and among
the Rocky and the neighboring mountains.   Santa Fé
has an altitude of nearly eight thousand feet above the
level of the sea; and the Valley of Taos, one of the most
northern settled portions of the country, has an equal elevation.   The central position of New Mexico, together
with its great elevation and great distance from either
ocean, exempts it from the fogs and damps that prevail
nearer the sea-coast.   The wind that blows from the Atlantic on the east and the Pacific on the west starts inland loaded with vapor, but, coming in contact with numerous mountain ridges on the way, condensation takes
place, and the moisture drops down in rain long before
it reaches the plains of New Mexico, which thirst in vain
for refreshing showers.   As a place of resort for invalids

there is probably no country on the continent equal to it, and if there was an easy, safe, and expeditious communication with the States, thousands would resort thither yearly for the restoration of their health.

While, as a general thing, but little rain falls, now and then there is a season that makes an exception to the rule, when the water comes down in torrents.   Such was the case in the summers of 1854–55, which will long be remembered by the inhabitants as unusually wet years. The rainy season began quite early the first year, and did not end till the first week in November.   Nearly every family in town suffered more or less, and both seasons several houses fell down.   The water poured through the mud roofs in streams as thick as a man's arm, and stood several inches deep in the rooms.   Several families were driven from their beds at midnight, and were obliged to seek shelter elsewhere.   Dry land was almost as eagerly sought after by the drenched inhabitants as by the dove from Noah's ark, and every conceivable place of refuge was resorted to.   One family, with bed and bedding, fled to the court-house, and there reposed securely in the arms of the law until morning.   The various expedients adopted to keep dry were amusing in the highest degree, and a faithful drawing of some of these scenes would place all other delineations in the shade.   Several pitched tents in their rooms, and others squatted under umbrellas.   One gentleman, being in succession driven from his bed and from under the table, as a last resort seated himself in an arm-chair with an umbrella over his head, and there remained until morning.   This state of things lasted three or four days.   A general feeling of ill-humor pervaded the community, and the countenance of every man you met bespoke disgust at the wet time they were having.

The flood of water failed to spare my premises, but

made an unceremonious entry into my quarters in the
dead hour of night, and came with a hearty good-will,
that showed it neither stood upon ceremony nor was a
respecter of persons.   In the first place, with a little show
of modesty, it insinuated itself through my roof in drops,
probably to try my temper for a ducking, but it soon increased into large streams, and kept up a steady running
the live-long night.   I immediately resolved myself into
a water committee of one to attend upon the leakage,
and mustered into service tubs, buckets, and various other vessels to catch the water in.   In a short time I carried out nearly a barrel; but the storm continuing and
the water increasing, I ceased my efforts to bail, and
quietly laid me down to sleep.   My sleep during the
balance of the night was disturbed by dreams of water-
works, and storms by sea and land; and when I awoke
in the morning I found my room in good boating order.
I made my escape by coasting around the wall, and
sought safety in drier quarters.

CHAPTER XIII.

RIDING THE CIRCUIT.

Duty of United States Attorney.—Arrangements for Travel.—Leave Santa Fé.—Pojuaque Creek.—La Cañada.—Los Luceros.—Crossing the Mountains.—Arrival at Taos.—Baile.—Situation of Taos.—Indian's Bride.—Revolution of 1847.—Court-house and Jail.—Lawyer smoking.—Kiowah.—Excursion to Taos Pueblo.—Kiowah's House. —Deputation of head Men. — Vaccination of Children: how they bore it.—We look at the Village.—Inside of Building.—Estufa.— Invited to Baile.—Fandangos and Music.—What took place at the Baile.—Egg-shells and Cologne.—Kit Carson.—Court adjourned.— We leave Taos.—Geological Formation of the Mountains.—View of the Valley of the Del Norte.—Arrival at Los Luceros.

THE United States Attorney for New Mexico is obliged to make the circuit of the Territory twice a year —spring and fall—to attend the sittings of the District Court in the respective counties, and look after the interests of his dear old " Uncle Sam." The spring term, the present year, was to begin at the town of Don Fernandez de Taos, seventy-five miles north of Santa Fé, the first Monday of March. The usual mode of travel is on horseback, as the roads in many places are quite impassable for carriages.

The evening before the day of starting I made the necessary preparations for the trip. Every thing that circumstances permitted me to carry were stowed away into a pair of ordinary-sized saddle-bags, consisting of law library, wardrobe, and barber-shop, which, being inventoried upon the spot, amounted to two shirts, two law-books, small Bible, two pairs of socks, writing materials, and shaving apparatus. These articles made up

DON FERNANDO DE TAOS.

my outfit for a journey of near a thousand miles and an absence of three months. These duties having been satisfactorily conducted, I threw myself upon the tender mercies of the God of Sleep, and was quickly captive in the land of dreams.

The next morning was as bright and clear as the most fastidious traveler could desire, and about nine o'clock our little cavalcade turned out of the Plaza and took the road to Taos. Our party numbered five persons : the governor, Judge Houghton, the United States marshal, your humble servant, and a Mexican, all well mounted. Giving the rein to our horses, we journeyed on at an easy pace through a sandy and hilly country. The sides of the hills are covered with a scanty growth of pine-trees, which cling with the tenacity of life itself to the barren soil. The sand lay deep and loose in the road, and for several miles we were not able to travel faster than a walk. On the way-side I noticed a feature peculiarly Mexican—a number of rude crosses, each with a pile of stones around it, thrown there by pious hands ; some had been erected to mark the spot where solitary travelers had been waylaid and murdered, and others pointed out the place where persons fell in the revolution of 1837.

In a ride of three hours we made the Pojuaque Creek, near the Indian pueblo of the same name—a little mountain stream that falls into the Del Norte. We halted here a few minutes to slake the thirst of man and beast, and to partake of a lunch of bread and meat, when we mounted and rode on. To the right of the road were observed some interesting sandstone formations, which, in the distance, looked not unlike the ruins of a town ; some resembled broken columns, single and in rows, ruined porticoes, and fallen pilasters. One locality, from its resemblance to a decayed building, had received the name of The Church : three sides were still standing, while the fourth, looking toward the south, had fallen. Here the sand-hills sink down into the valley, and the Del Norte comes in sight—a beautiful and clear, but not a broad stream.

We arrived at La Cañada—a mud village twenty-five miles from Santa Fé—about midday. The population is near three hundred. A small adobe church stands upon the Plaza, and a priest resides in an adjoining house to minister at the altar. In the history of New Mexico this little village has played a conspicuous part. It was always made the rallying-point for the Northern Indians in the various rebellions, and several severe battles have been fought in its vicinity. We tarried here but a few moments. We passed the two Indian pueblos of San Juan and Nambé, the latter lying a little distance off the road to the right, near the mountains. We learned that, a few days before, the council of Nambé had caused two of their number to be put to death for the supposed offense of witchcraft. The murderers were afterward arrested and tried at Santa Fé, of which a more extended notice will be given hereafter.

We continued up the valley until nearly dark, when we arrived at the hospitable ranch of Mr. Clark, at Los Luceros, where we stopped for the night. He welcomed us with genuine hospitality. We were ushered into the *sala*, where we found a cheerful fire blazing upon the hearth, which put new life into our benumbed bodies. For me the ride was unusually fatiguing, and when I dismounted it was with difficulty that I could walk into the house. For the first time I had backed a Mexican saddle, which, though pleasant to ride upon when you have become accustomed to them, generally punish the uninitiated for a few days. I thought to myself that, if thus crippled in the first day's ride, there would be nothing of me left long before the circuit should be completed.

In a little while supper was announced, when we were seated at a well-filled board, presided over by Mrs. Clark in person, contrary to the general custom of Mexican ladies, who do not eat with their guests.   Soon after, the *colchones* were spread upon the floor, when we retired, and slept soundly until the morning.

We were in the saddle betimes the next morning and on the road to Taos, yet forty miles distant.   We continued up the valley for six or eight miles, when the road inclines to the right to pass the mountains, while the river turns to the left and is soon lost from view.   The wagon-road winds round through the depressions in the mountains, while the bridle-path, which we followed, leads in a more direct route over some of the highest peaks. The first four miles of the way was through a little valley, until we arrived at the village of El Embudo, when we commenced the ascent in earnest, here steep and difficult. The distance across is about six miles by a single mule-path ; and, in many parts of the way, a slip of two or three feet would send the unfortunate wight tumbling headlong hundreds of feet below.   The path is winding in its course, and in some places too steep for the rider to keep the saddle.

From the summit of the peak we crossed the view is neither romantic nor picturesque, but dreary and forbidding in the extreme.   All around lie piled rugged mountains, then covered with snow, and the wind howled in dismal and piercing blasts through the dwarf pines.   We found the descent much more difficult than the ascent, the path being filled with ice, and very slippery ; and not feeling safe in the saddle, we dismounted, and led our horses down the slope.   We reached the valley below in safety, and halted to lunch on the bank of a small stream that flows through it.

As we descended the mountain we had an extensive

view to the north, and could plainly see the white houses of Taos, nearly twenty miles distant. To the northwest we could trace the *arroyo* through which flows the Rio del Norte, which appeared like a great black zigzag line drawn upon the plain. It is from two to five hundred feet deep, and entirely hides the river from view. Our course now lay through a rolling and broken country until we entered the Valley of Taos, with no improvement in the appearance. The sun went down while we were yet five miles from our place of destination, and the coming darkness caused us to ride more slowly. We entered Taos about nine o'clock, cold and much fatigued.

The governor and myself dismounted at the quarters of Major Blake, U. S. A., upon the faith of a previous invitation, and threw ourselves upon his hospitalities. In a short time a welcome supper was spread for us, of which we partook with a hearty good-will. We had hardly swallowed our meal when we received a pressing invitation to attend a *baile* a few doors distant, and though neither of us could more than walk, we wended our way thither under the escort of the gallant major. Arriving there, we were ushered into a crowded room, where we found all the fun-loving people of Don Fernandez assembled, including the *gente fina*,* and those that were any thing else than *fina*. The floor was filled with merry dancers, and the two-handed orchestra was dealing out to them a terrific compound of catgut and rosin. Those who tripped upon the "light fantastic" appeared to enjoy the fun amazingly, and half the strength and suppleness expended in any business of life could not fail to make a fortune in quick time. I observed no difference between this and numerous similar gatherings I had witnessed in the country, if we except the new faces.

* This expression has the same meaning in Spanish as the word *élite* in French.

and strange whisky-bottles. Not being in a condition to enter into the festivities, we returned to our quarters at an early hour, and were soon enjoying a little of that delightful article which Sancho Panza declares, and we take his word for it, " covers one all over like a cloak."

The town of Don Fernandez de Taos, the county seat of the county of Taos, is situated in the beautiful valley of the same name. The valley is one of the most productive in the Territory, and yields a large surplus of grain. It is mountain locked upon every side. The town was settled by the Spaniards at a much later period than many other portions of the Territory. The name of the first settler is said to have been Pando, who for some time was the only inhabitant of the valley. It is related of him that, in order to obtain the friendship of the wild Indians, who were troublesome, he promised his infant daughter to one of the chiefs in marriage. When she grew up the Indian came for his bride, but the maiden did not fancy her red lover, and refused to marry him. This so much incensed the tribe that they attacked the settlement, and killed all but the young woman, whom they carried into captivity. She lived with these Indians (said to have been the Camanches) several years, when she fell into the hands of the Pawnees, who sold her to a trader of Saint Louis, at which city she died some years ago. Ten thousand acres are said to be under cultivation in the valley, the whole of which is irrigated by small streams that come down from the mountains. The town has a population of near two thousand, and is built of adobes without order. In the centre is a plaza, upon which the best houses and most of the stores front.

During the troubles of 1847 Taos was conspicuous for its opposition to the Americans. The Mexicans and Pueblo Indians rose on the nineteenth of January and mur-

dered Governor Bent and six others.   They then marched with a force of several hundred toward Santa Fé, gathering additions to their numbers as they advanced.   General Price, having obtained information of their movements, marched a strong force to oppose them, which
met them the next day strongly posted near La Cañada.
The enemy were driven from their position at the point
of the bayonet with considerable loss, and retreated to
Taos, where they strongly intrenched themselves in the
Indian pueblo.   The troops followed in their steps, crossing the Taos mountains in two feet of snow, and attacked them on the afternoon of the third of February.   The
action continued that afternoon, all the next day, and
until the following morning, when the enemy sued for
peace.   They lost several hundred in killed and wounded, while ours was about fifty.   Among the Americans
who fell in the action was the brave Captain Burgwin,
of the United States dragoons, who was killed in the
charge upon the church, in the thickest of the fight, a victim of his own chivalry and daring.   In all the qualities
of a soldier and a man he had no superior in the service,
and left behind him an enviable reputation.   The military post near Taos bears his name—Cantonment Burgwin.

The District Court commenced the next morning after
our arrival, and here, for the first time, I had an opportunity of witnessing the working of our judicial system
among a strange people.   At the hour of eleven I wended my way to the court-house, which I found to be a
low, rude mud building, and less comfortable than the
cow-stables in some of the States.   I entered the sanctuary of justice, and took my seat upon one of the three
chairs that had been provided for the officers of the court.
Being now inside and fairly seated, the first thing to be
done was to take a survey of the premises, which was

accordingly made while the marshal was opening the
court in due form at the door.   The room was about
forty feet long, fifteen wide, and eight high.   There were
neither boards nor carpet to hide the earthen floor, which
was damp and cold.   On the south side were two windows, about two feet square each, and, instead of glass,
they were supplied with cotton cloth nailed across the
frames, which answered the double purpose of shutting
out both light and dust.   In addition to the three chairs,
there were as many old benches for the accommodation of
the bar, officers, parties, witnesses, jurors, and the lookers-on, and those who were not fortunate in the scramble
for seats had the felicity of leaning against the wall—
none of the best for Sunday coats—or sitting upon the
earthen floor.   The roof was none of the tightest, and
through the openings, which were neither "few nor far
between," could be seen the "stars in the quiet sky"
smiling down upon our deliberations.   This was dealing
out justice under a heavenly influence.   At the west end
of the room was the crowning glory of the house, de-
cidedly the most ornamental feature in the establishment,
for there the altar of justice was seated.   A small nook,
some eight feet by four, was partitioned off for the judge;
the front was trimmed with a few yards of flashy Mer-
rimac, and, as a matter of comfort, a couple of boards
were laid down for a floor.   The little place that held all
that was mortal and immortal of his honor much resembled a sentry-box, but was inferior in point of equipments.   A small pine table in front was used by the
clerk, marshal, and lawyers.   When I first entered the
room, and saw on one side a number of persons squatting
upon the ground, and upon the other a man to whom all
eyes were turned, fastened up in a cage, I was not certain that I had not made a mistake and intruded into a
sanctuary of the Grand Llama of Thibet, who was now

seated in his box, and about to receive the adoration of his subjects, instead of entering a court of justice.

While we are about it we might as well examine all the county buildings; and as we have a moment's leisure before operations commence, we will peep into the jail, and see what kind of a place is provided for those who are lucky enough to be boarded and lodged at the public expense. This necessary appendage to a court-house is a small room adjoining it upon the east side, and a prisoner confined there would be about as safe as when picketed out on the Plaza. The county at this time must have been minus both funds and credit, for the door, instead of being locked, was *securely* fastened with a twine string. Opposite the jail was another small room for the use of the grand and petit juries, and if both should have occasion to sit at the same time, one would be obliged to hold its session on the Plaza. With such a place to secure criminals, there were frequent jail deliveries, and it was but seldom offenders had justice meted out to them.

We have now seen all the sights, and will return into the house. The judge is upon the bench officially, and the wheels of justice are set in motion. The proceedings were in the same routine as in the courts of the States, except the use of a sworn interpreter to render all that was said into both languages. During the trial of a cause, I was considerably amused to see a member of the bar arise and ask permission of the judge to smoke in court; leave was granted him, when he pulled from his pocket a very Democratic-looking pipe, filled it with the noxious weed, and puffed away, apparently very happy.

On Tuesday the governor was visited by Kiowah, the war-chief of the Pueblo of Taos, and received a pressing invitation to come out to his village and see his people, which was accepted, and the following day was fixed upon for the excursion. At this time the small-pox was prevailing among the Pueblo Indians to an alarming extent, and Governor M. being authorized by the department to have the different pueblos vaccinated, determined to make this visit the occasion of administering the white man's *Great Medicine* to the Taosites. Kiowah was informed to that effect, and directed to have all the youngsters ready on the morrow. We started early the next morning for the pueblo, being accompanied by Major Blake and Lieutenant Johnson, U. S. A., and three or four citizens. A ride of three miles across the valley in a northwest direction brought us to the pueblo. Kiowah stood ready to receive us, clothed in his newest and best buffalo robe, and with a broad grin upon his amiable-looking countenance. Dismounting at his threshold, we followed his lead up the outside ladder into his house. He ushered us into a small room, with a ceiling so low that the tallest of our party could not stand upright. The floor was covered with a stiff, untanned bull-hide—a substantial carpet, by the way—and the owner's taste in the fine arts was exhibited in a few colored wood-cuts hanging around the wall. In one corner was the bed of the old warrior, even more imperishable than the carpet: a space, large enough for two persons to lie down, was built up of masonry and covered with bull-hide, upon which the renowned Kiowah was accustomed to repose himself after the fatigues of the camp.

We had not long been seated when a delegation of the head men of the village came in to pay their respects to the governor, and a greasier and more Indian-fied set of notables it was never my good fortune to behold. They had donned their comeliest attire for the occasion. Each one was wrapped up in a buffalo robe, covering him from his head to his heels, and made fast by a cord around the waist; and the costume was complete with the addition of a pair of skin leggins and moccasins. The paint-pot had been well patronized that morning, and their faces were bedaubed with this necessary article of an Indian toilet in the most approved style. As they entered, each one saluted us with a shake of the hand, when they seated themselves upon the floor, and main-tained a profound silence until they were addressed. We held a short confab with our red brethren through the means of an interpreter, and, as is always the case among civilized and savage, each party gave the other congrat-ulations upon their interview, and in turn pledged their "most distinguished consideration."

The war-captain was now requested to have the chil-dren brought in, in order that they might be vaccinated. Notice to this effect was sent around the village, and in almost less time than is required to write it the room was crowded with anxious mothers, bearing their un-washed jewels to offer up to the Great Medicine. The operation commenced immediately. At first the little vagabonds seemed to vie with each other as to who should be first operated upon — their native curiosity creating the desire. They seemed not to have imagined that the operation could possibly hurt, but they very shortly received a lesson that opened their eyes as well as their mouths. The first delegation stood it like young heroes—pride or something else keeping them from cry-ing—and matters seemed to be moving along with great harmony. Presently, however, a dirty little chap, whose tear-bags were hung close to his eyes, came up to be op-erated upon, and at the first entrance of the needle into his arm he broke out into a regular white-baby yell, that fairly made the room echo. Silence was now at an end. The cries of this one seemed to have a magic effect upon the others, and in almost less than no time there was a convocation of human sounds which embraced every pos-

sible tone in the scale musical—flats, sharps, and natu-
rals. After this there was no more voluntary martyrdom
to vaccination, but the fathers and mothers had to bring
them up by main force, and hold them while being op-
erated upon.

The vaccination being concluded, we accompanied Kiowah to take a look at the village. The population is
near fifteen hundred, and, except the war-captain and a
few others of the head men, they all live in two large
buildings, of which a description has already been given
in chapter sixth. We wended our way to the building
that stands upon the west side of the creek that runs
through the pueblo. As we approached, the several
stories were covered with Indians, young and old, who
swarmed from within like bees from a hive. On the
very top was a sentinel pacing his rounds, whose duty it
is to keep a sharp look-out day and night.

Not satisfied with an outside view, I determined to enter to see what was going on in the interior of this half
fortification and half dwelling-house. With this object
in view, I mounted the first ladder I came to, and ascended to the terrace above. This was covered with poles,
and the room below did not appear to be used as a dwelling. I then ascended a second ladder to the next higher terrace, which was covered with mud, and dried hard,
and on the top was a small hole, the only entrance to
the apartments below. I squeezed myself through it,
and, passing down a ladder, landed in the middle of a
room about eight feet square, which seemed to be the
shoemaker-shop of the village ; and the mender of soles,
with his better half by his side, was hard at work about
finishing a job. A small hole in the side of the wall let
in a little additional light and air to that which came
down the companion-way. In one corner was a small
fireplace, and a chimney that extended four feet above

the terrace carried off the smoke. I passed into several of the rooms, all about the same in point of size and appearance. Each appeared to be adapted to a single family, and they were scantily furnished with a few earthen vessels, and some bull-hides and dressed deer-skins for bed and bedding. This single building was said to contain seven hundred inhabitants, and is strong as a place of defense. When the ladders are pulled up, there is no way of entrance except by digging through the walls, which would be attended with great danger with an enemy above you.

Near this building, and a little way to the north, stands the *estufa*, or council-chamber, where grave affairs of state are discussed. It is a large single room, and is set apart for this purpose. The other large building stands on the opposite side of the creek, and the old church, where the severe battle was fought during the rebellion of 1847, is a few hundred yards to the west. Scattered around are a number of conical-shaped ovens, with a small hole near the top and a larger one at the bottom. Having now completed the object of our visit, and thanked Kiowah for his kindness, we mounted our horses and rode back to Taos, where we arrived in time to dine.

During the afternoon session of court, a nicely-folded billet was placed in my hands, which politely informed me that my services were needed that evening at a *baile* to come off at the house of one Señor Martinez, who, being the brother of the *Cura* of Taos, is reckoned to rank among the *gente fina* pretty high up on the list. My first thought was not to accept the invitation, inasmuch as I am of no earthly use in such an assemblage, the education of my heels, unfortunately, having been neglected in my youth, and, consequently, I lack all knowledge of the *Devil's Hornpipe*, *Pigeon Wing*, and kindred performances. This disability renders me a non-combatant in the strife, and seemed a legitimate excuse for remaining at home; but as the entertainment was mainly gotten up because of the strangers in town—a humble way of extending to them the freedom of the place—I finally concluded to go as a quiet "looker-on in Venice."

In New Mexico the general name of all assemblies where dancing is the principal amusement is *fandango*, which is not, as many suppose, a particular dance. Those gatherings where the better classes "most do congregate" are called *baile*, or ball, which differs in no other particular from the fandango. All New Mexicans are exceedingly fond of dancing, and, in fact, it seems almost as much a passion with them as with the French. Every class and rank in society participate in the amusement, and very small children are seen whirling in the waltz and tripping in the dance with the same gusto as their more mature companions. They dance and waltz with beauty and ease to the music of the guitar and violin, and sometimes these instruments are accompanied by a small drum, called a *tombé*. Some of the musicians play with considerable skill, and at times I have listened to performers who would have been deemed respectable any where. It is customary for one or more of the players to accompany the instruments with his voice, singing impromptu words which he adapts to the music and the occasion. Most of the persons in the room receive in turn a passing compliment in his doggerel, and when the notice is particularly flattering he expects a *real* (twelve and a half cents) in return, and will not refuse a quarter. They have a happy faculty of rhyming, and sometimes convulse the room with the aptness of their hits.

When the evening came on, I "fixed up," as the

phrase goes, as well as my scanty wardrobe would allow, to attend the *baile*. At the fashionable hour—for fashion does prevail to some extent in New Mexico, in spite of its being so far removed from the world—under the guidance of our kind host, we took up the line of march for the place of amusement. We found a large number assembled in the *sala*, many of whom were pointed out as the genuine *upper crust* of Don Fernandez, being well baked for upper crust, as a large majority of them were done very *brown*. The amusements of the evening had already commenced, and at the time of our arrival they were going it strong on the *cura*.* The host met us at the door, and, bidding us welcome, conducted us to seats at the head of the room.

There are manners and customs prevailing at these bailes at some periods of the year very different from any practiced in other sections of the Union, and this evening I saw a performance so entirely new that I became more convinced than ever that I was a Gringo. During the season of Lent there prevails a custom of the baile-going people providing themselves with egg-shells filled with Cologne water, and other sweet-smelling articles, which they break over the heads of their friends as a matter of fun, and the operation is looked upon as a capital joke. I had not been long in the room, and in the recess of dancing, when I observed three pretty girls coming toward the place where the governor and myself were sitting, with countenances beaming with fun, as though they were bent on some mischief. They approached within touching distance, and before we had time to stand on the defensive, or were even aware of their object, smash! dash! went the egg-shells over our heads in quick succession, and down our faces streamed the *eau de Cologne*. Like the episode of the boys and the

* A favorite Spanish waltz.

frogs, the current of fun seemed to run in one direction, and on this occasion there was no question about the young ladies having it. Satisfied with their gallant exploit, they marched composedly back whence they came, and quietly took their seats. This looked very much like storming the citadel.

There is a twin custom upon such occasions, which is, that you may kiss the fair assailants, provided you can catch them and inflict the penalty before they regain their seats. But in this instance they were out of harm's way before I had time to take any steps toward so delicate a performance, or even the deluge of Cologne permitted to open my eyes. As there was no help for such a misfortune, I submitted to my fate with the most commendable resignation, wiped away the flowing Cologne, and straightened up my drooping shirt-collar. I now thought of making a campaign into the enemy's country, by way of retaliation for the foray just related, and began to look around to seé how the land lay. I had no difficulty in singling out one of the three who had just paid us a visit, and accordingly made my arrangements "to carry the war into Africa." Armed and equipped as the custom in such matters required, I marched boldly up to the point of assault, and, in a manner that should become a gallant knight, broke the egg-shell over her head, much to the detriment of sundry lace furbelows, and she, too, was soon afloat in a sea of Cologne. I had not the pleasure of any further acquaintance with the fair maiden than the rather abrupt introduction forced upon me just before ; but want of ceremony seemed not to make any difference, and she bore the operation like a heroine, and welcomed the egg-shell with a musical *esta bueno*—it is good. During the course of the evening a second deputation of beauties paid me a visit for a similar purpose ; but by this time I had become somewhat initiated into the baile customs of Lent, and received the sweet-scented assault as kindly as could be. These little episodes do not in the least interrupt the dancing, which goes steadily on the while, and the merry-makers seem hardly conscious that a drop of Cologne is wasted upon the occasion.

The musician occupied a platform in one corner of the room a little raised above the floor, and the dancers, when not participating in the amusement, were seated on benches ranged around the wall. From some cause, the old *guitarero*, the leader of the orchestra, did not this evening, as usual, accompany the instrument with his voice, chanting his impromptu verses, and, unless his reputation had gone before him, no one would have judged him to be the *poet laureate* of the village. The first evening of our arrival in Taos, at the ball we attended for a few minutes, when this old musician saw the governor in the room, he made him the subject of his most eloquent verses. The substance of his eulogy was that he had known and played before many governors in his day, but that the one then present was a little ahead of them all, and was just the greatest governor that had ever been in New Mexico. Such a complimentary notice could not be overlooked nor go unrewarded, and his excellency had to pay a fee according to the terms of the panegyric.

While at Taos, I saw for the first time and made the acquaintance of Kit Carson, the celebrated mountaineer. I was standing in front of Major Blake's quarters, when I saw a small-sized, modest-looking person approaching, who, I was told, was the famous mountain-man of whom I had heard so much. He is about five feet eight inches in height, rather heavy set, and a little bow-legged; he is a mild, pleasant man in conversation, with a voice almost as soft as that of a woman. He has brown eyes and dark hair, with a face somewhat hard-featured from long exposure among the mountains. He was dressed plainly, and his whole personal appearance was entirely different from what I had imagined this celebrated trapper and hunter. There is nothing like a fire-eater in his manners, but, to the contrary, in all his actions he is quiet and unassuming. His has been a romantic, roving life, and his personal history embraces as much of wild adventure and hair-breadth escapes as that of any man in the Union. He has been fairly cradled among the Rocky Mountains and upon the desert plains that lie in the heart of the American continent, and is familiar with the fastnesses of the one and the trackless pathways of the other. He has endured all imaginable hardships with a steady perseverance and unflinching courage. A history of his adventures would make one of the most interesting volumes ever presented to the public.

The court adjourned Saturday morning, and as I had nothing more to detain me, I made preparations to return to Los Luceros, whence I must go the following Monday morning to Chamita to attend the court at that place. The governor and myself started off in advance of the balance of our party, who were not yet ready to leave town. We missed our way riding out of Taos, and for more than an hour were wandering through the valley, crossing arroyo after arroyo, and uncertain in what direction to turn, when at last we struck the main road, and journeyed on without interruption. We were soon overtaken by three Mexicans, who traveled with us, whose accession was quite welcome, inasmuch as the road was considered dangerous, being within the track of the Jicarilla Apache Indians. We lunched beside the same stream, near La Cieneguilla, and then commenced the passage of the mountains. We found the road less difficult than before. The weather had moderated meanwhile, and thawed away much of the ice and snow; we made the ascent without difficulty, and by the middle of the afternoon had safely descended into the valley of El Embudo. The day was more propitious than before, and as we crossed ridge after ridge, we caught sight of some views among the distant peaks not altogether unpleasing. Looking to the southwest, we had occasional glimpses of the Del Norte, like a small thread of silver glittering in the sun and winding its lone course through the narrow openings in the mountains.

I had better opportunity on my return to notice more particularly the mountains, and amid the almost universal desolation that presented itself, I saw some things that were interesting. They exhibit many signs of having, in past time, undergone great changes. In some places there are the remains of large craters of extinct volcanoes, with scoria and lava lying round about; at other points were strong indications of eruptions, where the primary formations had been thrown up upon the surface. At one place clay slate—an early formation—had been disrupted, and the strata now lie at every possible angle to the horizon. Some of the highest peaks are covered with boulders great and small, besides other water-washed stones, which indicate a previous submergence, or else these stones were cast up by volcanic action from a lake beneath. Here is a rich and interesting field for the skillful geologist, and as yet wholly unexplored.

In the immediate vicinity of El Embudo there are found some curious sandstone formations, caused by the action of the rain and atmosphere, and similar to those near La Cañada. On the right of the valley, passing south, stands a natural sandstone pillar, near a high ledge of the same material. It appeared about forty feet in height, circular, at least six in diameter, and from the road resembled a piece of chiseled work. The main ledge has been worn away at least fifty feet from the pillar, and there it stands, solitary and alone, like a giant sentinel watching over the destiny of the quiet little valley that spreads around. From this point the road runs through deep arroyos some two or three miles until you arrive at the little turn of La Holla, at the head of the valley of the Del Norte. Here this stream, one of the longest in America, is not much larger than a bubbling brook, and clear as crystal, and not until it has flowed more than a hundred miles through a loose and rich soil does it assume that thick, muddy appearance, which makes it distinguished above all other rivers on the continent.

Looking south from the highest point of the mountains as we crossed near La Holla, we obtained a fine view of the valley for some miles. It was almost the close of day, and right in front, like a ball of crimson and gold, the sun hung suspended near the mountain top, over which it reflected a thousand rays as it was about to bid the world good night. The glistening river flowed on at the base of the rugged mountain range, and the noise of water, falling over ledges of rocks in the stream, came up to us in soft murmurs, like nature's own music. Dotted here and there down the valley were the rustic houses of the rancheros, and an occasional cluster marked a small hamlet. Since we had passed up, the people had commenced preparations for the spring crops, and some were yet at work in the fields. The *acequias* had been opened for irrigation, and here and there, like veins on the bosom of mother earth, we could trace the little silver-like threads of water meandering through the freshly-plowed ground, carrying life to the newly-sown grain. The dead silence around impressed the scene favorably upon the mind, and gave evidence of the close of the busy week, and the approach of that day of rest when both saint and sinner can cease from his labors. We rode leisurely down the valley, and just before dark arrived at the rancho of Mr. Clark, where we were again welcomed with his accustomed hospitality.

CHAPTER XIV.

RIDING THE CIRCUIT—*Continued.*

I REMAINED at Los Luceros until the following Monday morning, and passed a quiet and not unpleasant Sabbath under the hospitable roof of Mr. Clark. The governor left for Santa Fé early on Sunday, where he arrived safely the same afternoon. During the day the judge and the balance of our party arrived from Taos, and remained at the rancho until the morrow.

The distance from Luceros to Chamita, the county-seat of Rio Ariba, where court was to commence the next day, is twelve miles, and we were under way for that point early Monday morning. We forded the river opposite the rancho, and after following down the stream for some distance, we turned to the west and struck across the sand hills. In the river-bottom the farmers were afield preparing the earth for seed-time; some were letting the water on the ground from the acequias, and others were engaged with hoe or plow breaking up the soil. In the space of thirty acres I counted as many plows in motion, true patterns of the homely implement used in the time of Moses and the Prophets, and almost " without note or comment." Each one was drawn by a pair of raw-boned oxen made fast by the horns, and in slow and measured tread they moved across the field to the gentle pricking-up by a villainous looking goad. We crossed ridge after ridge for about two hours, when, from the top of a high sand-hill, we espied our place of destination, a dirty little mud village built in a straggling manner along the eastern shore of the Chama River. Descending from the heights, we rode through a sandy bottom for about a mile, in sand nearly knee-deep to the horses, when we arrived at the town.

We found Chamita great in public houses, both in name and the quality of the accommodations, and hence we were not obliged to throw ourselves upon the tender mercies of a single establishment. Their names were all scriptural, being called the *Pontius Pilate House*, *Centurion Hotel*, and *Herod House*, and each had earned something of a reputation for the manner in which they provided for the guests that chance or necessity threw in their way. Being a stranger to the virtues of these several places where travelers are usually " taken in," I had no choice between them, but followed the lead of the judge, and gave my patronage to him of the Pontius. The host was on the *qui vive*, and received us as we dismounted at the corral gate; our animals were given in charge of a peon, when the master led the way into the house. We entered through a low door, and, traversing a narrow passage, were ushered into a room about twelve feet square. We found three other persons already quartered in it, but as there was no other vacant room in the house, we had to accommodate ourselves there as well as possible. The furniture was meagre, consisting of three small beds, a bench, and one chair, all of which carried with them the prestige of great age; and a small window, with panes of foliated gypsum, let in a few rays of light from the west. In this little crib of a place five full-grown men were obliged to quarter, and the reader may be well assured there was but little room to spare.

As a matter of course, the arrival of strangers in the house raised a sort of hubbub among the inmates, and all the Pilate family, old and young, male and female, were agog to see what offered new. Peeping out of a door which led into the narrow passage-way were the hostess and her daughter, who in personal appearance fully sustained the reputation of the establishment. They had their faces besmeared with the crimson juice of the *alegria* plant, and looked most frightful and disgusting. A thick coating covered the whole face, which gave them the appearance of wearing masks, with the eyes, nose, and mouth uncovered. This was the first exhibition of the kind I had seen, and it struck me as such a filthy and singular custom, that I was not slow to inquire the cause of it. Afterward I noticed the same in all parts of the Territory, and found it to be a common and cherished practice among the village and country beauties. It is done for the purpose of protecting the skin from the sun, and they will remain in this repulsive condition two or three weeks upon the eve of a grand baile or feast at which they may desire to appear in all their freshness and beauty. The cream of the matter is, that in most instances the complexion of the wearer is about the color of seasoned mahogany, and upon which all the sun from the north to the south pole could make no impression. Besides *alegria*, they make use of clay and starch in the same manner, and at times you will see these three colors displayed upon the visages of as many members of the same family. Perchance this belle of Chamita had been doing penance in a smeared face for several days, in order to appear in her most witching charms during the session of the court; and who knows but that ambitious thoughts had crept into her maidenly heart, and that she even hoped to be able to captivate one of the *Gringos* who might quarter at the Pontius Pilate? How do my fair countrywomen like this improvement in a lady's toilet?

Having laid claim to a squatter's right in the little room allotted for our quarters, and deposited there our baggage, we set out for the court-house, as it was about the hour when the administration of justice should begin. A trudge through deep sand for nearly half a mile brought us to the spot, where we found a considerable number of people awaiting the coming of the court. A majority of those assembled were wrapped up in blankets that had served them for bed and bedding the night before, while a few of the better class wore coats. When the judge drew near, every hat was doffed in the twinkling of an eye, and a most profound salutation made. The court-house was entirely void of accommodations, being a private house rented for the occasion at the rate of one dollar per day. Court was duly opened, but in a few minutes adjourned for dinner.

At about two o'clock in the afternoon five hungry men were seated around the little deal table in the travelers' room at the Pontius Pilate House, patiently waiting for the food the host had promised to wayfarers. Presently the maid of all work, who had been christened after the Virgin of Guadalupe, made her appearance, trencher in hand. How well the dinner was in keeping with the house! The bill of fare consisted of two small plates of boiled rice, about two pounds of badly-cooked meat, half way between a stew and a boil, a little bread, villainous coffee, and muddy water. We fell to work in good earnest, and, as keen appetites do not stand upon ceremony, we made the food before us disappear with wonderful rapidity. It was always a weakness of mine to know the name of every article of food placed before me, more especially when the dish is new and strange. In this instance I could not make out to which of the animal creation the meat belonged, and propounded the query to my neighbor, who gave it as his opinion that it was the tender part of a young puppy. This might, under ordinary circumstances, have been a damper upon the appetite, but now it had no other effect than to lay an embargo upon whistling, and stop discussion upon dogs while we were eating. Each man was furnished with a knife, but, there being an inadequate supply of forks, we were obliged to borrow and lend this useful article of table furniture.

In the afternoon court was again in session, but, as there was no business to employ my time, I amused myself, while sitting upon a log in front of the house, making a drawing of a Mexican plow that stood near. From the primitive simplicity of this implement, it might have come out of the ark, and in early times turned up the virgin soil of Palestine.

When bedtime arrived our host and hostess made the necessary arrangements to provide us with bed and bedding for the night. Three of our number took possession of as many little beds, the fourth taking to a mattress upon the floor. As bad luck would have it, or, more properly speaking, no luck at all, I was the last to be supplied with bed-clothing, and, by the time the host reached my corner, he had neither sheet, quilt, nor blanket. I felt a little curious to know how he would supply the deficiency, and provide me with the necessary covering. It occurred to me that, as I was the representative of Uncle Sam, perhaps I was to be provided with extra accommodations in the " spare room." The ingenuity of our host, however, quickly remedied the difficulty, and that, too, in a manner I little expected. Casting his eyes first at my unprovided bed, and then around the room, as much as to say, " What can be done for this man ?" his countenance at last brightened up at a happy thought that struck him.   He immediately put his new revelation into effect by going to the table and stripping off the cover, which he deliberately spread upon my bed, and left the room.   Here is seen the misfortune of being the last one served, and the force of circumstances made me submit to " Hobson's choice—that or none."   I have no doubt the poor man thought he was doing me a favor, and, taking that sensible view of the case, I wrapped myself up in the table-cloth and lay down to sleep.   The next morning I was somewhat exercised in mind to know how he would supply the place of the table-cloth, never imagining that he would make my poor bed-cover do double duty.   The host, however, entertained no such scruples, for, at the proper time, the identical cloth was taken from the bed and transferred to the table where it belonged, and

> " Thus it contrived the double debt to pay,
> A sheet by night—a table-cloth by day."

This episode terminated my residence at Chamita, and, having no further duty to discharge, I returned to Santa Fé the same afternoon, where I arrived about five o'clock.

The United States District Court commenced in Santa Fé the following Monday morning, the twentieth instant.   There was a long criminal docket, but of the whole number of cases there were but two of any interest, one being an indictment for the crime of murder, and the other a case of perjury.   The murder case presented some new features, such as are rarely met with in modern times.   Four Indians, of the pueblo of Nambé, were indicted, during the term, for the murder of two of their own number.   It was proved, on the trial, that the two murdered men had been accused of the imaginary offense of witchcraft, which consisted in eating up all the little children of the village, and their accusers alleged that they saw them pulling the bones of their victims from their mouths and nostrils.   The village assembled in council, upon the charge being made, to adjudge the case and award the punishment.   They condemned the accused to death, and, at the hour of twilight the same day, they were conducted a little way beyond the border of the village and shot.   They were made to kneel down, side by side, by the constable of the pueblo, and were both killed at the same fire.   Four only were indicted, because the participation of these in the killing could be more clearly shown than that of the others.

The scene at the trial was rather an interesting one. The accused were arraigned about twilight, and the struggle between the expiring light of day and that from the candles gave a dusky and indistinct appearance to every thing in the court-house.   They sat side by side within the bar, clothed in blankets and leggins, and with painted faces.   They seemed fully impressed with the novelty, as well as the danger, of their situation.   The room was densely crowded with Americans, Mexicans, and some Indians, eager listeners and lookers on.   The defendants severally pleaded not guilty, and put themselves upon "God and the country for trial."   The majority of the witnesses sworn and examined were Indians, and their evidence was given to the court and jury through the medium of two interpreters, being first rendered from the dialect of Nambé into Spanish by an Indian of the pueblo of San Juan, and then into English by the regular interpreter of the court.   The most important witness for the Territory was the governor of the pueblo, the following being the most material portion of his testimony:

" The four men (defendants) came and reported to me that they had killed Louis Romero and Antonio Tafolla, in accordance with the order of the pueblo. It was done in the beginning of this month (March). They only said they had killed them; did not see them after they were killed. They were killed not quite a league from the pueblo, in a north direction. They killed them at twilight. I saw them going out with the deceased; they had a shot-gun. Juan Diego carried the gun. I saw them when they came back to report to me. They were killed by order of the pueblo and the head men of the pueblo. I am the governor of the pueblo, and Juan Diego is the *fiscal* (constable) of the pueblo. It was the duty of the fiscal to execute the orders of the pueblo; they commanded him to kill these two men. The bad acts spoken of were that they were detected in the act of witchcraft and sorcery: they had eaten up the little children of the pueblo. It has always been our custom to put a stop to and check bad acts. We have not exercised this custom of killing witches since the Americans came here, because there had not been such doings before. This act was done by the command of myself and the whole pueblo."

This simple-minded Indian thus confessed the whole matter, as though the killing of the two men was a matter of duty instead of a crime; and his conduct is evidence that himself and the whole of the pueblo believed these two men were really witches. The defendants were acquitted because the venue was not clearly proved, as the killing took place upon or near the line between two counties, and it could not be shown upon which side of the line it occurred. This case showed a re-enactment of the scenes of Salem, in the heart of the continent, and in the middle of the nineteenth century.

The other case, that of perjury, involved some new and

interesting points, and brought in question the treaty of Guadalupe Hidalgo between the United States and Mexico. In the eighth article of that instrument there is a clause which provides that all Mexicans living in the territory ceded to the United States might, if they desired it, retain the rights of Mexican citizens by making their election to that effect within one year after the ratification of said treaty. There is nothing said as to the manner in which this election should be made, and the whole matter appears to have been left to the governments to prescribe, or to the persons interested to decide upon. In accordance with said provisions, Colonel Washington, in the spring of 1849, while acting as civil and military governor of the Territory, issued a proclamation calling upon all those who desired to make their election to do so in the manner therein pointed out. They were directed to appear before the probate judges of their respective counties on or before the first day of June following, and then and there to make their election in writing to retain the rights of Mexican citizens or lose the privilege. The clerk of the Probate Court was required to attach a certificate to the record in which the names were enrolled, and to send the same to the Secretary of the Territory, who was directed to have them published, and to send a copy to each county. The law was substantially complied with in these particulars, a large number availing themselves of this privilege. Here the matter ended for the time being.

At the fall elections in 1853, many whose names were found on this record as having elected to retain the rights of Mexican citizens offered to vote, and, upon being challenged, swore that they were citizens of the United States. Several of those who voted under these circumstances were afterward indicted for false swearing, and upon the trial of the first case called, out of some forty in all, these questions came up. The record was offered in evidence to prove that the defendant was a Mexican citizen, and that in swearing at the polls that he was a citizen of the United States he had perjured himself, and became liable to the pains and penalties in such cases made and provided. The court, after listening to lengthy arguments upon both sides, overruled the offer, declared the book not a legal record, and of course not evidence—that the proceedings on the part of Colonel Washington were illegal and without authority, and that those who had made an election in this manner had not parted with their rights as citizens of the United States. This decision disposed of the indictments pending, all of which were *nol. pros'd.* One reason given by the court for this decision was that the record of Santa Fé county had been signed by a deputy clerk instead of the clerk of the Probate Court himself, as the proclamation required. This was the case, but in our opinion it does not materially alter the question.

This disposition of the question of citizenship took a large number by surprise, even those who were parties in interest, and some considered it no better than judicial heresy. The two contracting powers undoubtedly intended that those who desired to do so might retain their ancient allegiance, and as no mode was pointed out by which this was to be accomplished, it is only reasonable to suppose that the particular manner of making the election was to be left to the persons who were interested, so that it should be done in some public and notorious way. A large majority of those who made this election considered that by so doing they retained all the rights of Mexican citizens, and acted accordingly. In evidence of the good faith on their part, several of them afterward came voluntarily into the District Court and made formal application to become naturalized. This is evidence that they considered themselves aliens, and it may be inferred that the court was of the same opinion, because, if they were already citizens, they could not avail themselves of our naturalization laws. Before the court, in the argument in question, I maintained, on the part of the Territory, the legality of the election, and argued that a notorious and public act of this kind, done under the sanction of a treaty, although neither power had prescribed a particular form of said election, was valid to all intents and purposes, and should be recognized by the court. Thus, by this decision of the court, at a single stroke, several hundred people, who were aliens of their own free will, were raised to the dignity of citizens of the United States, *nolens volens*, and a solemn treaty stipulation rendered inoperative.

The wording of the treaty itself seems to determine the question. It provides that the class of persons referred to shall *retain* their rights as Mexican citizens if they shall make the election within a limited time. Now a person can not *retain* what he has already parted with ; and if the Mexican population had become citizens of the United States immediately upon the ratification of the treaty, their former rights would have been entirely gone, and, in order to possess them again, they would have to be *regained* instead of *retained*. This provision of the treaty seems clearly to indicate that, during the period of a year, the right of citizenship of the Mexican population living in the acquired territory would, as it were, remain in abeyance ; and, instead of being clothed with either American or Mexican nationality, they were candidates for either the one or the other, according as they might elect to remain Mexican citizens, or, by not making an election, show their intention, and in reality become citizens of the United States. The limitation mentioned was for the purpose of allowing them time to determine whether they would part with their old or assume a new nationality; and, until they had done one or the other, the question of citizenship was undecided, and they were free to make such decision in the premises as they might desire. If the two contracting parties had deemed that some prescribed form was requisite to carry out the provision of the treaty, it is not likely they would have failed to perform their duty in so important a particular. The fact that neither government took any steps to determine the form of such election would seem to argue that they deemed the parties interested the best judges of the manner in which they should make the same. As the question here involved is of grave import, it would be well to have it settled by the highest judicial tribunal in the country. Citizens should not be allowed to part with their allegiance except in the most solemn manner, nor should aliens be permitted to enter our political sanctuary except through the channel pointed out by the Constitution and laws of the United States.

The next place at which the District Court was held was in the town of San Miguel, the county seat of the county of the same name, fifty miles east of Santa Fé. The judge and members of the bar, six or eight persons in number, left town on Sunday, the second of April, mostly mounted and well armed, on account of recent Indian depredations in the part of the country through which it was necessary to pass. We took the Independence road, and passed through the Apache cañon, elsewhere described, stopping by the wayside now and then to rest the animals, or take a shot at the small game that crossed our path. About midway of the cañon a general halt was made, to wait until the wagon which contained the judge and the rations should come up; and in the mean while a council of war was held as to the propriety of lunching at that point, which was decided in the affirmative by a unanimous vote. When the eatables arrived the attack was made upon them in due form. The supply of bread and meat was spread upon the ground—a couple of newspapers answering the purpose of table-cloth—supported on either side by a jar of pickles and a flask of " red eye." Water was obtained from a small spring close by, but the quality was not such as to be recommended to those who pass that way. The repast finished, we resumed the road, nor drew rein again until we arrived at Pecos, where we stopped for the night with an American who has squatted upon a piece of public land.

As we rode up to the *Hotel de Pecos*, for such the road-side cabin was duly christened by one of our number, " Pete," the landlord, stood ready to welcome us. Our animals were turned over to the care of his male help, while the host conducted us into the establishment. The cabin contained two small rooms, about ten feet square, with a little back kitchen ; but a traveler should never judge by the size of a house of the number likely to find accommodations, for upon this occasion it seemed, like a Philadelphia omnibus, never quite full. The first arrival numbered seven persons, which was soon followed by the marshal and his deputy ; and, I presume, if as many more had presented themselves, the good-natured host would have found accommodation for all, even had he been obliged to suspend some from the beams of the cabin. We had no fault to find with the manner in which we were lodged and fed ; and among the luxuries set before us were Irish potatoes, a vegetable found upon few tables in the country. The evening was passed, as was usual in riding the circuit, in conversation, singing songs, and in telling anecdotes, and at an early hour we sought the humble beds the host prepared for us.

We were in the saddle the following morning at eight

o'clock, but not before we had partaken of a substantial breakfast. We followed the bridle-path over an arid plain, under the brow of a high mesa which stretched along upon our right. On the left the view was bounded by ranges of mountains, whose rugged peaks shot far up into the clear blue sky. We halted about midway of the distance to lunch beside a little spring that flowed out between the crevices in the rocks, where we disposed of the remnant of yesterday's meal. Just before reaching this spot we passed the Apache trail, when the market-price of good white scalps fell as much as fifty per cent. in value, and we increased the speed of our horses several knots an hour. We who were mounted reached San Miguel about twelve o'clock, but the wagon did not arrive until nearly two. The whole distance from Santa Fé the country is mountainous and barren, and we passed but three houses on the way.

San Miguel is an adobe town of about a thousand inhabitants, situated upon the west bank of the Rio Pecos, a small but beautiful stream, which empties into the Del Norte a long way to the south. The river is skirted by a valley varying from one quarter to a mile in width, and, being dammed at various parts, irrigation is rendered comparatively easy, and also less expensive than in some sections of the country. As this was the time of planting the spring crops, the people were busy at work in the fields, some breaking up the ground with their wooden hoes and plows, while others were putting in the grain, or trailing the little currents of water from the acequias through the fields. This is the place where the Texan prisoners were first confined after their capture, and whence they were marched for the city of Mexico. The spot was pointed out to me where Howland and two others were shot, at the southeast corner of the Plaza. Three others of the prisoners, one of whom was Kendall,

were also led out to the place of execution, and the file
of men who were to settle their final account was already
drawn up, when they were rescued by the kindness and
intrepidity of a Mexican gentleman named Gregorio Vi-
gil.   He threw himself between the Americans and the
soldiers, and forbade the latter to fire upon unarmed men.
He was then a man of influence, and this conduct prevented the execution and saved them from death.   He
still resides in San Miguel, in reduced circumstances.
Such magnanimous conduct should be held in grateful
remembrance by every American.   San Miguel not being supplied with public houses for the accommodation
of travelers, those who were obliged to be in attendance
upon the court had to quarter round the town upon the
citizens.   I considered myself fortunate in obtaining a
seat at the table of a German trader in the place, and
rented a room to sleep in on the opposite side of the
Plaza.   We paid two dollars a day for our food, which,
for the price, should have been much better than it was ;
nevertheless, it was a decided improvement upon the fare
of the Pontius Pilate House at Chamita.   The standard
dish was stewed mutton, followed by boiled rice, and now
and then a compound which the cook, in the innocence
of her heart, meant for stewed chicken, but which was a
slander upon the divine art of the *cuisine*.   We had no
substantial ground of complaint, and, upon the whole,
found ourselves much better provided for than we had
expected.

The court continued in session five days, but the business transacted was of minor importance.   The public
buildings, as in the other counties I had visited, I found
in a very dilapidated condition, and void of all accommodations for the administration of justice; and it was a
matter of congratulation that the weather was dry, so
that we experienced no inconvenience from the leaking

propensity of the court-house. The only pastime I observed in the evening was gambling, of which the inhabitants seemed passionately fond. Monte was the favorite game, and considerable sums were lost and won.

We returned to Santa Fé on Saturday, where we arrived about sundown. During our absence matters and things had assumed quite a warlike appearance on account of the active hostilities then going on between the troops and the Apache Indians. General Garland and staff had come up from Albuquerque, and for the present established the head-quarters of the department at Santa Fé. Troops and munitions of war were being forwarded to the seat of hostilities in the north, and both the civil and military authorities were making preparations to carry the war on vigorously.

I remained in town until the Monday morning following, when I started for Peña Blanca, where the court for the county of Santa Ana was to meet that day. The distance is twenty-five miles, and I started with a single companion. We followed the main road some six miles, when we turned to the right into a bridle-path, a nearer way for horsemen. A ride of an hour and a half brought us to a *mesa* that lay in our route, at least two hundred feet above the valley. The slope rises at an angle of about forty-five degrees, and is covered with loose blocks of amygdaloidal trap rock, as black as night and hard as adamant. This mesa system is one of the remarkable features in the physical formation of New Mexico, and worthy the attention of the scientific. In this case, while riding over a plain, you come to another plain that rises up before you some two hundred feet, with an ascent so steep as to be impassable except at one or two points, and in all parts of the country we find such formations. The overlying rock of the slope is different in character from any other seen in that vinity.

We dismounted and led our horses up the zigzag path, when, once upon the top, we mounted again and rode onward. The plain above is some five miles in width, and almost as level as a board. The atmosphere was as clear as a bell, and there seemed hardly any limit to the distance we could see with the naked eye. We galloped across the plain, and as we approached the western side the valley of the Del Norte opened to our view, and in the distance we could see the river glittering in the sun. We found the opposite side of the plain bounded by the same slope as where we had ascended, but of greater length, and steeper. The descent was both difficult and dangerous, and in some places it required great care on the part of our animals to descend without falling. Here there are three separate slopes before we reach the valley below, being separated by small plateaux of a few hundred yards in width. Having arrived safely at the foot of the last descent, we mounted and rode forward to our place of destination.

Peña Blanca is but an insignificant Mexican village, built in the valley of the Del Norte, about half a mile from the river bank. Two or three large landowners reside here, and have respectable dwellings, while the balance of the houses are the rude mud huts of their peones. I made my quarters at the house of Don Tomas Cabeza de Baca, one of the *ricos* of the place, who lives surrounded with a throng of peones somewhat after the manner of the feudal lords of the Middle Ages. Dismounting at the main entrance of the corral which incloses the whole establishment, I resigned my horse to the care of a servant, and followed the lead of Don Tomas into the dwelling. Crossing a large court-yard, we ascended a flight of steps to the second story, and landed upon a portal looking toward the *placita*. Thence we passed through a large hall into a smaller room, which,

I was politely informed, was at my disposal. The apartment was a plain one. A single bed stood in one corner, and several mattresses were rolled up along the wall for seats ; a rough pine table and bench stood at the foot of the bed, and the earthen floor was without carpet or rug. Along the south front of the building extends a portal overlooking a large garden and vineyard, affording a fine view of the valley and the river.

It was about noon when I arrived, and I had hardly finished my toilet when dinner was announced. The meal was a true Mexican dinner, and a fair sample of the style of living among the better class of people. The advance guard in the course of dishes was boiled mutton and beans, the meat being young and tender, and well flavored. These were followed by a *sui generis* soup, different from any thing of the kind it had been my fortune to meet with before. It was filled with floating balls about the size of a musket bullet, which appeared to be a compound of flour and meat. Next came mutton stewed in *chili* (red peppers), the dressing of which was about the color of blood, and almost as hot as so much molten lead. This is a favorite article of food with the Mexicans, and they partook of it most bountifully. I tasted all the dishes that were placed before me, out of respect to the host, and in so doing laid aside all epicurean scruples, and the fear of being burned up alive. We were again served with stewed beans, and the repast was concluded.

As I have already stated in a previous chapter, the two main articles of food with the Mexicans are stewed beans, called *frijoles,* and a thin cake made of corn, called *tortillas.* The beans are boiled in the first place, sometimes with ashes to take off the hull, and then stewed with lard or tallow, and, when well seasoned with red peppers, are fit for use. Thus prepared they are quite palatable, and strangers soon acquire a taste for them.   The corn for the *tortillas* is boiled, with a little lime in the water, until the outer husk or shell is peeled off, when it is ground upon an oblong stone called a *metate*, a domestic utensil handed down from the aboriginal inhabitants.   The meal is then properly mixed and seasoned, and cooked upon small sheets of iron or copper. They are baked very thin, and always served up hot. These two articles are invariably eaten together, and assist to put each other out of sight.   A piece of the corn-cake is torn off, doubled up in the shape of a scoop, and then filled with beans, when both are swallowed together, thus eating your spoon at each mouthful.   Another dish peculiar to the country is the *atole*, made of corn-meal, and very similar to the mush in common use in the States.   Besides those already enumerated, there are other dishes, some of which have come down from the ancient inhabitants of the country.   The *chili* they use in various ways—green, or *verde*, and in its dried state, the former being made into a sort of salad, and is esteemed a great luxury.   They have also a dish called *olla podrida*, composed of various kinds of meats boiled up together, and which form a sort of *omnium gatherum* in the culinary art.   At their meals they drink water, coffee, or chocolate, but are more moderate in the use of these beverages than the Americans.   The chocolate is peculiarly fine, and excels that prepared in the United States.   Among the peasantry it is almost a thing unknown for the family to sit at a table and take their meals.   They generally gather around the fire-place, with their beans and corn-cake in their hands, and seldom make use of knife, fork, or spoon.

Court continued at Peña Blanca only two days, and but little business was transacted, and we returned to Santa Fé on Wednesday morning.   In my rambles around the village I came across an old-fashioned Spanish grist-mill, the first one of the kind I had seen in the country, which was something of a curiosity in a small way. The building was not more than ten or twelve feet square, with one run of stone, turned by a small tub-wheel by the water from a neighboring *acequia*. The upper stone was made in the form of a basin, with a rim around it some four inches wide, and fits down over the lower stone, made fast to the floor, and is about eighteen inches high. The grain is mashed by the revolution of the upper stone, and the meal falls down into a box built around the lower one. The hopper was made of bull-hide, and fastened to the beams overhead. The old miller was hard at work in his little mill, and I have no doubt he considered his simple apparatus the perfection of machinery.

PLAZA OF ALBUQUERQUE.

CHAPTER XV.

RIDING THE CIRCUIT—*Continued.*

I REMAINED the balance of the week in Santa Fé after my return from Peña Blanca, which afforded me an opportunity of witnessing the ceremonies of Passion Week. This season, so universally observed in Catholic countries, commenced on Saturday, the ninth instant, and, with the mass of the people, the entire week was kept as a holiday, the time being divided between amusements and the church. During this period the religious fervor is aroused to a higher point than at any other season of the year. The day most observed with pomp and parade is Good Friday, or *Viernes Santo.* The afternoon before a large assemblage collected in the *Paroquia,* or parish church, where appropriate services were celebrated by the bishop, whence a long procession afterward issued, which marched around the Plaza and through some of the principal streets. A large wooden cross, carried upon the shoulders of four greasy fellows, and to which was nailed an image of the Savior, headed the procession. It was surrounded by a band of women with candles in the hand, intended to represent the ten virgins. In addition, there was a goodly array of carved images, including the Virgin Mary, Mary Magdalen, and Saint John. After making the circuit of the town, they returned to the church whence they had started. The following day, being Good Friday, another procession started from the parish church, but somewhat different in its appointments from the previous one. It was preceded by a man mounted on a horse, intended to represent a centurion, who was surrounded by a Roman guard armed with spears, forming as villainous-looking a group as I had seen for a long time. The horse was led by two grooms, dressed in the same garb as the guard, who, to make him prance and show off in good style, pricked him constantly with short goads. Then came the dead body of Christ in an open coffin, on which were a number of small wooden images, with the usual accompaniment of saints and priests, and, while they marched, a choir of boys sang sacred music. The exercises closed with service in the church, and a torch-light procession in the evening.

I can not refrain from bearing testimony against these religious processions. The image of the Savior, and others of a similar character that held a prominent place in the exercises, were disgusting to the sight, and failed to create in my mind other feelings than those of pity for the worshipers of these unmeaning bits of ill-carved wood. Some of the *virgins* were known as among the most notorious females in town, but character seemed no requisite to fill a prominent place in the exercises. These parades are not seen in the States, and the sight of such an exhibition in the streets of our large cities would shock the feelings of all religious denominations. It is one of the practices of a darker age that still clings to the worship of the people of New Mexico; but I sin-

cerely hope the bishop will cause such public display of
saints and images to be discontinued among the other
reforms he may bring about in the Church.

I left Santa Fé on Sunday morning, the sixteenth of
the month, for the town of Albuquerque, where the first
session of the District Court in the third judicial district
was to commence the following day.   Our party numbered eight persons, composed of members of the bar,
marshal, and servants—mostly mounted.   I was detained near an hour after the others had started, and was
obliged to ride at a rapid gait the first few miles to overtake them.   About the time I came up with them my
horse stumbled, and threw me several feet headlong into
the road, and with force sufficient to cause me to see several full-grown moons and stars of the first magnitude.
The distance from Santa Fé to Albuquerque is about
seventy-five miles, south, and most of our road lay down
the Valley of the Del Norte.   The first fifteen miles we
traversed a plain, level and dry, which brought us to the
cañon of the Rio de Santa Fé, six miles in length.   This
is a narrow passage between opposite mesas, in some
places at least two hundred feet deep, through which runs
the little River of Santa Fé, seeking an outlet into the
Del Norte.   The same mesa bounds the cañon on the
right that we crossed on the road to Peña Blanca, but
here the slope is almost perpendicular.   In some points,
after rising up at an angle of sixty degrees for about a
hundred feet, the side of the mesa starts into a perpendicular rampart, formed of vertical rows of stone like artificial masonry.   Where the formation is an ash-colored
clay, disposed in layers, the action of water and the atmosphere has caused it to assume many interesting appearances, and at one place the part just visible above
an intervening point resembles the entablature of a Grecian portico, which distance mellows down into nearly

perfection of outline. We lunched midway of the cañon, and grazed our animals upon the few blades of grass that grew among the boulders.

Debouching from the cañon, we entered upon another mesa, which we crossed, and then descended into the Valley of the Del Norte near the Indian pueblo of Santo Domingo. The village lies a little way off the main road, on the bank of the river. The houses are two stories high, built of adobes, with the usual form of terrace. The roof, supported by pine logs, is nearly flat, covered with bark and dirt. Like the other pueblos, the houses are entered by ascending to the roof by means of a ladder in the first place, and then through a hole left as a sort of companion-way to the rooms below. The *estufa* is built in the usual form, and is entered through a trapdoor in the roof.

Leaving Santo Domingo a little to our right, we continued down the valley. A few miles below we passed the pueblo of San Félipe, situated upon the west bank of the river. Near the present village are seen the ruins of the old pueblo, upon a high bluff bank some two hundred feet above the water. On either side of the river runs a chain of hills, those on the west side extending inland in extensive mesas. The valley is mostly uncultivated, except here and there a few acres susceptible of irrigation. In front of us we could trace the serrated ridges of the Saudia Mountains, yet several miles to the southeast. Before sundown we arrived at the little village of Algadones, where we found quarters for the night, with fare at a reasonable price.

When we came to saddle up the next morning, we found that our horses, during the night, had broken out of the corral, and we could now see them making for the mountains as though the Evil One was after them. A party of mounted peones were sent in pursuit, who, after a considerable chase, succeeded in heading them off and bringing them back.   We rode out of town at half past six, and held our way down the valley, with thirty miles before us for the morning's travel.   The first village we passed through was that of Bernalillo, owned and inhabited principally by the Pareas, an old and wealthy Spanish family.   Here the valley widens, and a greater amount of land is under cultivation, which, from appearance, is tilled with more than usual care.   The acequias were in good order, and the means of irrigation abundant.   The improved mode of farming observed here may be attributed to the introduction of American implements of husbandry within a few years.

At this place we enter the vine-growing region of New Mexico, which extends down the Valley of the Del Norte to some distance below El Paso.   Throughout this extent grapes of a superior quality are cultivated.   When pulled fresh from the vine the flavor is very fine, and they are thought to be equal to those imported from Spain and the Mediterranean for table use.   It is impossible to tell how much wine is made yearly, as there is no means of arriving at the quantity, but it will reach several thousand gallons.   It is manufactured altogether for home consumption, and very little, if any, finds its way into the United States—at least, it never gets into the market.   It is a good article, and is said by those who are judges to be superior to many of the wines that are imported from Europe.   That made in the Valley of El Paso has become quite celebrated, and is thought to be a better article than is manufactured elsewhere.

The mode of cultivating the grape is different from that pursued in the United States, but whether such treatment is required from the nature of the vine I am unable to say.   The vine is not trailed on frames, as is usually the case elsewhere, but is kept trimmed close to

the ground.   In the spring of the year, the branches
which have grown out the past year are cut off close to
the parent stock, which is rarely more than four feet
high.   The vines are thus trimmed annually.   They are
set out from the cuttings, which are laid down in narrow
trenches four feet apart, and one end is allowed to pro-
trude through the earth about six inches.   They begin
to bear the third year after they are planted.   In the
fall of the year, and before frost sets in, the main stock
is covered with earth, as a protection against the cold
weather of winter, but which is removed as soon as the
spring opens, and preparatory to trimming.   In the neighborhood of Bernalillo, and at various other points down
the valley, we saw numerous vineyards, some of them
several acres in extent, and in all the vines looked thrifty.

There are two kinds of grapes grown in New Mexico,
the Muscadel and a common grape, both of which are
said to have been brought from Spain.   The former is a
light red, and the latter about the color of the native
Fox grape found in the United States.   They are smaller and sweeter than the Isabella grape, and are more
juicy.   Two kinds of wine are made from them, white
and red.   In the Rio Abajo the vintage begins about the
tenth of October, but earlier at El Paso.   The grapes
are picked from the vines and carried to the vats, where
the juice is pressed out of them.   The vats are made of
bull-hide while green, and, to keep them in shape while
drying, they are filled with dirt, which is thrown out
when they have become thoroughly dried.   The top is
covered with the same material, perforated with small
holes, upon which the grapes are thrown as they are
brought from the vineyard, and trod into a pulp by the
feet of the peones, the juice running into the vat below.
The pulp that remains is made into excellent vinegar.
The vats are then covered with plank, the cracks being

smeared well with mud to keep out the air; and the juice is allowed to remain thus sixty or seventy days, when it has become wine, and is drawn off into casks, and put away for sale or use. These grapes are said to produce a better article of claret wine than that imported from France, but the want of bottles to put it in, and the absence of facility to send it to market, prevent its manufacture in any quantity. I believe these grapes could be cultivated with success in the vine-growing regions of the United States, and I hope that some one interested in the culture will try the experiment. Instead of being planted upon the hill-side, as is the case in most vine-growing countries, they are cultivated in the bottoms, close to the streams, where they can be irrigated. No climate in the world is better adapted to the vine than the middle and southern portions of New Mexico, and if there was a convenient market to induce an extensive cultivation of the grape, wine would soon become one of the staples of the country, which would be able to supply a large part of the demand in the United States, instead of importing it from Europe.

While writing of grapes and wine, we have been slowly pursuing our way down the valley toward our place of destination. The country appears to improve as we advance southward, the hills recede farther from the river, more land is under cultivation, and the mode of farming appears in advance of that in the northern part of the Territory. In some few places the old plow, of Jewish memory, has been thrown aside, and a more modern implement introduced in its stead; but they still patronize oxen, which drag their lazy bodies along the furrows at the slowest possible speed. As we passed through the Indian pueblo of Saudia, the young Indians were running about the village naked, amusing themselves shooting with the bow and arrow and kindred sports, while their industrious fathers were at work in the fields.   We next made the Mexican village of Los Ranchos, formerly the county seat of Bernalillo, which extends along the road about half a mile, and is composed principally of large farm-houses.   It is in the midst of a tolerably good agricultural country, and considerable attention is paid to the cultivation of the vine. Soon after passing the Ranchos we caught a glimpse of the church steeples of Albuquerque, four or five miles to the south, which we held in view until we arrived there.   As we neared the town we met a crowd of country people returning from market—Mexican rancheros and Pueblo Indians.   Some were on foot, trudging along under a load of articles they had purchased with the proceeds of their marketing, and others were astride the ever faithful burro, which they urged forward by an incessant thumping of the heels, and a little gentle pricking with a sharpened stick.   We entered the dusty streets at a gallop, when our party separated to their respective places of accommodation.

I found comfortable quarters in the building used as the military head-quarters of the department.   Before I left Santa Fé, Major Nichols, assistant adjutant general of the army, tendered me the use of his rooms while I should remain in Albuquerque, and gave me a letter of introduction to Mr. David Garland, which contained the request that he would place them at my disposal.   During the week I passed there I received many kind attentions from Mr. Garland, my host, to whom I yet feel under obligations.

The town of Albuquerque is venerable with age, whose settlement dates back about two hundred and fifty years, to the time the Spaniards first obtained a foothold in the country.   It is situated a few hundred yards from the river bank, and in one of the most productive regions of the country—the Rio Abajo—where is found a large portion of the wealth of the Territory. In times past it received much importance from being the head-quarters of the Armijo family, for many years the first in point of influence in the country. The name of the founder of the town has not come down to us, but it is supposed to have been named after one of the dukes of Albuquerque, who was viceroy of Mexico soon after its conquest, probably the same who commanded the Spanish forces in France in 1544 as the ally of Henry the Eighth of England. The population is not more than fifteen hundred, a few families only being the descendants of the *ricos* of other days. The town is irregularly laid out and badly built. In the centre is a plaza of some two or three acres in extent, and into which the principal streets lead. The houses are generally grouped about without order, and the best are but indifferent mud buildings, some of the more humble ones being partly in ruins. As a place of residence it is far less pleasant than Santa Fé. At some seasons of the year high winds prevail, when the sun is almost obscured by the clouds of fine dust that is whirled through the air, and which finds an entrance into the houses through every nook and cranny. Then there are flies and musquitoes, which swarm in and out of doors in untold millions, which neither day nor night allow man or beast to live in peace. The weather is oppressively warm in the summer season. The water used for all purposes comes from the river, and is so muddy that you can not see the face in it until it shall have settled several hours. The difference in altitude between this town and Santa Fé is nearly three thousand feet, which accounts for the diversity of climate in the two places. The army depôts are located here, which causes a large amount of money to be put in circulation, and gives employment to a number of the inhabitants.

I had no more than time, after my arrival, to dispense with a little of the dust of travel, and make the necessary ablutions, before my presence was required in court, then about to open the session. I took my way to the eastern edge of the town, and in a modest-looking mud building found quite a throng assembled, and the judge upon the bench. The court at this place continued in session during the week; but as the details of legal proceedings can not be otherwise than wearisome to the reader, I will not claim the attention to their recital. There were five separate indictments found for the crime of murder, which does not speak well for the morals of the county. One little circumstance I will mention, which shows the actor to have been either a fool or a knave, or a little of both. A man was indicted for stealing fifteen mules, and as he could not be then tried, he was directed to confer with his attorney about giving bail for his appearance at the next term. He treated the whole matter as a good joke, and hardly thought it worth while to look for security for his future appearance. He said he understood the whole matter, and knew well why they had placed his name upon the books of the court: they wanted somebody as defendant in the case, and had only used his name for the sake of convenience, but that they might as well have chosen some one else. The poor fellow did not appear to realize the position he occupied, but most likely came to his senses after he was convicted and " sent below" for two or three years.

The dullness of a week's hard work in the court-room was somewhat enlivened by a dinner given by Mr. Garland in the mess-hall at head-quarters, and which was attended by the court, members of the bar, and officers of the army on duty at that post. As all such assemblies are in duty bound to be, it was a " feast of reason and a flow of soul." The usual quantity of witty things were said, and the customary attention paid to the delicious viands, both from respect to the gentlemanly host and in obedience to manly appetites. Each succeeding dinner-party being an exact type of its "illustrious predecessor" in all essential particulars, and as most of my readers, at some period in their life, have been present at such an entertainment, they will be good enough to imagine the whole proceedings, and thereby save me the trouble of writing them down.

From Albuquerque we continued down the valley to Tomé, the county seat of Valencia county, the next point at which the District Court is held. I started for that place about the middle of the afternoon of the twenty-third instant, Sunday, in company with Judge H., my old traveling companion. The day was clear, but one of the strongest winds of the season was blowing up the river, almost fierce enough to lift us from our horses. The valley increases in width as we advanced, but in that section it is mostly adapted to grazing purposes. About sundown we arrived at the rancho of Mr. Baird, where, by previous invitation, I tarried all night, while my companion continued on to Peralta, a few miles farther down. Several other gentlemen, on their way to court, arrived before dark, and also remained over night at the rancho. We were all treated with genuine Southern hospitality, and passed a pleasant evening with our host and hostess.

We took an early start the next morning, as we had a ride of thirty miles to make before reaching Tomé. Our course lay nearly due south along the bank of the river, which here rolls toward the Gulf of Mexico in a deep and muddy current. On the eastern side runs a ridge of rocky hills, bare of vegetation, while on the west the country is more level, with mesas extending back from the river. Numerous flocks of sheep and herds of cattle were feeding upon the excellent pasture the valley here affords, under the charge of shepherds and herders. With each flock there was one or more of the invaluable shepherd-dogs common to the country, some of which appeared to discharge their duties with as much intelligence as their biped companions. We passed a few ranchos, an occasional hacienda, and one Indian pueblo, that of Isleta. A few miles from Peralta we came to the residence of Doctor Henry Connelly, an American, who has resided in the country ever since 1828. His house is a large establishment in the old Spanish style, and the buildings for his peones and other purposes which surround it make up quite a little village. He has acquired wealth and influence, and is at this time a member of the Legislative Council. About a mile below Doctor Connelly's we passed what is known as the *bosque*, a large tract of fine timber, mostly cottonwood, something very rare in New Mexico. Wood is exceedingly scarce all over the country. The valleys are generally bare of it, and that found upon the mountains consists of a growth of scrub pine called piñon. The country is said to have been well wooded when the Spaniards first settled it, but in many parts it has been entirely cut off, and in some instances without leaving even a tree for shade. Cottonwood principally grew in the valleys along the water-courses.

Some time before we reached our place of destination we could see the green trees that shade the Plaza of Tomé, and the spire of the church above the level of the valley. It was about noon when we arrived, and I found comfortable quarters awaiting me at the house of a fair widow, having been secured through the kindness of Judge Benedict. The court being already in session, I had only time to dismount and lay off pistols and spurs, when I was obliged to go thither. I wended my way to a small one-story mud building, where I found his honor in the act of instructing the grand jury in the *modus operandi* of presenting offenders to the kind consideration of the court. The room was long and low, and had a platform slightly elevated at one end for the judge, a small table for the members of the bar and clerk, and three benches for the rest of the world. The light of heaven that was shed upon the proceedings struggled manfully through two small and dirty windows, and partly dispelled the gloom within. I remained in court until the adjournment for dinner, when I repaired to my quarters, and while the cook is giving the finishing touch to the red peppers and fried beans about to be served up, I will introduce the reader to the town of my whereabouts.

Tomé, the county seat of Valencia county, is a village of not more than four hundred inhabitants, with the usual number of burros and dogs. The situation is rather picturesque, and in this particular compares favorably with any Mexican town in the country. The valley spreads out several miles between mountain ranges that bound it on both sides of the river. The soil appears naturally fertile, and, wherever cultivated, produces good crops. The Plaza is shaded and ornamented by a number of fine old cottonwood trees. The hand of Time has lain heavily upon Tomé, and a change has come over its appearance. In former days it was one of the most prosperous towns in the Rio Abajo, and was the scene of annual festivals, when hundreds of people from far and near flocked thither for purposes of religious worship and amusement, and feast and fun were kept up for several days. In the course of time, the hostile Nabajos made descents upon the town, and carried many of the inhabitants into captivity. From this period we may date its decline. The people deserted their houses for a more secure home, the trade fell off, and the religious festivals were no longer celebrated there.   The best buildings have tumbled down and gone to decay for want of a keeper, and the grass is growing green in many a yard where happy hearts once sported.   Of late years the place is looking up a little, but it is still dilapidated in appearance.

By this time the cook has completed the preparations for dinner, and the viands are smoking upon the table. We found the eatables at the house of our fair hostess superior in quality to those placed before us in the generality of Mexican houses, and the cooking was more after the American manner of doing such things; and then it was something of a relief not to see the omnipresent *chili*, like the shortcomings of one's ancestors, staring you in the face at every meal.   The plates were clean, which was not always the case elsewhere; and then, as an additional comfort, each person was provided with a knife and fork.

The business of the court occupied the entire week up to about ten o'clock on Saturday morning, but nothing of much importance or interest was transacted.   We were all somewhat amused at one circumstance that took place.   Two indictments for trading without license were tried, in both of which the jury rendered a verdict of "Not Guilty," and fined the district attorney fifty dollars for prosecuting, at which rate it would be dear work attending to the "pleas of the crown."   If there is any truth in the old adage, " Set a rogue to catch a rogue," the composition of the grand jury at the present term was most admirable.   They had been chosen, as his honor informed them in his charge, because of their honesty and integrity, to ferret out crime committed in the body of the county of Valencia; and, according to the standard, the selection was well made, for just before they adjourned one of their number picked the pocket of the interpreter and made off with the spoil. From the first Monday of March up to the present time, about eight weeks, while conducting the pleas of the Territory in the District Court, I had tried, or caused to be indicted, fourteen persons for the crime of murder in different offenses, and, according to the testimony, eight of the cases were the result of liquor.

The people of Tomé were not unmindful of the rites of hospitality while we remained in their village, and on Tuesday evening a *baile* was given for our amusement at the house of one of the most respectable inhabitants. The *sala* had been decorated for the occasion, and the Paganini of the village had been called into requisition. As is customary upon such occasions, a table well supplied with liquors stood in one corner of the room, where all who were so disposed could regale the inner man with a little *spiritual* comfort. It is quite the custom, after each set, for the gentleman to take his partner to the table to treat her, and it is rarely the case that the fair sex are averse to imbibing.

I made my adieus to the fair hostess of Tomé a little before noon, and, in company with one traveling companion, started for Socorro. Our course still lay down the Valley of the Del Norte, upon the east bank of the river. For the first fifteen miles the appearance of the country was about the same as that hitherto traveled over. As we went south, the mountains called *Las Sierras de los Ladrones* rose in view in the distance, and served as a landmark until we reached our place of destination. At Casa Colorado we struck a young desert, an excellent pocket edition of the great African Zahara, over which we journeyed for about four miles. A high west wind was blowing at the time, and there was no grass upon the ground to keep the sand where it belonged : it drifted about like snow in a winter's storm ; the particles were fine and dry, and the atmosphere was so filled with them as almost to obscure the sun. The sand blew into our faces like hail, and our poor animals, at times, would stop, refusing to face the storm. In many places the loose sand was piled up in conical-shaped hills, several feet in height, and the finer particles were constantly whirling around them. For the distance this region extends, it is as perfect a desert waste as can be, and we were right glad when we reached the southern border, and once more had a hard road under our horses' feet.

We traveled that afternoon to La Hoya, about twenty-five miles from Tomé, and remained there for the night. The country nearly the whole way is too barren to be susceptible of cultivation, and the only fertile spots are occasional small patches in some of the valleys close to the river. It was near sundown when we entered the town, and as we rode in the whole canine population saluted us from the roofs of the houses, and, as is always the case with Mexican dogs, the more secure they are the more impudent they become. We stopped at a house where two other Americans, who had preceded us, were staying.

Supper was over when we arrived, but the landlord had the table respread in a short time, and some simple food placed upon it. I had lain down upon a colchon to rest, and could but watch and be amused at the operation of getting supper. First and foremost came the master of the house with a few small pieces of bread wrapped up in a dirty cloth; next the maid-servant with a pitcher of coffee; then followed a second with a large dish of *chili colorado*, a compound of red peppers and dried buffalo meat stewed together, flaming like the crater of Vesuvius ; and a third servant, with the knives and forks, closed the procession. These articles, with a few corn-cakes, made up the repast; and hunger, which is the best of sauce, enabled us to eat them with a relish.

La Hoya is situated on the east bank of the Del Norte, a few hundred yards from it, and contains some four hundred inhabitants. In times past the Nabajo Indians used to make frequent descents upon the town, and our host exhibited, with much pride, a bow, quiver of arrows, and a lance which he captured a few years ago in one of the encounters after having slain the owner. Mattresses were spread in the *sala*, and, being travel-wearied, we retired early, and slept soundly until morning.

We were astir on the morrow at early dawn. The host, with his " man-servants and his maid-servants," had *chili, tortillas,* and coffee prepared for us by the time we were ready to partake, when, the meal swallowed and bill paid, we mounted and rode away. We took the beaten track that leads toward the south, and traveled at a brisk gait through a sandy and barren country. In a ride of fifteen miles we came to a small village on the Del Norte, opposite the town of Limitar, and near the point at which we wished to pass to the west bank of the river. Two of us rode directly to the ferry, while the balance of our party tarried in the village. The river was quite high and rapid, and the only means of crossing was in an old canoe made out of a cottonwood log, the horses being obliged to swim. We divested them of their saddles and bridles, and tied the *cabestro* (a long hair rope) around their necks to guide them while in the water. We had some difficulty in getting them to take the water ; but, once fairly in and striking out for the opposite shore, we converted them into a convenient motive power, and made them drag canoe and passengers to the other side, where we arrived in safety. Our efforts to induce our animals to enter the stream reminded us of those made use of upon a certain occasion when

Æsop got in a stubborn mood and refused to take the boiling flood. His master seems to have adopted an effectual plan to accomplish his end, for he says, if the old poets can be believed,

"I bored a hole in Æsop's nose,
  And through it run a string;
I led him to the river bank,
  And kicked the bugger in."

Arrived upon the opposite bank, we paid old Charon his fee, saddled up our dripping animals, and rode away to Limitar, where we stopped for dinner and siesta at the late residence of General Manuel Armijo.

General Armijo was the most distinguished man that New Mexico has ever produced, and for many years before the Americans occupied the country he held the highest position in the Territory. His rise from the lowest obscurity to great distinction among his countrymen is one of those rather romantic occurrences that mark the course of every people. He came up from the lowermost round in the ladder of Fame, and, solely by the force of his native genius, eclipsed all his compeers in the race. His origin was so humble as to be almost unknown. When a boy he tended sheep and goats upon the mountains, and grew up a *pastor*, without education and without friends. It is said of him by some of his countrymen that, when a shepherd, he would steal the sheep and goats of his employers, and in some instances would sell them to their owners two and three different times. In this manner he is said to have obtained a start in the world, and his talent helped him to the goal. He taught himself to read and write long after he had grown up to man's estate. He was the governor and commander-in-chief of the province at the time the American army entered the country, but he gave up his power without a struggle. He died in the winter of 1854, leaving considerable wealth behind him.

The *mayor domo* of the establishment received us in the court-yard and conducted us into the house, where we were welcomed by the owner of the establishment, a son-in-law of the deceased general. As is customary with a Mexican gentleman, he placed every thing at our disposal, but we well understood that nothing farther was donated to us than accommodations for ourselves and horses. We were ushered into the main *sala*, where servants soon made their appearance with water for the necessary ablutions and the accompanying toilet fixtures.

The room exhibited a singular mixture of modern elegance and barbaric taste. In one corner stood an elegant canopied brass bedstead, after the most approved Parisian style, while in close contact was another clumsily made of pine and painted a dirty red; heavy wooden benches seemed misplaced beside velvet-covered chairs and a beautiful Turkey carpet; and the time-stained wooden beams that supported the roof were reflected in twenty gilded mirrors that hung around the room. Dinner was served up with more than the usual style of the country, and the respective dishes were as palatable as could be desired. Besides water and coffee, we had native wine and whisky upon the table. After dinner was concluded we all indulged in a siesta, which is as much in the programme of good manners at a gentleman's house in a Spanish country as genteel behavior in the drawing-room.

We resumed the road for Socorro at three o'clock in the afternoon, and reached that place about sundown. The balance of our party had overtaken us at Limitar, and we were also joined on the way by the marshal and his deputy, which increased our number to a respectable cavalcade. The marshal's deputy was a member of the Smith family, who relieved the tedium of the ride by the relation of some of his experience as a soldier in the country during the war. He stated that when the troops first came into that section of the territory in 1846, there was but little money among the country people, and that the circulating medium between them and the soldiers was buttons, which, being yellow and bright, had more value in the eyes of the simple peasantry than silver coin. When the soldiers wished to make a purchase, they would cut a button off their jackets and file off the eye, when it would pass current in all trading operations. The officers, discovering how easily the soldiers made their purchases, resolved to follow their example. One day a boy brought something into camp that Captain B., of the dragoons, wished to buy, but as money had no value in the eyes of the seller, at a considerable sacrifice he cut three or four buttons from a handsome fatigue jacket, and offered to the boy in exchange for his articles, but he refused to receive them because they were not as large as the buttons of the soldiers. The poor captain turned away in disgust, having mutilated his handsome jacket without gaining his point.

Now and then our friend Smith tried his hand at the healing art, and, being quarter-master-sergeant of the regiment, he always used horse-medicine in his practice. He was known among the peasantry, with whom his practice lay, as Doctor Simon. Upon one occasion he administered a stiff dose of saleratus and vinegar to an old woman for the rheumatism, and, strange as it may seem, she got well under his treatment. Her friends looked upon the cure as a most miraculous one. A few days after, her son visited the camp with a present of eggs and chickens for Smith, as a reward for curing his mother. He inquired for "Doctor Simon," but was conducted through mistake to Doctor Simpson, the surgeon of the regiment, whom he told that he had brought him something for doctoring his mother. The doctor, not being in the secret, denied curing the woman, but the boy insisted that he had, and that the medicine he had given her had " biled up." The interpreter here explained that the " Doctor Simon" alluded to was Smith, the quarter-master-sergeant, who was sent for ; and when he told them that the medicine that " biled up" was saleratus, all were surprised that the poor woman had not given up the ghost under the treatment. He divided the donation of chickens and eggs with Simpson, whose practice he had infringed, and was informed that in time to come he must not extend his professional services beyond the four-footed beasts for whom he was especially licensed.

In Socorro I took my meals at the house of Mr. Conner, an ex-Mormon, but lodged in another part of the town. The marshal and myself occupied the room together at a rent of fifty cents a day. It was a small and uncomfortable affair, with one door and one window, and before the latter dangled a dirty rag instead of glass. The floor was the bare, damp earth, and the furniture consisted of a small pine table, a rude bench, and two mattresses : the ornaments were a couple of family saints, a small piece of looking-glass set in tin, and a few paper rosettes stuck upon the wall. The remainder of the building was inhabited by two families, one occupying the wing across the court-yard, while the other lived in the *sala*. One evening I entered the *sala* to light my candle, and found the poor family seated upon the bare earthen floor eating their supper, which consisted of atole, without bread or meat. The room was cheerless in the extreme, and they did not appear to possess a single comfort of life. They were surrounded with filth, with hardly enough clothing to cover them, and yet in this condition live the great mass of the people of the country.

CHAPTER XVI.

RIDING THE CIRCUIT—*Concluded.*

THE town of Socorro is situated upon the west side
of the Del Norte, on a bluff bank some two hundred feet
above the river.   The name, in English, means *succor*,
and is said to have been so called from the following
circumstance: During the rebellion of 1680, a party of
Spaniards, retreating down the valley, hard pressed by
the Indians, here met troops from El Paso coming to
their assistance, and in commemoration of the event, the
town afterward built upon the spot was called Socorro.
The population is about five hundred, and at that time
the family of Mr. Conner were the only Americans in the
place.   The valley, in the neighborhood of the town, is
productive, the pasturage is unusually fine, and good
crops are raised.   The inhabitants are favored with good
clear water, and are not obliged to resort to the muddy
river.   About three miles distant is a somewhat remarkable warm spring that comes from beneath a range of
hills, and immediately below falls into a pool which forms
a fine place for bathing.

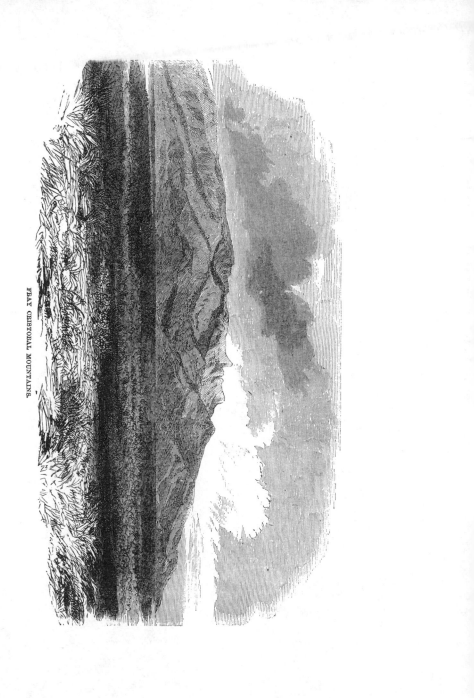

FRAY CRISTOBAL MOUNTAINS.

The court continued in session at this place until Friday without transacting any business of importance or interest. The court-house was in better condition than in most of the other counties, and the situation more pleasant. The front looked out upon the Plaza, while in the rear was a beautiful vineyard, which promised an abundant supply of delicious grapes. There was no jail in the county, nor had there ever been one. The only stirring occurrence during the week was the advent of a mad calf one evening upon the Plaza, followed by a crowd of men and boys yelling like so many fiends. They intended to stone the poor animal to death, but were prevented from carrying their cruel purpose into effect. I was afterward told, by a resident of the place, that the next morning the calf was killed, and the flesh distributed through the place for food.

The members of the bar invited Mr. Cardenas, the converted Catholic priest heretofore mentioned, to preach during the week, and on Wednesday evening he held forth in the court-house. The sermon was in Spanish, and he had a respectable audience as listeners, mostly Mexicans. The bar organized themselves into a choir, and during the exercises sang three hymns, one of which was that delightful old Church tune,

" How tedious and tasteless the hours,"

every word of which found its way to my heart, and carried me back to my boyhood days, and vividly revived a holy recollection of the best of mothers. I had not heard the hymn for years, and now to listen to it in a strange land, and under the peculiar circumstances which brought it forth, awakened thoughts and feelings that had lain dormant for years.

The evening before we left Socorro we rode out to the warm spring and bathed in its pleasant waters. The pool is some twenty feet long by fifteen wide, and eighteen inches deep. The temperature of the water is about that of new milk, and it is said to possess some medicinal qualities that render bathing in it conducive to health. This spring supplies the town, and by the time it arrives there becomes cool and pleasant to the taste. There are several warm springs in New Mexico, some of which are medicinal in a high degree; and if in the States, and they could be conveniently reached, they would prove a fortune to the owners. One, in the neighborhood of Las Vegas, is celebrated as effecting remarkable cures in cases of chronic rheumatism, and invalids occasionally resort thither.

The next point south of Socorro at which the District Court sits is the town of Las Cruces, the county seat of Doña Ana county, the distance between the two places being one hundred and fifty miles. Our party numbered six persons, who were obliged to continue south, the balance returning north. We all intended going down on the east bank of the river; but the water being too high for Judge Benedict to cross in his buggy, he and three others traveled on the west bank, while two of us crossed to the other side. The mail-party came along about the time we were ready to start, and we took the opportunity of traveling in their company for greater security. We crossed the river by fording, and joined them as they were hitching up. There were seven persons, all told, including three passengers—six Americans and one Mexican.

It was about noon when we left camp, and we drove that afternoon twenty-five miles to the rancho of Mr. Crabb, where we stopped for the night. Our road, as usual, lay along the bank of the river, sometimes through fertile bottoms, and at others among the sand-hills. We found accommodations at Mr. Crabb's. A few nights before, a party of Mescalero Apache Indians attacked his corral and carried off his stock, which caused us to keep a close watch upon the animals. The next day we drove to Fray Cristobal, sixteen miles, to breakfast, passing on the way the ruins of Valverde. Some years ago this place was a flourishing settlement, but the inhabitants were driven away by the Indians and have never returned. All the way down from Socorro the country is mostly barren, and we saw but one house.

Fray Cristobal is a simple camping-ground, and not, as the young traveler would most likely imagine before he arrived there, a respectable-sized village, where he could find entertainment for man and beast. The place is named after an old Franciscan friar, who lived in the country many years ago, and was so called because of the resemblance of the profile of the mountain to the outline of his face. The accompanying sketch shows a striking likeness to the human countenance, and must be recognized by every one who has passed that point. On the west bank of the river, between Socorro and the lower point of the Jornada, there are two military posts, Forts Craig and Thorn, one village, Santa Barbara, and an occasional rancho.

Fray Cristobal is the northern terminus of the *Jornada del Muerto*, or the *Journey of Death*, a barren stretch of country, which extends nearly a hundred miles to the south. It is almost a dead level, and without water except the little found in holes after a rain, and is bounded on each side by a range of mountains, that on the west shutting off all approach to the river. The only vegetation is a short, dry grass and a few weeds. It is, properly speaking, a table-land, and the shape is not unlike that of a canoe. The width is from five to thirty miles. The river here makes a long detour toward the west, while the road that crosses the Jornada runs almost due south. This desert has ever been the dread of travelers, and many a one has entered upon it and never been heard of afterward. It was formerly the range of the Mescalero Apaches, who in some instances cut off whole trains. In the winter season it is visited by terrific storms of wind and snow, and sometimes both men and animals are frozen to death before they can cross it. In the warm season it is very usual to make the drive in the night, particularly if the holes do not contain water, as it is easier for the animals. Our present camp-ground being at the mouth of the Jornada, the necessary preparations are made for crossing it: the water-kegs are filled, animals well rested, and the wagon examined to see that every thing is in good traveling condition.

We remained in camp from eleven in the morning until five in the evening, resting beneath the fine old cottonwoods, while the animals pastured upon the luxuriant grass that covered the river bottom. Having completed our arrangements, we left camp and commenced the passage of the Jornada. The road for the first five miles gradually ascends until it reaches the plain, where it becomes smooth and hard, and superior to any turnpike I have ever seen. The night was beautifully clear, and in the soft atmosphere of that southern latitude the stars shone out with great brilliancy. Every thing rested in profound quiet, and no noise was heard but the clatter of our horses' hoofs and the rumbling sound of the wheels upon the hard road. The mountains could be distinctly traced in the moonlight, and but for their serried peaks, to remind us that we were upon terra firma, it would have required no great stretch of the imagination to believe ourselves at sea. A tall soap-weed grows upon the Jornada, which more than once in the night I mistook for Indians. They are about the height of a man's head, with a bushy top, and are well calculated to deceive the unwary traveler. We made sixty miles of the distance by three o'clock in the morning, when we halted and turned our animals out to graze for a couple of hours. I made my bed on the leeward side of a bush, and, in spite of the chilliness of the atmosphere, I slept soundly until I was awakened by the conductor to continue the ride. We hitched up between five and six, and completed the balance of the distance to the river by eleven, stopping meanwhile to breakfast beside a hole that contained a few barrels of filthy stuff we were obliged to call water.

We halted to dine and graze our animals at Robledo, the southern terminus of the Jornada, where we remained until four in the afternoon, and then drove into Doña Ana. We stopped here for the night. The stage drove into a large corral (in plainer English, cow-yard), and, as there was no public house in the village, or other place where travelers could find accommodations, we spread our blankets among the mules, and slept as soundly as though we had been provided with more sumptuous quarters. This is a modern-built Mexican town, with a population of some five hundred; the river bottom here is broad and fertile, and well watered and cultivated.

At Doña Ana resides Mr. P. M. Thompson, a young man of enterprise, whose life is full of romance. He is a native of New Jersey, where his friends still reside; but, at the age of twelve years, he ran away from school at Morristown, and joined Black Hawk's Indians about the close of the war between them and the United States. He was adopted into the family of White Hawk, a brother of the chief, and in all respects was brought up as an Indian; his face was painted, and he was taught the use of the bow and arrow, and other accomplishments of the red men. He remained with them until the war with Mexico, when, being in Saint Louis upon a visit, he enlisted in the army and went to New Mexico, where he was afterward discharged. We drove the next morning to Las Cruces, where the stage stops to change the mail. This was properly the end of my journey, but, as a week would intervene before the meeting of the court, I concluded to continue on to El Paso, forty miles below. I tarried at Las Cruces but a few moments, when I resumed the road in company with one of the passengers, who bestrode a mule belonging to the stage. Four miles brought us to the silver-smelting furnace of Mr. Stephenson, where we stopped a few minutes to examine the works, and look at some of the specimens of the precious metal obtained from the ore, when we mounted and rode to Fort Fillmore, four miles farther on.

Fort Fillmore is a large and pleasant military post, and is intended to garrison a battalion of troops. The form is that of a square, the quarters of the officers and men inclosing the open space within on three sides, while the south is open toward the river. The buildings are adobes, but comfortable. A farm at that time was attached to the post, since discontinued, on which were raised vegetables for the troops. There is also a well-selected post library for the use of officers and men, which is an evidence that the government does not overlook the mental wants of her soldiers. The post was garrisoned by three companies of the third United States infantry, under the command of Major Backus, an officer of experience and merit. I was received by the officers with the politeness that always characterizes them. Among others, I met Dr. S., surgeon at the post, the son of a distinguished citizen and valued friend of my native state, whose acquaintance I made with more than ordinary pleasure in that distant region.

We left the fort for El Paso about eleven, in advance of the mail, as we were desirous of arriving there that evening. The country is uninhabited until you arrive within four miles of the Pass, where you find three or four houses by the road side. There is evidence of former settlements along the valley, but the fields have gone back into a state of nature, the buildings tumbled down, and the acequias filled up, the whole having been laid waste by the Indians some years ago, and never resettled. A few miles below the fort we passed the battlefield of Bracito, where Doniphan fought a severe action with the Mexicans during the war. At four we stopped an hour upon the river bank to graze our animals. It was nearly sundown when we reached Frontero and entered the sand-hills. Here the country becomes very hilly and barren of verdure, except a few cactuses and a sparse growth of stunted pines and mesquite. The sun went down while we were winding among the hills, and we were left to finish the journey in the dark. Slowly traveling the tortuous course of the hilly road, we descended again into the river bottom, and between eight and nine o'clock we arrived at the hospitable mansion of Judge Hart, who made us feel at home the moment we had passed his threshold.

Our wearied animals were given into the care of the *mayor domo*, while their no less tired riders were taken charge of by our host. By the time we had made our toilets supper was announced, of which we partook with unusually keen appetites. After supper we retired to the library, and passed some time in most agreeable conversation. During the evening several gentlemen came in for the purpose of organizing a Masonic lodge, but as neither my companion nor myself had ever been initiated into the mysteries of the order, we were not allowed to participate in the ceremony. Our host excused himself to attend his brethren, and we, at the same time, claimed the privilege of amusing ourselves in our own way, and therefore went to bed. In spite of the near proximity to the place where the mystic rites of the order were being enacted, I had no troubled dreams of spooks or fiery gridirons, nor saw the ghost of the murdered Morgan ; but the God of Sleep, with gentle kindness, sat upon my weary lids until the sun had climbed far up into the heavens the following morning.

El Molino (the Mill), the residence of Judge Hart, is rather romantically situated upon the east bank of the Del Norte, three miles above the Mexican town of El Paso, and a short distance below where the river forces its passage through the mountains.   The house is built in the Mexican style, is large and convenient, and within were found every luxury and comfort of home.   At this point there is good water-power, which he has taken advantage of and erected a large flour-mill.   Judge Hart is a native of Kentucky, and settled at this point at the close of the war, in which he served as an officer.   Mrs. Hart is a Mexican by birth, a Chihuahuanian, but of fine Spanish blood, and is a lady of refinement and intelligence.   Having something of a literary turn, he has collected together a good selection of books, and there, removed from the great and busy world, he spends his time between business and the pursuit of letters.

I awoke refreshed, and, after a substantial breakfast, felt in a condition to follow whithersoever our host might lead in the pursuit of amusements or sight-seeing.   Toward noon we rode down to Magoffinsville, three miles below, to pay our respects to Mr. M., the proprietor, whom I found living quite in nabob style in a large Spanish-built house, that reminded me somewhat of an old mansion of the feudal ages.   Fort Bliss had lately been established here, and, for want of barracks, the officers and men were quartering in the buildings of Mr. M.   The present garrison was four companies of the

FORT BLISS, TEXAS.

eighth infantry, under the command of Lieutenant Colonel Alexander.

Here begins the somewhat celebrated Valley of Paso del Norte, which extends south thirty or forty miles, until the mountains again close down upon the river. The width varies from a half to three miles, and at a few points it is wider. The land is fertile, well irrigated, and produces fine crops. It is particularly productive in wheat, and it has been estimated that this narrow strip of land, lying on both sides of the river, would produce, under proper cultivation, enough to support a million of inhabitants. The valley would grow the grains and vegetables, while the hills and mountains would supply good pasturage for numerous flocks and herds. The climate is delightful, and even excels that of New Mexico. It is a region of perpetual spring and summer, and most of the tropical fruits and plants flourish as though it was the land of their nativity instead of their having been transplanted from a still more genial clime. The grape, in its variety, grows in great abundance, and vineyards, from which delicious wines are made, are scattered all along down the valley. In writing upon this subject, De Bow, in his Industrial Resources of the South and West, says, " The most important production of the valley is grapes, from which are annually manufactured not less than *two hundred thousand gallons of perhaps the richest and best wine in the world*. This wine is worth two dollars per gallon, and constitutes the principal revenue of the city. The El Paso wines are superior in richness, and flavor, and pleasantness of taste to any thing in the United States, and I doubt not that they are far superior to the best wines ever produced in the Valley of the Rhine or on the sunny hills of France. Also a great quantity of the grapes of this valley are dried in clusters, and preserved for use during the winter. In this state I regard them *far superior to the best raisins that are imported into the United States.*" Grapes and wines are the most valuable productions of the valley; but next to the cereal grains in point of usefulness may be mentioned the *lechuguilla*, a plant that grows upon the almost barren mountain-sides among the stunted pine and cedar trees. The blades are very fibrous, and, when pounded, washed, and scraped, are manufactured into ropes and many other useful articles.

If the proposed Atlantic and Pacific rail-road should be constructed through Texas, El Paso will be an important point on the route, and it will be the means of settling this whole valley with an enterprising population. The place of crossing is just below the mill of Judge Hart, which is said to be the most eligible point for the purpose upon the river.

The Mexican town of El Paso del Norte, in the State of Chihuahua, is situated upon the western bank of the river, and nearly opposite Magoffinsville. It was settled some two hundred and fifty years ago, and was originally the seat of a Spanish mission. There is a difference of opinion as to the origin of the name it bears. Some maintain that it was so called because here the river passes the mountains, while others contend that it was because the fugitive Spaniards *passed* to this place from the north in 1680, when driven out of New Mexico by the Indians. The former is probably the correct origin of the name, as the town was founded many years before this rebellion took place. The settlements extend down the valley some ten or twelve miles, and the population is estimated at six thousand. The houses are so much interspersed with vineyards, orchards, and cultivated fields, that it presents more the appearance of a succession of plantations than a town. The *Plaza*, as the more compact portion is called, is near the head of the valley,

CATHEDRAL EL PASO DEL NORTE.

where is situated the old cathedral, custom-house, and other public buildings, and where the trade of the town is carried on. Just below the point where the river passes the mountains a dam has been thrown across the stream, in order to turn the water into a large acequia, which runs the length of the valley, and irrigates the gardens, fields, and vineyards. El Paso is the centre of a considerable trade with the northern states of Mexico, Texas, and New Mexico, which is principally carried on by means of pack-mules.

I remained during the day and night the guest of Mr. Magoffin, and was never treated with greater politeness and kindness. The next morning I went over to El Paso with a party of gentlemen to see the town. We rode down to the ferry, when we stripped the saddles and bridles from our horses, which we put into the boat, and made the animals swim across. Safely upon the other side, we saddled up again and rode into town, the custom-house officer at the landing allowing us to pass without examination. These officers are accommodating fellows. The duty upon silver taken from Mexico to the United States is about eight per cent., but the merchants manage to get it across for about one half by making a *private arrangement* with the officer, who is always ready to "turn an honest penny." Each man has his price, and if one sum will not buy him another will. As we rode through the town I was struck with the charming appearance it presented. On every side were vineyards, flower gardens, orchards, and shrubbery, loaded with foliage, flowers, and fruit, and little canals carried water along nearly all the streets, and through the gardens and yards, adding to the pleasantness of the scene. Fruit-trees of all kinds, singly and in groves, were growing on every hand. The buildings are ordinary adobe houses, but such was the beauty and picturesqueness of their surroundings that they appeared much more pleasant than mud houses evér seemed before. When to these natural beauties we add nearly every delicacy and luxury that the heart of man can crave, and a climate that rivals that of Italy, it can easily be conceived that, as a place of residence, it is almost an earthly paradise. We stopped at the only public house in the town, and remained to dine. The landlord was a German or a Swiss, and is said to have been one of the cooks of Charles X. of France; but whether or not he learned the profession in a royal kitchen, his *cuisine* upon this occasion was quite incomparable, and far exceeded my expectations. His soup, meats, and other dishes, of which there was a variety, I have seldom seen surpassed in the first hotels in the United States. If cooks were ennobled nowadays, he should certainly be dubbed *Master of the Kitchen*, and be allowed to wear a golden spit at his button-hole as a badge of his rank. Upon this side of the river I found every thing purely Mexican, and even the near proximity of the Americans, without the advantage of their institutions, had failed to start the inhabitants from the Rip Van Winkle sleep in which they have slumbered for centuries. I imagined that I could see a difference, even in the donkeys and beggars, between those of El Paso and the same race of quadrupeds and bipeds who inhabit the soil of New Mexico. A small guard of soldiers was stationed in the town to aid the government officials in carrying into effect the mandates of his serene highness. We returned to the Texas side of the river before sundown, when, making my adieus to the kind host at Magoffinsville, I continued up to El Molino, and again became the guest of Judge Hart.

I took my departure from El Molino on Saturday, the thirteenth instant. I was favored with the company of a party of officers returning to Fort Fillmore; we numbered eight persons, including the wife and daughter of Colonel Alexander. The day was clear and pleasant, and we made the distance to the fort by four in the afternoon, without hinderance on the way. I remained at the post until the following Monday, quartering with Dr. S. With the exception of those who have their wives with them, the officers formed a common mess, and appeared to live on the most agreeable terms with each other. I dined with Major Backus and family on Sunday, and made the acquaintance of his wife and daughter, whom I found to be pleasant and intelligent persons, and who had shared the major's camp and garrison life in New Mexico for three years. The troops turned out on Sunday morning for inspection and parade, and the band discoursed sweet music at different times during the day.

On Monday morning I rode up to Las Cruces, to give my attendance at the United States District Court, which was to begin its sessions that day. The county seat of Doña Ana is a modern-built Mexican village, and, in Yankee style, stretches mostly along one broad street, with a population of about a thousand souls. On the opposite side of the river is the famous Mesilla Valley, which has caused such a hubbub in the political world. It lies along the west bank of the Del Norte, some thirty odd miles from north to south, with a width of from a quarter to two miles, being bound on the west by a range of barren mountains. The glowing accounts that have been written about the beauty and fertility of La Mesilla are not sustained by the reality, and were gotten up by those who were entirely ignorant of the subject. The population is much less than represented. At the first election held after the Gadsden purchase the number of votes polled was two hundred and thirty-five, and at the

Congressional election in 1855 the number was between five and six hundred, making the population, at the highest estimate, not more than about twenty-five hundred. But a small portion of the valley is cultivated, and that by means of irrigation, the water being brought from the river in acequias. In point of fertility, the soil is about equal to the remainder of the Territory; but I would not exchange a good Pennsylvania farm of a thousand acres for the whole valley for agricultural purposes.

The term at Las Cruces was a slim affair, so far as matters of interest were concerned; yet there were enough unimportant cases to occupy the time of the judge until Friday afternoon. Two indictments were standing upon the criminal docket for offenses committed in the Mesilla; but as this valley was not then considered as belonging to us, and within the jurisdiction of our courts, these cases were disposed of in a summary manner. Before this territory (La Mesilla) was reacquired under the Gadsden treaty, it was a source of constant annoyance to our authorities. The villains who found a home there would slip across the river, commit offenses, and return before they could be apprehended; and the rascals from this side would flee to the other after the commission of a crime—and both were equally safe, there being no treaty between us and Mexico for the rendition of fugitives from justice.

During our attendance upon the court, the judge, bar, and officers found accommodations at the public house of a Mr. Bull, where, for two dollars and fifty cents a day, we got tolerably good living. In the interval of business many amusing anecdotes were related, one of which, told by Judge B., is too good to be lost. In the county of S., in the State of Indiana, the two associate justices were, upon one occasion, holding a term of court, when a motion was made to dismiss a case, or, in common legal parlance, to throw it out of court. This brace of modern Lycurguses listened to the argument of counsel pro and con with the gravity of a badger, and, after it was concluded, made up their minds that the case should be thrown out of court, and, in accordance therewith, one of these worthies directed the clerk to throw the papers out of the window.

After court adjourned on Friday evening I rode down to the fort and passed the night there. The commanding general of the department had arrived during the afternoon, and, as the sun was about going down, the band came upon the parade and played some delightful airs in honor of his presence. This is one of the most delightful seasons to listen to music, and he who can not appreciate the " concord of sweet sounds" at such a time must be a much greater scamp than the Bard of Avon writes him down.

I returned to Las Cruces the next morning, and the same afternoon we turned our faces homeward. Our party was now a dozen strong, being joined at Doña Ana by the mail and a Chihuahua merchant traveling north, where we slept the first night. The second day we made about eighty miles on the Jornada, and at three in the morning we lay down to sleep upon the cold, hard earth for a couple of hours, while our animals rested and grazed. I had a severe chill during the time, but it was not strong enough to keep apart my heavy eyelids. The *Journey of Death* safely passed, we continued up the valley of the Del Norte without accident, and arrived at Santa Fé on the twenty-sixth day of May.

Thus I completed the judicial circuit of the Territory. The distance is nearly a thousand miles, and the country we traveled mostly composed of barren mountains and sandy plains, and in many parts traversed by hostile Indians. The accommodations were meagre enough, unless we had the good fortune to stop with an American family, or to partake of the hospitality of the officers of the army, and several times we had to lie in the open air. I saw enough to be satisfied that the office of United States Attorney for New Mexico is no sinecure, and one trip should satisfy any reasonable man, unless he has an overweening desire to become a modern Wandering Jew, or a new-fangled Don Quixote traveling hither and thither in search of legal or other adventures. The trip afforded me an excellent opportunity to see the country and the people, and also to observe how our judicial system works among a population just tasting of its effects. Every thing convinced me that they are an orderly and respectful people, and I have observed better decorum among them in the court-house than I ever noticed in the States in the most intelligent community. In every instance I was treated with great kindness, and hardly saw an instance of rude behavior during the whole of my absence.

CHAPTER XVII.

TRIP TO THE NABAJO COUNTRY.

One of the most interesting excursions I made in New Mexico was a visit to the country of the Nabajo Indians in the summer of 1855, who inhabit a region that lies between the rivers Colorado and San Juan, about two hundred miles west of Santa Fé. Governor Meriwether had been appointed sole commissioner to make treaties with the various Indian tribes of the Territory, and upon this occasion he went into the Nabajo country to treat with them, whither I accompanied him in the capacity of private secretary.

We left Santa Fé on the afternoon of the fifth of July, and encamped for the night at Delgado's Ranch, fourteen miles from town. Our party numbered five persons, the governor, his son, myself, and two servants. General Garland had made arrangements to accompany us, but, being detained by official business, he did not join us until after our arrival at Fort Defiance. We stopped the second night in the *bosque* (wood) near Algodones, and the next morning drove into Albuquerque in time to dine. We remained here until the noon of the next day, partaking of the hospitalities of Captains Rucker and Gibson, U. S. A., when, learning that General Garland would not be able to overtake us, we concluded to move on, even at the risk of traveling the whole distance without an escort.

It was near mid-afternoon when we resumed the road. We drove down the Del Norte three miles to the government ferry, where we crossed to the west bank of the river. The ferry is kept by an old Mexican in the employ of the quarter-master's department at twenty-five dollars per month, but who is allowed to charge for ferrying over citizens. The means of crossing was a rickety old scow, that could accommodate but one wagon at a time. The passage was somewhat difficult on account of the high wind, but we made the opposite shore in safety. We drove about two miles down the river, when we turned to the west, intending to drive to an acequia we supposed ran at the foot of the sand-hills that bound the valley, and encamp. We traveled until about dark, but, finding no water, we retraced our road, and made our camp for the night within a mile of a small Mexican village we had passed soon after we left the river. We were a mile from the river, which distance we had to drive the animals and carry the water we used for drinking.

I was deputed to go on a foraging expedition, and for that purpose returned to the village. I went from house to house, making diligent inquiry for those articles necessary to supply our larder, but received several *no hai's* (there is none) before I was able to find the objects of my search. I purchased enough eggs to fill my pockets, three half-grown chickens, and a good-sized log of wood for fuel. As I rode back to camp, with the chickens dangling from my saddle-bow and the wood upon my shoulder, I looked not unlike some modern Robin Hood returning from a foray. The lateness of the hour and the weight of our eyelids vetoed cooking, and so we lay down to sleep after partaking of a cold snack.

We broke up camp at five o'clock the next morning. As we were about hitching up, our animals treated us to a stampede, which detained us an hour. From the river bottom we ascended a gradual slope of some four miles to a sandy and undulating mesa, over which we traveled in a direction nearly northwest. By noon we had made about thirty miles, when we halted to lunch and graze near a small sulphur spring. Our camp was in a little dell, inclosed by rocky headlands, in some places showing almost a perpendicular escarpment of rock. Many large rocks lie upon the surface, mostly of a fine sandstone, formed in strata of not more than half an inch in thickness, and placed in as regular layers as though they had been laid by human hands. Nothing could be clearer than their formation in water, according to the modern geological theory, but how they came upon these high headlands, many miles from any stream, I do not pretend to know. We left the mesa before we had traveled half the distance, and entered a valley which had the appearance of having been the bed of a lake. The northeast side, near which ran our road, showed evident signs of having been washed by a large body of water. The rock is a soft laminated sandstone, full of holes and small caverns. Near the top, about where the old water-line appears to run, it has been scooped out underneath, until the upper part forms an overhanging ledge, much the same as we notice in a rock-bound coast upon which the waves incessantly break. The water appears to have subsided to about half its depth and there remained stationary some time, as a second ledge has been formed about midway

392 NEW MEXICO AND HER PEOPLE.

of the slope. The opposite side of the valley was too distant to be examined, but, from the glimpse I was able to obtain of it, the formation appeared different, the slope being overlaid with trap rock. The small river Gallo runs through the valley, but at this season of the year is almost dry.

We took the road again at five, and traveled ten miles, when we encamped for the night near the bank of the little river. We found a few stagnant pools in the bed of the stream, the water being almost strong enough to turn the stomach of an elephant. We afterward discovered that a crystal spring flowed near us, which at that time would have been more delicious than the nectar of the gods. Near our camp were living a Mexican family, perched in a rude hut upon the rocky bank of the Gallo. A few patches of corn in the valley, and a small flock of goats and sheep, made up their worldly goods and means of living. When we awoke in the morning, we had the satisfaction of knowing that the mules belonging to the baggage-wagon had stampeded during the night, and gone to parts unknown. Their tracks in the sand showed that they had turned their faces homeward. The teamster was dispatched in pursuit, while two men were left in camp to await his return, the governor and myself continuing on our way. Up to this point we had traversed almost a desert country, as dry as powder, sandy, and bare of trees. The only stream we crossed was the Puerco, now without a drop of water in its bed, but at some seasons of the year one of the most rapid and dangerous rivers in the country.

In a drive of five miles from the camp we came to the Indian pueblo of Laguna, where we unhitched and remained until the baggage-wagon came up. As we entered the village, the inhabitants were getting in motion for the day; some of the young maidens were in the pens milking the cows and goats, while others, with earthen jars upon their heads, were carrying water from the stream. Being athirst, I followed the steps of the water-carriers to the holes in the bank of the creek, but found the water a brackish, nauseous compound, hardly fit for man or beast; but, instead of drinking the stuff, I visited the goat-pens, and purchased a cup of new milk fresh from the fountain-head. On the opposite side of the town there is a clear and beautiful spring which boils up from beneath a sand-bank. Before Mr. Gorman's family came to live at the pueblo, the Indians would not touch the water, alleging as a reason that they knew the devil was in it, because it boiled up so. Seeing that Mr. Gorman's family used it with impunity, they concluded they might possibly be mistaken about Old Nick being in it, and commenced to use it themselves, which they have ever since continued to do.

Mr. Gorman is a Baptist missionary, and has resided at the pueblo some two years and a half. They have elected him a member of their community, with all the rights and privileges of a full-born Indian. He sits with them in the *estufa* in council when affairs of state are discussed, and preaches to them on the Sabbath in the village church, and, upon the whole, he is exercising a good influence over this simple-minded people.

The pueblo of Laguna stands upon a rocky knoll on the west bank of the Gallo, and at the distance of a few hundred yards presents rather a picturesque appearance. The population is reckoned at about a thousand souls. It is built without order, and the houses are generally small; none of them are more than two stories high, and the upper story recedes from the lower, so as to form an uncovered terrace. They are generally of mud, though a few are built of stones. The rooms are small, low, and badly ventilated, and a few small pieces of foliated

gypsum set in the thick wall admits the light.   The entrance is by means of ladders from the outside to the
roof, when you descend into the interior through a small
hole just large enough to admit an ordinary sized person.
They pull the ladder up after them on to the roof or terrace, and thus render themselves secure from intruders.
The rows of houses are separated by narrow lanes.   In
the centre of the village is a small plaza, surrounded by
two-story houses, with three narrow places of entrance,
within which they hold their dances and feasts.   They
dress pretty much the same as the other pueblos ; but,
according to custom, a large number of the children were
running about naked.   This is a modern pueblo, and is
said not to be more than two hundred years old, and one
of the head men gave me the following account of its first
settlement : That, a long time ago, their ancestors were
at the point of starvation where they then lived, and that
four men were sent out to seek a place for a new home.
In their search they arrived at the place where Laguna
now stands, where they found good water and fertile
land.   They returned and gave the information to their
people, and in a short time they changed their residence,
and the whole of them removed to this point.   It is also
said that, at the time of the rebellion of 1680, the inhabitants fled to Zuñi to escape the fury of the Spaniards.

   The children of Mr. Gorman have acquired the Indian
dialect so as to speak it with almost the same fluency
as their mother tongue.   Taking Master James, about
twelve years of age, with me as interpreter and guide, I
wended my way to the pueblo on a tour of sight-seeing.
We first went to the house of the cacique, which we entered by ascending an outside ladder to the terrace, across
which we passed into the building.   In the room were
seated several Indians upon the floor, all employed in
some useful occupation.   The cacique himself was paint-

ing a new *tinaja* (earthen pot), which he was covering
with numerous rude figures in black and red.   None of
them rose from the floor to welcome us, but gave the
usual guttural salutation and continued at their work.
Young Gorman chatted with them a few minutes, when
we bade them good-by, and climbed down the ladder into
the street again.

Having expressed a desire to see their god Montezuma, my young guide led the way to the house where the
famous deity is kept.   This is the most cherished, and
probably the only one still retained of all their ancient
heathen gods.   It is greatly in vogue in a dry time,
when it is brought forth from the sanctuary, and, with
dancing and other rites, they invoke it in favor of rain,
but whether it has ever been able to bring refreshing
showers to the parched earth is a question open to discussion.   We picked up one of the head men on the
way, who accompanied us.   We ascended a ladder as
before, and entered a small and badly-lighted room,
where we found a shriveled-up old Indian, entirely naked,
except a small cloth about his loins and moccasins upon
the feet.   Master James made known the object of our
visit, and told him we were not Mexicans, and would
neither injure nor carry away the god, which assurance
was necessary, as none of that race are permitted to look
upon it.   A conference was now held between the man
that accompanied us, the old keeper, and an old hag of
a woman who had come in in the mean time, and in a
few minutes we were informed that we could see Montezuma.   The old woman was dispatched to bring it in,
who returned after a short absence, carrying something
in her arms, wrapped up in an old cloth, which she placed
carefully upon the floor.   The cloth was then removed,
and their favorite god stood before our eyes.   I was
much disappointed in its appearance, it being a much

ruder affair than I was prepared to see. I had expected to see something in imitation of man or beast, but there was presented to our sight an object that neither resembled any thing upon the earth, in the heavens above, or in the sea beneath, and I felt that it could hardly be sinful in the poor ignorant Indians to fall down and worship it.

The god Montezuma is made of tanned skin of some sort, and the form is circular, being about nine inches in height, and the same in diameter. The top is covered with the same material, but the lower end is open, and one half is painted red, and the other green. Upon the green side is fashioned the rude representation of a man's face. Two oblong apertures in the skin, in the shape of right-angled triangles, with the bases inward, are the eyes; there is no nose, and a circular piece of leather, fastened about two inches below the eyes, represents the mouth; and two similar pieces, one on each side, opposite the outer corners of the eyes, are intended for the ears. This completes the *personnel* of the god, with the addition of a small tuft of leather upon the top, which is dressed with feathers when it is brought out to be worshiped upon public days. The three Indians present looked upon it with the greatest apparent veneration, who knelt around it in the most devout manner, and went through a form of prayer, while one of the number sprinkled upon it a white powder. Mateo, the Indian who accompanied us, spoke in praise of Montezuma, and told us that it was God, and the brother of God. After contemplating this singular spectacle for a few minutes, we withdrew, quite astonished at what we had seen. Who would have believed that within the limits of our Union, in the middle of the nineteenth century, there was to be found such a debased form of heathen worship?

We were entertained most hospitably by Mr. Gorman

UPPER COVERO.

and family, with whom we tarried until about twelve, noon, when we resumed the road. We drove thirty miles that afternoon, and encamped for the night at the Hay Camp, on the banks of the Gallo. We followed up the valley of this stream, the country presenting the same general appearance of having once been submerged in water, in some places the surface being covered with numerous water-washed boulders. We halted at the small Mexican town of Quivera, or Covero, long enough to fill our water-kegs and replenish our failing stock of provisions. A half-grown pig, chained in the cavity of a large rock, appeared to have the best quarters in the village, and in personal appearance he was by far the most respectable-looking inhabitant of the place. Leaving the village, we entered upon an extensive plain, barren except near the town, where a few fields of grain and vegetables are cultivated by means of irrigation. Upon our right loomed up old Mount Mateo, with heavy clouds now and then clustering around his bald peak, threatening to drop down rain upon the traveler beneath. In ten miles we came to the Gallo, which we crossed, and continued up the south bank until we reached our place of camping. Soon after crossing the stream we struck a very remarkable lava formation, probably one of the most curious in the world. It appears to have come down the valley in a broad stream of liquid fire until it became cool and ceased its flow. It follows the general course of the stream, and is many miles in length. In some places some obstruction appears to have dammed it up, at which points the stream has widened. The lava is as black as ink, and in appearance as fresh as though it had just cooled and ceased running. It came from the northwest, and some miles beyond this point are the remains of an old crater, from which this current of fire must have flowed.

The sides of the valley differ in no essential particular from the description already given. The strata are exposed toward the summit, and the opposite sides have such a uniformity of formation as to argue having been forced asunder. Here the action of fire predominates, and the basin does not appear to have been filled with water to a greater depth than about thirty or forty feet. At this height the rocks are water-washed, and those of a soft sandstone have been hollowed into caverns, and some rounded into boulders. The strata have been disrupted in some places, but mostly lie horizontally. The alcalde of Laguna joined us during the evening, having been sent by the governor of the pueblo to guide us to the fort. The interpreter of the Nabajo Indian Agency also came into our camp during the night, and accompanied us the balance of the journey.

We broke up camp at five and a half o'clock the next morning, and continued on up the valley of the Gallo. During the day we saw lava of a much older date than that already mentioned, and of an appearance entirely different. We stopped at *Agua Azul* (blue water), twenty miles from the Hay Camp, to lunch and graze the animals. Here we found good grass, and purchased a sheep of a Mexican herder, which we cooked for dinner. Thence we traveled that afternoon thirty miles farther to a small laguna, where we arrived about ten o'clock at night. We had intended encamping at a spring twelve miles beyond Agua Azul, but, having passed it undiscovered, we were obliged to continue on to the next water. About sundown we crossed the great backbone of North America, the ridge that divides the waters of the Pacific and Atlantic, and began to descend the western slope. At this place the rise to the culminating point from either side is so gradual that you are hardly aware when you have reached the highest point of the ridge, and, to assure yourself of the fact, you have to look at the direction of the water-courses. Toward the west we could see the reflection of the setting sun upon the clouds away below us.

Our afternoon drive was exceedingly fatiguing, and the animals became so much wearied before we reached the camping-ground that it seemed doubtful whether they could hold out until they arrived there. Our two guides went ahead to search for the water, and signal us if they should find it. After a while we saw, far ahead, a small red light, resembling a bloody star, which seemed to recede as we advanced, like the deceitful Will-o-the-Wisp. Finally it appeared to stand still, then grew larger, and at length we made it out to be a fire which the guides had kindled upon a rocky knoll to direct us to the water. We reached the laguna weary and worn, and, after a hasty supper, we laid down to sleep, with the wolves around us howling a lullaby. Our route to-day lay through valleys and depressions in the mountains; on the right the headlands are bold and abrupt, while on the left they have been worn down into gentle slopes, covered with a growth of cedar-trees.

We were on the road by sunrise the next morning, and made the fort by nine the same evening—distance about fifty miles. The country gradually descends as you go west, and the water flows toward the Pacific. In the valleys we saw wild sage and a little short, dry grass growing, and some of the hill and mountain sides are covered with small cedar-trees, but, with this exception, the whole country is a barren waste. About five miles from the fort, and at the entrance of the valley that leads up to it, is seen rather a curious formation of sandstone. There is a whole colony of large pillars and cones, some of which are more than a hundred feet high, with smooth sides, and more or less tapering to the top.

We enter the valley through what resembles a natural gateway, between opposite sandstone ridges, that do not approach nearer than three or four hundred feet of each other. It is probable that this was once a continuous ridge, which, by some great convulsion of nature, was forced asunder. At one point the broken crags resemble a ship under sail. About half way up the valley to the fort there rises up an immense mass of trap rock, to the height of at least two hundred feet, which resembles, at a distance, the spires and minarets of an old cathedral or mosque blackened with age. The reception from Major Kendrick, the commander of the post, and his officers, could not have been more kindly bestowed, and gave us the assurance that we were entirely welcome.

Fort Defiance is built in the heart of the Nabajo country, to keep that numerous tribe of Indians in awe. The location is one of the most eligible ones that can be found in all that region, being at the mouth of *Cañoncito bonito* (pretty little cañon), a favorite spot with the Nabajos, and near fertile valleys and good water. The cañon is about half a mile in length, with almost perpendicular rocky sides, which in one place are four hundred feet in height. The bottom is not over three hundred feet broad, level and grassy, and a small stream of water flows through it toward the fort, being fed from two springs near the head of the cañon. This post was built some years ago by Major Backus, since much improved by Major Kendrick, and at this time was garrisoned by three companies, one of light artillery and two of infantry. The quarters of the officers and men are built around a large parade, some three hundred by two hundred yards, covered with a fine coat of grass. Some of the buildings are of mud, and others of pine logs, and all comfortable enough, barring occasional leakage in the rainy season. The officers' quarters are upon the north side, and front

CAÑONCITO BONITO.

upon the parade. The stables of the artillery horses are a little to one side, on the west; they are roomy and comfortable, and the horses are cared for in the best manner. Besides the battery of six-pounders, there are also six pieces of mountain howitzers. Every thing about the post appeared in fine order, and bore evidence of good and wholesome discipline.

The next morning after our arrival at the post a party of us rode up to *Laguna Negra*, fourteen miles, to see the Indian agent, and learn when he could have the Red Men assembled for council. We made the distance in three hours, keeping up the valleys, and saw little of interest on the way. At one point in the route there is a singular formation of trap dike, such as is seldom seen. In a narrow valley there rises up an immense mass of red sandstone, through which runs a perpendicular section of trap not more than four feet in width, and which appears as though it had been placed there by a mechanic. The trap dike can be traced some distance on either side of the valley, like a belt extending across the country.

Laguna Negra (black water) is a pretty little sheet of water among the mountains, and is one of the places much resorted to by the Nabajo Indians. The water is of a dark hue, but cool and deep. We found Agent Dodge with his tent pitched upon an eminence overlooking the lake, and around were about a hundred Indians, some engaged in their usual sports, and others quietly sitting upon their horses. The governor held a short talk with the head men, and Monday, the sixteenth of the month, was fixed upon as the time for meeting them in council, and forming the proposed treaty. The chiefs promised to have their warriors present at the appointed time, the majority of them then being among the mountains within a short distance. We dined with the agent.

A dirty squaw, who seemed to be the mistress of the kitchen, baked a corn-cake in the ashes, roasted the side of a sheep on a stick before the fire, and made a pot of coffee. These we ate sitting upon the ground, and, as soon as we had done, our red brethren took our places and finished the repast. We returned to the fort the same afternoon.

General Garland, with Captain Ewell's dragoons, reached the fort on Saturday afternoon, the fourteenth, and was received by a salute from the field battery. The next day the whole garrison was paraded under arms, and reviewed and inspected. The following morning, Monday, the sixteenth, being the day fixed upon for the Indian council, the governor, two or three officers, and myself proceeded to the lake under escort of the dragoons. Before we arrived there a large number of Indians met us and accompanied us in, the throng increasing in numbers as we neared our destination. We pitched our tent near the shore of the lake, and the dragoons were picketed close by. At one o'clock we assembled in council. A small space, intended for the chiefs and Americans, had been inclosed with cedar boughs, but the crowd rushed in, and by the time we had taken our seats it was crammed full. The crowd of Indians upon the ground was very great, being estimated at two thousand, all mounted and armed warriors except a few women and children. As a general thing, they were tolerably well dressed, mostly in buckskin. Before any talking was done, tobacco was passed round to the head men, who quickly made themselves cigarritos, and went to smoking with great gravity and gusto. The Indians of New Mexico never use the pipe, but smoke an ordinary Mexican cigar instead.

Order having been restored in some degree among this democratic rabble, the council proceeded. The governor, through the medium of two interpreters, told the Indians that he had been sent there by their Great Father in Washington to hold a talk and make a treaty with them, in order that we might live in peace and friendship with each other. He then explained the terms of the treaty he desired to make with them: that they were to be confined within a certain district of country, while the balance of their land was to be ceded to the United States, for which they would receive annuities in goods for some twenty years; that they would be compelled to live in peace with the whites and neighboring Indian tribes, and to cultivate the soil for a living, etc. When the provision for the rendition of those guilty of crime was mentioned, one of the chiefs remarked that it had always been their custom, and that they would prefer to continue it, to pay for offenses committed instead of giving up the offenders. They were told firmly, in reply, that such was not our manner of doing business, and that no terms of the kind would be agreed to. In conclusion, they were requested to consider upon what had been said to them, and to give their answer in the morning. When we returned to our camp we found it surrounded by hundreds of Indians, and some dozen or more greasy fellows were occupying our tent, and smoking in a manner ridiculously cool and independent, but they soon made tracks after our arrival. The sergeant of the guard on duty had attempted to drive them out before our return, when one fellow drew an arrow upon him, but, sooner than have a collision, he had allowed them to remain in quiet possession of the tent. The majority of the Indians remained on the ground over night, and were fed at the agency. In the evening there was a rumor in camp that the bad men of the tribe intended to attack us during the night, but we viewed it as an idle tale, and lay down to sleep with the same feeling of security as though there had not been an Indian near us. The night passed quietly away, and we awoke safe and sound the next morning.

The Indians were seen gathering together in great numbers as the morning wore away, and soon there were as many assembled as yesterday. They were galloping to and fro along the valley in tens, and twenties, and fifties, and on the border of the lake, half a mile distant, large groups were collected together, as though engaged in deliberation. Our camp was again surrounded by hundreds, who would sit so immovable upon their horses that man and beast seemed but one animal. Early this morning a delegation of Indians from the pueblo of Zuñi came into camp, as they alleged, to see the governor, but really upon a begging expedition. They were accompanied by the governor, and also the officer whose duty it is to look after the sun and moon, the latter being necessarily an owlish-looking individual. His office is doubtless a sinecure, but, if such a one existed under our government, with a fat salary attached, it would command the first talent in the republic. The general, with the light battery, arrived in camp about nine, and took up a position near us.

The council opened about noon. During the morning the chiefs had been in conference with their people, considering the propositions made to them the day before. Having determined to accept the terms offered, some twenty of them came to our camp and announced the fact, and said they were ready to proceed with the business. They took their seats in a circle upon the ground, appointed one of their number spokesman for the whole, and then lit their cigarritos for a smoke. About the opening of the council, the head chief, named *Sarcillas Largas*, sent his medal and official staff to the governor, with a message that he was not able to govern his people, and desired to resign his office. His resignation was accepted, and the assembled chiefs were requested to select a man to fill his place. The choice fell upon *Manuelita*, a good Indian, and who was duly invested with the dignity of office. He would not receive the staff the other chief had surrendered, nor allow the medal to be suspended from his neck by the same string, giving as a reason that his people had a superstition about such things, and that, if he should receive them, he would soon lose his influence over the tribe. His explanation of the matter was deemed satisfactory, and the governor gave him his handsome steel cane, and supplied the medal with a new string.

Being ready to proceed to business, Manuelita, in the name of his people, told the governor that his talk of the day before was good, and that they were all agreed to the terms he proposed. The treaty was now read, and interpreted to them article by article; but when they came to the fourth, Manuelita said his people claimed a much larger district of country, and that they were in the habit of going to the mountain of Polonia, outside of the reservation, to worship the spirits of their fathers, and that some were averse to giving up this sacred spot. The governor explained to them, from Park's map, that this mountain would fall within the country reserved to them, with which they were satisfied. They desired permission to get salt from the Salt Lake near Zuñi, which was conceded to them. After the various articles had been read, interpreted, and agreed to, they were duly signed by the chiefs, and witnessed by the officers and a few other Americans present.

After the conclusion of the council, a considerable amount of presents was distributed among the Indians, when a scene of confusion took place that was highly amusing. The chiefs told the governor that they would make a proper division of the goods if he would turn the same over to them, which was accordingly done; but, instead of dividing them among the Indians, they threw them into the crowd pell-mell, when a general scramble took place. The reader can imagine the scene, when a wagon-load of goods is thrown among near two thousand wild horsemen, and each one bent upon getting all he can. What riding and pitching there was! Here you would see a fellow, with a piece of muslin, riding toward the mountains at full speed to hide his prize, and two or three others in hot pursuit, with their knives flashing in the sun. The fugitive being overtaken, a severe struggle takes place for the spoil. The muslin has become unwrapped and stretched to its full length, each party tugging to obtain the lion's share, when, as the opportunity offers, each horseman cuts off as much as he can, and gallops away with his well-earned prize, after leaving the original possessor but a small portion. Some were seized and made to disgorge by main force, while others effected a safe retreat with what they obtained in the first instance, and returned to the scene of contest for more. Others were unhorsed in the struggle, and both parties contended on foot until one or the other proved victorious. Brass kettles, knives, tobacco, muslin, looking-glasses, and various other articles changed owners with a magic quickness, and always *nolens volens*, as far as the late holder was concerned. When the contest was over, some were almost loaded down with goods, while others, less fortunate, were empty-handed. How like a commentary upon life was this struggle of the wild Nabajo horsemen for a few dollars' worth of presents! Before the Indians left the ground, the light artillery performed various evolutions, much to the astonishment of the natives. We remained in camp that evening, and returned to Fort Defiance the next morning.

In many respects the Nabajos are the most interesting tribe of Indians in our country, and their history, manners, and customs are not unworthy an investigation. They appear superior in intelligence to all the other North American tribes, and differ from them in their habits and traditions. They live in the very heart of the continent, and from time immemorial have roamed over both the Pacific and Atlantic slopes. They have ever been known as a pastoral and peaceful race of men, and live by raising flocks and herds, instead of hunting and fishing. They own some two hundred thousand sheep, and more than ten thousand head of horses, and at times one single chief is worth as much as fifteen thousand dollars in stock, owning thousands of sheep and hundreds of horses. They raise corn, wheat, beans, pumpkins, melons, peaches, wild potatoes, etc. They sometimes grow as many as sixty thousand bushels of corn in a single season, and the present year (1855) they are supposed to have five thousand acres under cultivation. They number about twelve thousand souls, and can muster twenty-five hundred mounted warriors. They are industrious and laborious, and the men, women, and children are generally kept employed. They manufacture all their own wearing apparel, and make their arms, such as bows, arrows, and lances; they also weave a beautiful article of blankets, and knit woolen stockings. They dress with greater comfort than any other tribe, and wear woolen and well-tanned buckskin. The skin breeches come down to the knee, where they are met by blue stockings that cover the lower half of the leg; the breeches fit tight to the limb, and the outer seams are adorned with silver or brass buttons. The coat reaches below the hips, with a hole at the top to thrust the head through, and open at the sides; it is made of wool, woven in bright colors, and is fastened around the waist by a leather belt, highly ornamented with silver when the wearer can afford it. They wear numerous strings of fine coral, and many valuable belts of silver, and generally appear with a handsome blanket thrown over the shoulder in the style of a mantle.

The Nabajo Indian is seldom seen on foot, a horse being as indispensable to him as to an Arab of the desert. They manufacture their own saddles and bridles, bits, stirrups, etc., as also the looms on which they weave their handsome blankets, which are quite an ingenious affair. It is a noted fact that they treat their women with more respect than any other tribe, and make companions of them instead of slaves. A Nabajo never sends his wife to saddle his horse, but does it himself if he has no peon. The modern doctrine of "Woman's Rights" may be said to prevail among them to a very liberal extent. The women are the real owners of all the sheep, and the men dare not dispose of them without their permission; nor do the husbands ever make an important bargain without first consulting their wives. They admit women into their councils, who sometimes control their deliberations; and they also eat with them. They are mild in disposition, and very seldom commit murder; but they consider theft one of the greatest human virtues, and no one is thought to be at all accomplished unless he can steal with adroitness.

Their form of government is so exceedingly primitive as to be hardly worthy the name of a political organization. In this respect they are far behind the other tribes of the country. The democratic doctrine prevails among them, and the will of the majority always governs. They have no hereditary chief, but one is elected from time to time, who surrenders his authority at pleasure, when a new one is chosen in his stead. There are a few rich families in the tribe, who form the aristocracy, and possess a little additional influence, but neither age nor rank commands the same respect as among other tribes.   In their councils they are little better than a tumultuous rabble, and lack the dignity and decorum we generally see among Indians.   The tradition of their origin is that, a long time ago, they came up out of the water a great distance to the north, and they believe that when they die they will return into the water whence they came. They have another tradition by which they account for the Nabajos being a more numerous race than the whites. They say that in the beginning a beaver dug a great hole in the earth, out of which came seven Nabajos and five white men, and therefore they believe they are the most numerous people.   Very conclusive reasoning!

CHAPTER XVIII.

TRIP TO THE NABAJO COUNTRY—*Concluded.*

THE religious belief of the Indians is somewhat un-
usual for Indians. Their god is a woman, who they
believe places the sun in the heavens every morning, and
they say that the moon is carried around the sky upon
the back of a mule, whose ears they can plainly see. They
have a number of prophets, who profess to receive revelations from the woman who has charge of the sun, and
which, at stated periods, they communicate to the people. They also prophesy as in olden times, and thus
exercise a considerable influence in the tribe. They
have certain fast-days, during which they neither eat nor
drink, but strictly observe the practice of total absti-
nence. Their habitations are a kind of lodge, made of
poles and grass in a very rude manner, and the reason
they give for not living in houses is, that when they first
came up out of the water, they left this matter with the
women, who preferred to live in lodges. When a person
dies in a lodge, they pull or burn it down; and when a

man quarrels with his wife, which is seldom the case, he generally kills some person in his grief. They have a superstitious dread of approaching a dead body, and will never go near one when they can avoid it. They also have a great antipathy to a hog, and they will neither eat the flesh nor allow one to come into the nation.

Their form of marriage ceremony is peculiar and primitive. When a man and woman desire to become " bone of one bone and flesh of one flesh," they sit down on opposite sides of a basket, made to hold water, filled with *atole* or some other food, and partake of it. This simple proceeding makes them husband and wife ; but the contract sits so lightly upon them that they have the privilege of separating and seeking new companions the next day. The husband, at the time of marriage, makes a present of horses to the bride's father, and she takes him home to live with her. In person they are a little above the medium height, and well made ; their complexion is a dark brown, but they have not the same high cheek-bones as the Indians of other tribes. They have several native blacksmiths, who work in iron with considerable skill. The rich men own a number of peones, generally Mexican captives, whom they employ in tending their flocks and herds. Some of them marry into the tribe, and from choice remain with them all their lives. Every thing connected with their religion is of the most primitive and crude belief imaginable, and I have serious doubts whether they have any tangible conception of a Supreme Being, nor have I been able to learn that there is any word in their language which means God.

The reader has probably queried ere this as to the origin of these Indians, so far in advance of all the other nomadic tribes in the arts and civilization. Were I disposed to indulge in speculation alone, I might, with some degree of plausibility, claim them as the descendants of the lost tribes of Israel. Their tradition that they came up out of the water a long way to the north—being a peaceful and pastoral people—drawing their subsistence from flocks and herds, instead of hunting and fishing, as other tribes; their aversion to the flesh of the hog; that when they die they will return into the water whence their fathers came, instead of believing in the usual heaven of Indians—good hunting-ground and an abundance of game; their having prophets, who prophesy and receive revelations; and their strict observance of fast-days, when they abstain from eating and drinking, and also their keenness in trade. Furthermore, their better treatment of women, their greater skill in the mechanic arts, and improved personal appearance, all point them out as a superior race of Indians. It has long been the received opinion with many learned men that the lost tribes of Israel crossed from Asia at Behring's Strait and spread over the continent of America; and the only thing wanting to sustain this hypothesis was the failure to find satisfactory evidence among our Indian tribes to fix them as the descendants of the fugitive Israelites. In this view of the question, the evidence in favor of the Nabajos is stronger than can be adduced in behalf of any other tribe or people.

Speculation aside, who are probably the Nabajos? Mr. Gregg, in his excellent work upon New Mexico, gives it as his opinion that they are the remnant of the Aztec race which remained in the north when that people migrated toward Anahuac. Among the reasons he advances in support of this position are their superiority in the manufacture of blankets, cotton textures, and embroidering in feathers. Their blankets are unquestionably a fine article, and they excel in making them because they have particularly cultivated this branch of industry; but they neither work in cotton, nor have I ever seen a particle of plumage-work among the many hundreds of them with whom I have come in contact. Humboldt fixes the country of the Nabajos as the region inhabited by the Aztecs of the twelfth century; but there is nothing found among them at the present day, nor seen in the ruins that remain in their country, that will compare favorably with the mechanical skill of the Aztecs. If they once inhabited villages, why have they become a wandering race, living in rude huts, and how came they to lose the knowledge of constructing large edifices, which is the case if their ancestors lived in the villages whose ruins now cover the country? If the Nabajos have any connection with the ancient races of Mexico or Central America, they must be of Toltec instead of Aztec origin. If the stream of migration had flowed from the northwest through New Mexico, as is maintained by some, we would find traces of them scattered along their line of march to the starting-point. But such is not the case. There are a few ruins of ancient villages on the north bank of the San Juan, but in all the regions to the north of that, as far as I have been able to learn, there is no evidence remaining that such a people ever passed over the country. From that river southward their line of migration can be traced by occasional ruins. This would seem to argue in favor of their Toltec origin, and that in ancient times they migrated from the south toward the north; and the reason of their ruins exhibiting less mechanical skill than that found among the Aztecs is probably because they changed their location before that people reached such a high state of civilization.

In opposition to this pro and con testimony as to the origin of the Nabajos, my own opinion is that they are only a branch of the great Apache family, that have inhabited the territory from time immemorial. The ruins found in the country in which they now live are undoubtedly the remains of the villages of Pueblo Indians, whose inhabitants have either become extinct or changed their location. We find much evidence among the records of the early Spanish governors of the existence of former pueblos, whose location at the present day is almost unknown. As late as 1692, the pueblo of Pecos contained a thousand inhabitants, but it has long since fallen into decay, and the remnant of the population have united themselves with another community. In the old documents in the secretary's office at Santa Fé, whenever any mention is made of the Nabajos, they are invariably spoken of as the "Nabajo Apaches," and do not appear to have been known under any other name; and the Pueblos were always so designated in contradistinction to the wild Apaches, who led a wandering life. When Coronado passed through the country in 1540, he did not see any other Indians than the Pueblos until he reached the plains between the mountains and the Arkansas, from which we may infer that the wild Indians did not then inhabit the country in which they now have their homes, but were subsequently driven in from the plains by a superior enemy or some other cause.

I regret that I had not leisure to examine the ruins found in various parts of the Nabajo country, and other interesting objects to be found there. The principal remains of ancient pueblos are found in the Valley of the Rio Chaco, a southern tributary of the San Juan. Some of the ruins are quite extensive, with chambers in a tolerably good state of preservation, and exhibit skill in the mechanic arts superior to that possessed by the Nabajos at the present day, and which are undoubtedly the remains of some of the pueblos which Coronado's people visited or make mention of.   One of the most wonderful exhibitions of Nature to be found in the country, or any where else in the Union, is the Cañon of Chelly, which is a natural passage through a mountain range twenty-five miles in length, and from one hundred to five hundred yards in width.   The sides are of solid rock, nearly perpendicular the whole length, almost as though they had been chiseled by the hand of art, and in many places they are five hundred feet high.   There are numerous lateral branches which are less stupendous.   A small stream of water runs through a portion of it, and in it are numerous cultivated fields and orchards of the Nabajos.   There are also the ruins of pueblos within the cañon.   There are several other smaller cañones, but they sink into insignificance when compared with that of Chelly.

In conclusion of my notice of the Nabajos, I give a vocabulary of a few of the words in most common use among them.   The spelling of the syllables is, of course, entirely arbitrary, but I have endeavored, as far as possible, to make them represent the true sound of the words.   Their language has never been reduced to writing, and therefore we can do no more than approximate to the proper pronunciation in English.   The list of words here embraced was furnished to me by Captain H. L. Dodge, the agent for the Nabajos, and a young Indian named Armijo, a son of one of the principal men of the nation, and may be relied upon as mainly correct.

Vocabulary of upward of sixty Words in Nabajo and English.

Nabajo	English	Nabajo	English
Thlie	one.	Has-ta	six.
Na-che	two.	Sotz-sitz	seven.
Tah	three.	Sa-pe	eight.
Tee	four.	Nas-ti	nine.
Ich-la	five.	Nez-na	ten.

Cla-za-ta.........	eleven.	Clos-na-ta	wheat.
Na-che-ze-ta ...	twelve.	Pah-li-ki.........	dollar.
Tah-za-ta........	thirteen.	Pah	bread.
Tee-za-ta	fourteen.	Tu-aj..............	water.
Ich-la-ta	fifteen.	Na-ta-nay	governor.
Has-ta-za-ta.....	sixteen.	Jay-uh............	sunrise.
Sotz-sit-za-ta....	seventeen.	Skin-ni	brother.
Sa-pe-za-ta......	eighteen.	Eh-ki.............	white shirt.
Nas-ti-za-ta	nineteen.	La-ki.............	white.
Nat-teen	twenty.	Cla-zin	black.
Tah-teen	thirty.	Clit-so	yellow.
Tee-teen	forty.	Lat-che	red.
Ich-la-teen	fifty.	Clee-be-gel	saddle.
Has-ta-teen......	sixty.	Clee-ma-sas-tah	bridle.
Sotz-sitz-teen....	seventy.	Ah-ka-chuh	candle.
Sa-pe-teen	eighty.	Cle-cha...........	big dog.
Nas-ti-teen	ninety.	Klong	prairie dog.
Nez-na-teen.....	one hundred.	Cla-ja	pantaloons.
Tooh	water.	Claj-ek-la-ki	white drawers.
Ne-yel	air.	A-ja-lan-siques.	how do you do?
Ich-car-go........	day.	She-sol-ka.......	good-by.
Pa-ma	mother.	A-pin-da.........	good morning.
Schi-za	father.	Ya-dey-uh.......	good evening.
Clee	horse.	Ja-da-nagan	where do you live?
Na-ta.............	corn.	Za-sho-se-kis....	are you well, my
Na-ta-na	captain.		friend?
Es-ta-na..........	woman.	Tah-tol-geh	what is the name
Ta-na.............	man.		of this place?

About a hundred miles west of the Nabajos, and upon the great tableau between the rivers San Juan and the Colorado Chiquito, are found the seven villages of the Moqui Indians. They are about midway in the wilderness between the Rio Colorado of the west and the Del Norte. A bute or *mesa*, with a flat top, rises up several hundred feet, upon which the Moquis have built their villages. The sides of the mesa are nearly perpendicular, and the top can only be reached by means of a stairway cut in the rock. Around the base lies their arable land, where they cultivate grains, fruits, and vegetables, and pasture their flocks and herds. During the day they attend their crops, and watch their sheep and goats in

.he valley below, but when night approaches they retire up to their villages, where they rest secure. They are a mild and peaceful race of people, almost unacquainted with the use of arms, and not given to war. They are strictly honest. They dress in cotton and other garments of their own manufacture. The females are said to be good-looking and of symmetrical persons ; they are neat and cleanly in their habits, and well treated by the men. The latter do all the work in the fields, while the former attend alone to the labor within doors. Their manufactures in woolen, cotton, leather, basket-work, and pottery exhibit considerable skill. The women have a peculiar style of dressing their hair, and the rank and condition of each may be known by the manner in which she wears it. The married women wear it done up in a club at the back of the head, while the virgins part it in the middle behind, and bring it round to either side, something in the form of a rosette, and nicely smoothed and oiled.

The houses are built much in the same manner as those of the other pueblos, some being constructed of stone and mortar, and others of mud ; they are two and three stories high, and comfortable. They cultivate by means of irrigation, and their crops sometimes fail by reason of the mountain streams giving out ; but, to avoid a famine, they always keep on hand a considerable supply of provisions. They are kind and hospitable to strangers, and when one approaches their villages they watch his movements from the tops of the rocks and houses. Now and then their more warlike neighbors, the Nabajos, come sweeping down upon them, and drive off their flocks. They offer but little resistance, but, gathering up all the movables they can carry, they retreat to their strongholds upon the mesa height. Among them are a few albinos, with perfectly white hair and light eyes, while the complexion of the balance is about the same as the other Pueblo Indians.

The Moquis have had but little intercourse with the American or Spanish population of New Mexico, and retain their aboriginal manners, customs, and religion. It is supposed by those who have examined the subject with the most care that they are the remains of the province of Tusayan, which was visited by a portion of the command of Coronado in the winter of 1540–41, on their way to the great cañon of the Rio Colorado. From the investigation I have bestowed upon the question, I am of the opinion that Moqui is identical with ancient Tusayan, for which conclusion reasons are given more at length in a previous chapter.

Some sixty miles to the south-southeast of Fort Defiance is situated the pueblo of Zuñi, on a small tributary of the Colorado Chiquito. The village contains some fifteen hundred inhabitants, and in all essential particulars does not differ from the other pueblos in the Territory. The houses are two and three stories high, and terraced, and the streets are narrow. It contains a Catholic church. The inhabitants cultivate the soil, raising a good deal of grain, and they possess numerous flocks and herds. There are several albinos in the village. The present town is in the valley, but the old pueblo was built on the top of a high mesa, almost inaccessible from below. A few miles to the east of Zuñi is a noted quadrangular mass of white sandstone, known as Inscription Rock, which has attracted much attention. It is nearly a mile in length, and more than two hundred feet in height. On the north and south faces are numerous inscriptions in Spanish of the names of persons who passed that way, with the dates. Some of them are deeply and beautifully cut into the plane surface of the rock, and reach back as far as 1606, two hundred and fifty years ago. They are cut upon the vertical faces, about the height of a man's head from the ground. Upon the top of the rock are the ruins of two pueblos, the size and shape of which, with the dimensions of the rooms, can be distinctly traced, and many pieces of painted pottery are lying round about. The inscriptions generally contain a short memorandum of the object of the visit, having been made either by travelers exploring the country, Spanish soldiers on the march to conquest, or by the early Franciscan friars penetrating the wilderness to convert the native heathens to the living God. What a field for sober reflection this rock presents to the mind, with its inscriptions, hieroglyphics, and ruined villages! It is a mute but eloquent historian of the past.

We left Fort Defiance to return home on the afternoon of Wednesday, the eighteenth of July, and traveled through the rain twelve miles before we encamped. We halted about sundown in a boggy valley, where we sank shoe-top deep in mud at every step. As we had about arranged our camp for the night, the mules and dragoon horses, near a hundred in number, became frightened at some imaginary scarecrow, and stampeded in the most approved style, and made their way back to the fort. A party of soldiers were sent in pursuit, who returned with the truant animals about three o'clock the next morning. Fortunately, none were injured, but all were greatly jaded. The rain continued to fall in torrents, and, take it all in all, it was one of the most uncomfortable nights I ever remember to have passed in camp. The next morning the clouds broke away soon after sunrise, and it remained clear the balance of the day. That evening we encamped at the laguna. During the day we passed, near the Ojita, one of the finest natural meadows I have ever seen. It must have contained several thousand acres, and was covered with a heavy growth of grass resembling barley.

The next day we lunched at Agua Azul, and encamped for the night at the Gallo. As we drew near the Gallo we saw a number of Indians about the valley whose conduct created the suspicion that they were returning from a marauding expedition, and had stolen property in their possession. When they got sight of us they began catching up their animals and flocks, and made for the mountains. Captain Ewell, with a detachment of dragoons, was sent in pursuit, but found, when he overtook them, that they were a party of Sandoval's Nabajos, who were about leaving the watering-place as we drew near. The next day we encamped near the Sulphur Spring, five miles east of Laguna. We halted a while at the pueblo, and partook of the hospitalities of Mr. Gorman and family; and the governor held a talk with delegations of Laguna and Acoma Indians, to endeavor to reconcile a long-standing difficulty between them.

The following morning our party divided, the general and escort proceeding to Los Lunas, while the governor and myself continued the direct route homeward. That night we encamped on the west bank of the Del Norte, a high wind preventing us from crossing. We passed over the next morning with no other mishap than my horse tumbling overboard into the river. Thence we continued up the Valley of the Del Norte, and arrived in Santa Fé on the afternoon of the twenty-third instant.

New Mexico, with all her barrenness of soil and unforbidding aspect to the stranger and new settler, is not entirely void of attractions. She has within her limits resources which, if properly developed, would vastly increase her importance to the rest of the Union, and add greatly to her wealth. If Nature has denied to her bounties lavishly bestowed upon portions of our beloved country, she has provided other gifts, which in some measure serve as a recompense in place of those withheld. I allude to her mineral wealth, which consists of gold, silver, iron, copper, and coal. The old Spanish records state that the leading object of the first adventurers into New Mexico was their thirst for gold, based upon the stories they had heard of the richness of the country. In those days a desire for the yellow metal was such that, in the search for it, men were willing to endure all manner of hardships and sufferings. The expedition of Coronado was mainly induced by the accounts that Baca and his men gave of the abundance of gold that could be obtained. One of the causes of the revolution of 1680 was the cruel treatment the natives received in the mines ; and, after the expulsion of the Europeans, it is said that they filled up the most valuable mines, some of which remain unknown to this day. In various parts of the country are found old abandoned mines, which have not been worked within the memory of man.

Gold abounds in several localities, but the mines that have been worked with most success, and are supposed to be the richest, are in the Placer Mountains, thirty miles southwest of Santa Fé. In the same region are washings which have been worked for some years, and a large amount of gold taken out. The mines at El Placer are said to have been accidentally discovered about thirty years ago, when work was immediately commenced in them. Mr. Gregg says that, from 1832 to 1835, when mining operations were the most flourishing, from sixty to eighty thousand dollars per annum were taken from them, and that, from the first discovery up to 1844, they yielded about half a million of dollars. There has been but little work done in them since the war with Mexico.

The three mines that have been worked at the Placer

are known as the Ortiz, the Biggs, and the Deavenport mines.   The shaft of the Ortiz has been sunk more than two hundred feet, and produced, with the rude labor bestowed upon it, about one dollar to the hundred pounds of ore, not much more than one third of the gold being extracted.   The Biggs mine is within a few feet of the Ortiz, but the shaft has neither been sunk so deep nor in so skillful a manner, and therefore not worked to as much advantage.   These two mines are on the same lead.   They were descended by means of pine logs with notches cut for the hands and feet, and all the ore raised was carried up on the backs of men.   The work was dangerous and laborious, and but little progress could be made.   The ore is quartz, but easily crushed.   The third mine, the Deavenport, is within a mile of the other two, lower down the same ravine, and of a different character.   The ore is dug out of the side of a mountain, is easily obtained, and the supply is inexhaustible.   There is no vein or lead, as in ordinary mines, but an immense mass or quarry of gold-bearing rock lies in the mountain side.   In most places it crops out at the surface. The ore is more easily crushed than the former, and every pound gives more or less gold, and frequent pockets of loose earth are found which yield with exceeding richness.   The ore of this mine is hardly as rich as the other two, but the facility with which it can be obtained renders it more valuable.

These mines, when in operation, were worked by the old-fashioned Spanish toroner, the rudest of all mining machinery, which consists in nothing more than two large flat stones attached to a horizontal beam, and drawn round by a mule upon a bed of flat stones.   The process of grinding the ore, as well as that of amalgamating, was slow and imperfect, and not more than one third of the gold could be obtained.   Yet, with this prim-

itive mode of working, the mines have always more than
paid expenses, and in some instances considerable clear
profit has been realized.   With modern machinery and
skillful management, they could not fail to yield a large
revenue over and above the expenses, and would be a
money-making operation.   Wood is abundant and convenient; water is scarce a part of the year, but a small
expense would remedy this, and give a plentiful supply
at all seasons.   Labor is cheap, and any number of
workmen could be obtained for about one half the wages
paid in the States.   All of these mines are richer than
many of those in Virginia and Georgia that are worked
with considerable profit.   In the winter of 1855, the
owner of the Deavenport mine put up two toroners, which
he worked ten days, and obtained very nearly two hundred dollars' worth of gold, about one half over and above
the expenses.   The weather was extremely cold, and
the water had to be heated before amalgamation would
take place.   I saw the gold that was obtained, which
was sent to a gentleman in the States interested in mining operations.   These three mines were examined in
the fall of 1834 by Mr. William Idler, of Philadelphia, a
man of science and much experience in gold mining, who
pronounced them all rich, and that they would pay well
if properly worked.

The diggings known as the New Placer, where gold is
taken out by washing, are on the opposite side of the
same range of mountains.   In 1844 a piece of gold was
found there which weighed at the Mint the value of
$1213, and other pieces have weighed as many as three
and four pounds when taken from the earth; and I have
seen several lumps in almost a pure state that weighed
within a fraction of three quarters of an ounce after all
the dirt was washed off.   The gold of New Mexico is
worth about nineteen dollars at the Mint, being of a finer

quality than that obtained from California.   In addition
to these mines and diggings, gold has been discovered in
the mountains near Saudia, at Abiquin, near El Embudo, near the mountain pass of Sangre de Cristo, and in
many other parts of the country.   Near the Placer
Mountains the whole earth seems impregnated with the
precious metal; and I have never seen a handful of surface dirt taken from the neighborhood of the mines that
would not yield more or less gold by careful washing.
From information and observation, I believe it to be one
of the richest gold-bearing countries in the world, and
capital only is wanting to make that Territory another
California.

Silver is found in various parts of the country.   The
most valuable mines that have yet been explored are in
the county of Doña Ana, near the little town of Las Cruces, which have been worked to some extent.   The ore
is obtained from a range of mountains to the east, where
it can be extracted with ease and at small expense, and
has been pronounced exceedingly rich.   Silver is also
found in the Saudia Mountains.

Besides the precious metals, copper, iron, lead, coal,
and some zinc are found in the country.   Some of the
copper contains gold in sufficient quantities to pay for
the extracting.   The lead is much blended with copper
and other hard metals.   Iron ore has been discovered in
various localities, but I am not aware that it has ever
been manufactured.   The coal is hard, burns well, and
is found cropping out upon the surface in various places.
Salt lakes are numerous in New Mexico, but the largest
are not more than a few miles in circumference.   The
salt is deposited in immense cakes, and is obtained by
scooping it up from the bottom.   The dry season is the
best time to gather it, and after being dried in the sun it
is ready for market.   Nearly all the salt used in the Ter-

ritory is obtained from the lakes. They are common to all citizens, and are resorted to at certain seasons of the year to obtain a supply of this necessary article. Mineral and warm springs are found in several parts of the country, some of which possess high medicinal qualities, as has been already mentioned. *Yeso* (gypsum) abounds in many places, and is used for whitewashing instead of lime, though limestone is abundant. It is found in foliated blocks of numerous layers, which, being separated, are used for window-glass by the country people.

These minerals compose the natural wealth of the country, and, in the absence of all commercial advantages, must be the basis of its future prosperity. To develop them to any considerable extent would be a laborious and expensive task under existing circumstances, and, indeed, it can hardly be looked for at present. The remote situation of the country, difficulty of access, and the few advantages it possesses combine to keep capital and enterprise away from New Mexico. Compared with other Territories, there are few inducements for emigrants to go there to seek new homes. There is but one thing that can possibly open a new era in the prosperity of New Mexico, which is the building of a rail-road through the Territory to the Pacific. It would give a new impetus to all her interests, and do more to develop her resources than all other causes combined.

Compared with the rest of the Union, New Mexico may be called a desert land, and a large portion of it is almost as unfitted for agricultural purposes as the plains of Arabia. In appearance it is the most ancient country I have ever seen, and looks as though it might have been worn out long before the rest of our earth was made. The mountains are mostly barren, barring a stunted growth of pine-trees ; the plains are almost as sterile, and the small fertile valleys are like angels' visits, " few and far between." The minds of the people are as barren as the land, with as little hope of being better cultivated. Congress has donated two sections of land in each township for school purposes; but so large a portion of the country consists of rocky mountains and barren plains that there is a poor prospect of the donation ever yielding much for the cause of education. In lieu of the land, Congress should make an appropriation in money, as an education fund, to be expended in such manner as they might direct—the principal to be properly invested, and the interest arising from it only to be expended. At the session of the Territorial Legislature of 1855 and '56, an act was passed establishing a common-school system, which, it is hoped, will work some good. It will raise a tax of some thirty thousand dollars, and provides for at least one school in each precinct of the Territory. The law is defective in many particulars, but it exhibits a desire, on the part of the people's representatives, to do something to enlighten the minds of the rising generation.

The mere expense of living is greater in New Mexico than in any other section of the United States, and prices are generally much higher than in California. Many articles of food, and every description of clothing, are brought from the States in wagons, a distance of nearly a thousand miles from the frontiers of Missouri. The trains arrive out in the summer, from June to August, and the wagons are usually drawn by oxen, six and eight yoke making a team. The trip is made in from forty-five to sixty days, and a large number of wagons usually travel together, for the sake of protection from the Indians. The usual freight is nine and ten cents per pound. There is no insurance upon the goods thus transported, because of the great risk. Some trains return to the States the same season, while others, which belong to

the merchants, winter in the Territory, and go in early
the next spring.   The goods are mostly delivered at
Santa Fé and Albuquerque, whence they are sold to the
traders and distributed through the country.   The value
of the merchandise thus brought into the country in a
prosperous season, including the freight paid, can not be
less than seven hundred and fifty thousand dollars, and
it may reach a million.   The circulating medium of the
country is gold and silver, and neither copper nor bank-
notes are known in trade.   A great quantity of silver
dollars and doubloons come from Mexico, and much gold
finds its way across from California.   The merchants
generally make their remittances to the States in drafts
obtained from the disbursing officers of the general government, which is a great convenience, and attended with
less risk.

The Americans in the Territory do not exceed five
hundred, exclusive of the troops, and are found in all
parts of the country.   They are engaged in every branch
of business, and exhibit the energy always manifested
by our countrymen wherever met with.   It may be asked whether the native Mexicans have been benefited by
the country coming into the possession of the United
States, and having our institutions extended over them.
From my observation, I believe they have been improved
in both a social and political point of view.   They live
under certain and written laws, and are protected in the
enjoyment of all their rights, instead of trusting to the
caprice of an irresponsible individual as before.   There
is a decided improvement in the style of dress and mode
of living; they wear a greater quantity of American
goods, and tea, coffee, and sugar are becoming more common in use among the peasantry.   Many are dispensing
with the *serape* (blanket) as an every-day garment, and
are wearing coats instead; and buckskin is giving way

to woolen and cotton goods, and moccasins to leather shoes. There is also an improvement in the mode of building, and their houses are made more comfortable than before.

I am now about to draw the volume to a close, and take leave of you, my readers. I have endeavored to give you a faithful picture of New Mexico as it now is, with its vices and its virtues. I have written nothing in malice, because I have no such feelings to gratify; and my only desire is to present a correct knowledge of the country and the people. Some of the sketches show a dark picture in a moral point of view, but they are nevertheless true. Let us hope that a brighter day may soon dawn upon this distant and benighted portion of our happy land.

THE END.